Forging
Legislation

Other books by Paul Light

The President's Agenda: Domestic Policy Choice from Kennedy to Reagan

Vice Presidential Power: Advice and Influence in the White House

Artful Work: The Politics of Social Security Reform

Baby Boomers

Forging
Legislation

Paul C. Light

Hubert H. Humphrey Institute of Public Affairs
University of Minnesota

W. W. NORTON & COMPANY
New York   London

The text of this book is composed in New Baskerville, with the display set in New Baskerville Condensed. Composition by PennSet, Inc. Manufacturing by Courier, Westford. Book design by Suzanne Bennett & Associates.

FIRST EDITION.

Library of Congress Cataloging in Publication Data

Light, Paul Charles.
    Forging legislation / Paul C. Light.
        p.   cm.
    Includes bibliographical references and index.
    1. United States. Dept. of Veterans Affairs—History.
2. Legislation—United States.   3. United States. Congress.
I. Title.
KF5118.V47F67   1992
343.73'01—dc20   91-18400
[347.3031]

ISBN 0-393-03038-5 (paper)

W. W. Norton & Company, Inc.
500 Fifth Avenue, New York, N.Y.
W. W. Norton & Company, Ltd.
10 Coptic Street, London WC1A 1PU

1 2 3 4 5 6 7 8 9 0

To my father,
Richard M. Light,
a veteran of both war and parenthood

Contents

approved by Congress and signed by the president into
public law.

Passage of the Department of Veterans Affairs Act was
not a legislative miracle, however. In fact, the story of the
act is rather like that of most other bills in Congress—neither
routine nor spectacular, rarely a front-page story, but often
an inside headline, moving forward, moving backward,
sometimes stalled, but uniformly disorderly. Indeed, just
about everything about the original bill was normal—normal length, hearings, and floor votes, even normal detours
and delays. Then came the chance for veterans reform, and
all chaos broke loose.

Thus, for those who want to learn more about the real
legislative process, the Department of Veterans Affairs Act
is an excellent place to start. For those who want to learn
more about how Congress involves itself in public administration or where $30 billion in veterans programs fits into
America's social safety net, it may well be the only place to
start. (For those interested in legislative miracles, I might
recommend my earlier book, *Artful Work: The Politics of Social
Security Reform.*)

Forging Legislation is based upon my work on Capitol Hill
during the One-hundredth Congress. I joined the Senate
Governmental Affairs Committee in January 1987. As the
professional staff member responsible for the Department
of Veterans Affairs Act, I followed the bill from the moment
it was referred to committee all the way to its enrollment
on parchment paper for delivery to the president—from
committee hearings, to the drafting of a new bill, committee
markup, Senate floor action, the House–Senate conference,
final passage, and a bill signing ceremony on a crisp October
morning just weeks before the 1988 presidential election.

Forging Legislation is told from the vantage point of a
Senate Governmental Affairs staffer, which means that I
may have missed some twists and turns along the subways
and corridors of Capitol Hill. Like the "fog of war" that
envelops a battlefield in confusion during war, there is a

Preface

THIS IS THE story of how an ordinary bill called the *Department of Veterans Affairs Act* really became a law and how it inspired some extraordinary politics. Designed as a political salute to America's huge veterans lobby, the elevation of the Veterans Administration to Cabinet status eventually became the legislative "hammer" behind the first major reform of veterans policy in fifty years.

Along the way to the president's desk, the act overcame attempts to amend it, redraft it, even kill it, but not the effort to link it to a second, much more significant bill giving veterans the right to sue their government. Ironically, it was a reform almost uniformly opposed by the big veterans groups that so desperately wanted their own Cabinet department.

To become a vehicle for reform, however, the act had to first survive the normal winnowing process that suffocates most other bills. And survive it did. After starting out as one of nine thousand *bills* introduced in the One-hundredth Congress (1987–88), it eventually earned its way to the House and Senate floor as one of four thousand bills *reported by committee*, and emerged as one of only seven hundred *act*

fog of politics that envelops the legislative process. Readers will simply have to trust that I knew my way through the haze, and that I had the good sense to ask key staffers, friends, and colleagues on Capitol Hill for additional information as I wrote this book.

Acknowledgments

I always save writing the acknowledgments until the very last moment, for this brief section is the most pleasurable part of writing a book. It signals the end of the project, and provides an opportunity to thank friends and colleagues for their support.

For their helpful comments at various stages of the project, my thanks to Charles O. Jones, Burdette Loomis, G. Calvin Mackenzie, and Barbara Sinclair. Special appreciation to my students in the Humphrey Institute's social welfare administration course, who critiqued the very first draft of the book; Don Fusting, who shepherded the project through every stage of the process at W. W. Norton; and Patty Peltekos, who edited the final manuscript. All improved the book through their efforts.

For their patience on Capitol Hill, my thanks to a host of colleagues on and off the Governmental Affairs Committee: Edye Thomas, Paul Bustin, Deborah Lessor, Michael Nacht, Michael Slater, and the long list of fellow staffers, including Bob Coakley and Bob Harris, who shared my office suite, Harry Broadman and Steve Ryan, who shared many of my issues (and occasional defeats). Thanks,

xiv   ACKNOWLEDGMENTS

too, to those on Glenn's personal staff, including Mary Jane
Veno, Pat Buckheit, Kathleen Long, and Celia Gainer. Special thanks to Len Weiss, the staff director, who invited me
to join the staff in the first place.

For their lasting good humor and endurance throughout
the project period, my thanks to a host of friends: Melissa
Hedden and Mickey Sue Prosser, my life-long friends from
the Governmental Affairs Committee; Lorraine Lewis, also
a life-long friend who provided constant friendship and
flawless legal advice as Committee counsel; Bob Katzmann,
my closest friend in Washington and colleague at the Governance Institute; and Judy Leahy of the Humphrey Institute, as well as her family, all of whom provided a bulwark
of support along the way.

For his faith and durable commitment to public service,
my special appreciation to Senator John Glenn. This book
could not have been written without his confidence in me.

Finally, for their support through every stage of the process, thanks to my wife and daughter, Sharon Pamepinto
and Katherine Pamepinto Light. They make it all worthwhile.

Forging
Legislation

1

A Separate Safety Net
(The Setting)

NINETEEN THIRTY WAS A very good year for America's veterans. While the nation suffered through the first full year of the Great Depression, virtually every living veteran received some new benefit.

It was as if Congress and the president had decided that veterans, and veterans alone, would be protected from the economic catastrophe. Spanish-American War veterans came first, followed in short order by Civil War veterans and World War I veterans, each winning their own separate packages. All in all, benefits went up $118 million, or almost 20 percent, as veterans cornered $700 million in a federal budget of barely $4 billion.

Congress did not limit its largess to combat veterans, however. For the first time in history, Congress also granted pensions to those *not* injured in war. Although these non-service "pensions" were substantially lower than existing service-related "compensation," Congress clearly broke with the past, entitling an entire new class of claimants. Within two years, over 400,000 nonservice-related World War I veterans were added to the benefit rolls, many with no disability other than poverty.[1]

Nineteen thirty was also a very good year for the veterans bureaucracy.* Under pressure to make sense of a patchwork of agencies and programs, President Herbert Hoover merged the Veterans Bureau, the National Home for Disabled Volunteer Soldiers, and the Interior Department's Bureau of Pensions into a single administrative behemoth called the Veterans Administration. In doing so, Hoover created the bureaucratic home for what would eventually become a separate safety net for every soldier who survived boot camp. But the VA, as an independent agency, operated outside the Cabinet circle, giving it ample freedom to link more closely with Congress.

It is a wonder the veterans groups do not celebrate Hoover's birthday every year, for by the end of 1930, one-fifth of the federal budget was earmarked for veterans, whether disabled in combat or not, while one-third of all federal employees worked at the VA. At the time, veterans represented only 4 percent of the population.

America had not suddenly discovered veterans in 1930. The nation had always accepted its moral obligation to those who "shall have borne the battle," as Abraham Lincoln called them, beginning with pensions for veterans of the Revolutionary War. Rather, as the number of wars America participated in began to increase, so too did the number of veterans and their competition for federal dollars. Veterans of the Civil War, the Sioux Indian War, the Spanish-American War, the Mexican border campaign, and World War I were all in line for benefits. As members of Congress began to view their jobs as life-long careers, they also began to worry about maintaining support back home. Suddenly, vet-

* I have chosen not to use the possessive of veterans when describing the veterans lobby, veterans programs, or veterans policy, in large measure because the Senate and House Veterans Committees no longer do so.

erans and their organizations became much more visible. And they knew it.

That a new era of veterans politics had dawned was obvious as early as 1919, when the newly created American Legion began lobbying Congress for a bonus for the nearly 3.5 million veterans who had served in World War I, a bonus that would have roughly doubled the entire federal budget of $4 billion. In spite of three presidential vetoes, the bonus became law in 1924, albeit somewhat less generous than originally proposed.[2]

The victory, and those that quickly followed, clearly established the veterans lobby as a political force to be reckoned with. Today, led by the "big three"—the American Legion, the Veterans of Foreign Wars (VFW), and the Disabled American Veterans (DAV)—and reinforced by a host of smaller, specialized groups such as the Vietnam Veterans of America (VVA) and Paralyzed Veterans of America (PVA), the veterans lobby has forged an "iron triangle" with the Veterans Administration and the House and Senate Veterans Committees. The iron triangle has protected veterans programs for fifty years.

Thus, even though the VA was created by the president, the veterans lobby quickly cast its lot with Congress. It was nothing more than good old-fashioned pork-barrel politics. Not only would members of Congress care more about taking care of *their* veterans back home, they would take ownership of the VA as a delivery system for local constituents, including the doctors, nurses, and construction workers who would either work or build the VA facilities. (In 1987, the VA had $9.4 billion of construction projects underway, all at the local level.)

Organized into thousands of local chapters always at the ready, the lobby clearly had its greater influence in the halls of Congress, not the West Wing of the White House. The message to local Legion posts and VFW halls was simple: if your VA facility is in trouble, don't hesitate to call your member of Congress, and if your member doesn't have a facility, don't hesitate to cause trouble. Not surprisingly, many of the VA's flagship facilities were built in the home districts of particularly powerful members of Congress, including a huge, new hospital complex in Martinsburg, West Virginia, home of former Senate Majority Leader Robert Byrd.

My first encounter with the veterans triangle was like stepping into a scene from *Journey to the Center of the Earth*, a movie in which a team of modern-day explorers stumble upon a long-lost world of dinosaurs and volcanoes.

In Ronald Reagan's Washington of anti-big government was an administrative civilization of unimaginable size and scope. Made up of 172 veterans hospitals, 229 outpatient medical clinics, 117 nursing homes, 189 Vietnam veterans "storefront" outreach centers, 58 regional benefit offices, and 111 cemeteries, the VA was operating at a total cost of $27 billion a year.[3]

In an age of budget cuts and personnel freezes there was a national hospital system staffed by 194,000 government doctors and nurses, a massive benefits program providing $15 billion in support to veterans injured both in war and peace, one of America's largest life insurance companies carrying $213 billion in coverage for some seven million policy holders, a huge home loan program holding $12 billion in mortgages, and an educational assistance program called the GI Bill helping 240,000 veterans go to school.

In a time of smaller government and privatization there was an agency of almost unimaginable size and scope, second only to the Pentagon in its total number of employees. At 250,000 full- and part-time civil servants, the VA was bigger than the combined departments of Commerce, Energy, Education, Housing and Urban Development, Interior, Labor, the Environmental Protection Agency, Small Business Administration, and National Aeronautics and Space Administration! Only the Department of Defense was larger, weighing in at one million plus, not counting the soldiers.

Finally, in an era of loosely knit "issue networks" composed of highly mobile interest groups and shadowy bureaucrats was an agency run by an iron triangle, a form of government long thought extinct.[4] Composed of the House and Senate Veterans Committees, the veterans groups, and VA bureaucrats themselves, the veterans triangle was anything but loosely knit.

"Just about every pivot point of the Iron Triangle is occupied by personnel who used to be part of another pivot point of the Iron Triangle," one veterans lobbyist explained. "You have former national commanders or service directors who now work at the Veterans Administration in very high positions. You have former VA employees who work for the Committees on Veterans Affairs. You have former committee staffers who work for the veterans' organizations."[5]

Despite its size and scope, the VA had a standard organization chart, or "wiring diagram," with an administrator and deputy administrator at the top, and a normal assortment of staff and line offices directly below. As a general rule, offices that provide support to other units within an agency are called staff, while those that provide direct services to clients are called line. Every agency needs a bit of both.

At the VA, staff support came from at least four different offices: a personnel office to hire employees, a budget office to keep track of spending, a general counsel's office to offer legal advice, and an inspector general's office to ferret out fraud, waste, and abuse. Less than 10,000 of the VA's 250,000 employees worked in the various staff offices. But their jobs were essential to the agency's success. No personnel office, no employees; no budget office, no spending; and so on.

Nevertheless, the VA's main mission depended on three line units and their 210,000 employees: the Department of Veterans Benefits, the Department of Medicine and Sur-

Figure 1. The Veterans Administration, 1987

Board of Veterans Appeals	Administrator	General Counsel
	Deputy Administrator	Budget Office
Inspector General		Personnel Office
		Office of Equal Opportunity

Department of Medicine & Surgery	Department of Veterans Benefits	Department of Memorial Affairs

Associate Deputy Administrator, Logistics	Associate Deputy Administrator, Congressional	Associate Deputy Administrator, Management	Associate Deputy Administrator, Public Affairs

gery, and the Department of Memorial Affairs. But just because the three shared the same line on the organizaton chart did not mean they were equal partners. The tiny Department of Memorial Affairs had achieved its status as an operating unit more through a symbolic mission—to operate the national cemetery system—than by budget or numbers of employees.

The real power and influence inside the VA resided in the Department of Medicine and Surgery. The doctors clearly had the most prestigious mission—"they save lives and wear white coats," one Department of Veterans Benefits employee remarked to me in passing. "The rest of us deliver the checks or dig the graves." On the unwritten organization chart, the Department of Medicine and Surgery was at or very near the top.

When reading the chart for the first time, I almost missed the Board of Veterans Appeals in the top left corner. Created in 1933, the board was the last stop in the VA's administrative appeals process. To the extent veterans felt wronged by a decision in the Department of Veterans Benefits, their only recourse was to challenge the agency through a maze of upward internal reviews, which ultimately ended at the board. Most other agencies had no need for such an adjudicatory body, since most agencies allowed their clients to take them directly to court.

The most amazing thing about the VA was not its size, but the diversity of its programs. In 1987, the VA offered more than sixty separate entitlement programs—meaning every eligible veteran was entitled to benefits. I had only to skim a sampling of the programs to get a sense of the enormous range of veterans benefits (all figures are for 1987):

Those who (a) served during war time or peace, and (b) were disabled as a result of that service were entitled to *compensation* ranging from $69 dollars per month to $1,355 depending upon the degree of disability. (2.2 million veterans received some form of compensation, with an average disability, or injury, rating of 20 percent.)

Those who (a) served only during wartime, (b) fell below a set income level, and (c) were able to prove permanent and total disability not connected to service—that is, even if it occurred after discharge—and not caused by "willful misconduct or vicious habits," were entitled to a *pension* of anywhere from $5,963 per year to $11,387 with an additional amount for each dependent. Anyone over the age of 65 was automatically considered "permanently and totally" disabled. (630,000 veterans received some kind of pension.)

Using a different formula for World War II, post-World War II, Korea, post-Korea, Vietnam, and post-Vietnam veterans, most veterans were eligible for GI loans for the purchase of a home, condominium, or mobile home, including a subsidized mortgage rate, no down payment, and a small "loan origination" fee usually far below what average home buyers had to pay. (Over 480,000 veterans held loans totalling over $34 billion on an average home price of $72,201, in the mid-range of the middle-class housing market.)

Under five programs directly administered by the VA and another three supervised by the agency, veterans were eligible for up to $50,000 in life insurance at standard rates. (These eight programs provided nearly $220 billion in coverage to 7.4 million veterans, making the Veterans Administration one of the largest insurance companies in America.)

Those who were disabled as a result of active service during war or peace were eligible for up to $35,500 to cover up to half the cost of building, buying, or remodeling their homes to accommodate their disability, another $5,000 for the purchase of a car or other vehicle or for adapative equipment, and an annual clothing allowance of $365.

During the first ten years following discharge, most veterans were eligible for a variety of educational and job-training programs, including a monthly allowance while seeking a high-school equivalency degree, college loans, tutorial assistance, tuition support (even for correspondence courses), or flight training, and on-the-job training, for which the VA paid one half of the entry-level wages. (These benefits totaled $788 million in 1987, down by one-fifth over 1986 as most Vietnam veterans finally exhausted their eligibility.)

Survivors of service-disabled veterans—their spouses, unmarried children under eighteen, and some parents— were eligible for Dependency and Indemnity Compensation (DIC) ranging from $498 a month to $1,274 for spouses, and lesser amounts for children and parents.

Families of veterans who had been entitled to either compensation or pensions were eligible for an allowance to cover burial costs, plus additional costs for transportation if the veteran died at a VA facility. They were also eligible for a small plot or interment allowance, and either free burial in one of the over one hundred veterans cemeteries, including a free headstone or grave marker, or a small headstone or grave marker allowance. (246,000 headstones were ordered from the VA, while over 50,000 veterans were buried in veterans cemeteries.)

By 1987, the bill for these and other VA benefit programs totaled almost $15 billion, including paychecks for 13,000 full-time personnel in the Department of Veterans Benefits. In theory, anyone who wanted to understand America's welfare state had to know something about the VA. In practice, few did.[6]

The sixty benefits programs are only half of the story, however, for the VA also ran the largest health-care system, public or private, in the United States. Working through a network of highly independent hospitals—the Department of Medicine and Surgery appeared to work under the motto, "If you've seen one VA hospital, you've seen one VA hospital"—the VA's 200-plus clinics served as feeder lines into its 172 hospitals, which, in turn, served as feeders into its nursing homes and domiciliaries. Again, I only had to page through a sampling of programs to grasp the breadth of services available in the VA health care network (all figures are for 1987):

> Care in any of these government hospitals, clinics, nursing units, treatment centers, and domiciliaries was guaranteed to *any* veteran with a service-connected injury (compensation) or nonservice connected injury (pension). Veterans not covered by compensation or pensions could also use VA hospitals, but were subject to a means test to determine their ability to pay for all or part of the cost.
>
> In most cases, veterans were eligible for limited travel allowances to and from VA health care facilities, including payment for disability-rating examinations. Veterans in remote areas received outpatient care from traveling teams and mobile clinics.
>
> Some homeless veterans were eligible for psychiatric care through a $5 million pilot program authorized under a 1987 statute.
>
> Most veterans were eligible for outpatient dental care at ninety-six hospitals or outpatient clinics. (146,000 veterans received dental services ranging from cleanings to oral surgery, denture fittings, and experimental titanium tooth implants.)
>
> Hearing-impaired veterans were eligible for audiology and speech programs at most VA facilities. (The Veterans Administration handled over 684,000 visits, and more than 56,000 veterans received free hearing aids—at a cost of $186 each.)
>
> Vietnam-era veterans were entitled to counseling at several hundred Vietnam Veteran Outreach Centers across the country. Established at the urging of Congress, the program was designed to help Vietnam veterans particularly those with post-traumatic stress disorder (PTSD), readjust to civilian life.

The Civilian Health and Medical Program of the Veterans Administration (CHAMPVA) provided funds for private care for dependents and survivors of some veterans. This was one of the few programs in which the VA actually paid "civilian" providers, in large part because the VA does not have the capacity to provide certain kinds of care to women and children—there was no pediatric or obstetric service in the VA hospital or outpatient system.[7] Moreover, because the VA had so little experience supervising private providers, CHAMPVA has been in almost constant turmoil. (CHAMPVA cost roughly $100 million.[8])

Every year, approximately 100,000 medical and nursing students at America's private and public universities received additional training at affiliated VA hospitals and clincis. Many of these private and public medical schools were located just across the street from the local VA facility, forging extremely strong political connections as a potential defense against VA budget cuts.

In 1987, the bill for these and other medical programs totaled roughly $10 billion, including the salaries of almost 200,000 full- and part-time employees in the Department of Medicine and Surgery. Under statute, Congress required the VA to keep 90,000 hospital beds in service, even if some were always empty.

Again, in theory, anyone who wanted to understand America's health system had to know something about the VA. In practice, few did, even though private hospitals were increasingly dumping poor veterans into the VA as soon as the profits ran out, thereby evading cost controls enacted in the early 1980s to slow health-care inflation.[9]

It was impossible not to be awed by this "cradle-to-grave" system—a system built, staffed, and operated entirely by the VA. Nevertheless, by 1987 Congress and its staff were starting to ask some very tough questions about who got the benefits and at what cost. The questions were prompted by a deluge of studies from the General Accounting Office (GAO), the investigative arm of Congress.

The answers were hardly comforting, for most of the VA's $30 billion did not go to those who bore the greatest costs of war at all, but to those with 20 percent disability ratings or less. Moreover, even those with 100 percent ratings were not necessarily severely injured. Recall that the VA automatically considered any veteran over sixty-five who applied for a pension as "permanently and totally" disabled, regardless of health.

Consider service-connected compensation as an example. According to the GAO, although all service-connected veterans had to be certified as having been injured while in the military, many in combat, roughly two-thirds were receiving compensation for problems rated 20 percent or less disabling, while nine in ten received compensation for problems rated 40 percent or less disabling.[10] Two-thirds were thirty years or younger when they first received their disability rating, and two-thirds had drawn their benefits for at least twenty years or longer.

At least some of these service-connected benefits were for injuries and diseases related more to the natural passage of time than to injuries received in service, what the GAO called the "ordinary diseases of life." Simply put, it was hard for the GAO to understand how diabetes, hemorrhoids, multiple sclerosis, and arteriosclerotic heart disease could be considered service-induced injuries.

Yet each year thousands of veterans were being certified for precisely those diagnoses. According to GAO estimates, 19 percent of veterans receiving service-connected benefits in 1986 had injuries *not* related to service, adding up to $1.7 billion in "compensation for disabilities that resulted from diseases that our physicians concluded were neither caused nor aggravated by service."[11] Indeed, according to the GAO, roughly one-third of veterans rated 100 percent disabled were suffering from the ordinary problems of aging. Consider two examples presented by GAO:

In 1971, 7 years after leaving the service, this Air Force veteran received a 30-percent rating for chronic obstructive lung disease; the rating was increased in 1975 to 60 percent. The veteran began smoking 10 years before entering the service and smoked 20 to 30 cigarettes a day. The veteran had pneumonia before entering the service and suffered other lung diseases (bronchitis, pneumonia, chronic cough, influenza, and emphysema) while in the service. The physicians reviewing the case [for GAO] felt that the veteran's smoking alone would not have brought on his condition whether or not he went into the service.

Within three months after his induction, this Navy veteran was hospitalized for a heart condition. Rheumatic heart disease was discovered dating back to his childhood, and he was subsequently discharged. He received a 60-percent rating for the heart condition after discharge, which, 30 years later, was raised to 100 percent. Our physicians believed that this veteran's heart condition, dating from childhood, was unrelated to his brief military service.[12]

Much as Congress could feel sympathy for these individuals, few members could easily justify costly service-connected benefits for illnesses clearly unrelated to service. In its response to the report, the VA correctly noted that it was not required to determine a *causal* connection between military service and a specific injury, merely to establish that an injury occurred between the time of induction and discharge. Nevertheless, the report, and those that followed on other VA programs, raised serious doubts about just who benefited most from America's separate safety net.

Just as most of the benefit dollars went to those with less severe injuries, so, too, did most of the hospital beds. Most patients were not those injured in service at all, but those with nonservice connected disabilities. In fact, the VA was, and is, best understood as a poor people's system that cares for those who would otherwise slip through the system into charity care. "The VA does serve a special clientele," writes health expert Harvey Sapolsky, "but most of its population is precisely the population that is said to be neglected by private medicine in America."[13]

In 1987, for example, only 13 percent of the VA's 1.4 million hospital admissions were veterans with service-connected injuries considered 50 percent or more disabling. Another 26 percent were those with service-connected injuries rated 40 percent or less disabling, and a whopping 51 percent were those with nonservice connected disabilities.[14]

Moreover, according to internal estimates, as many as one-third of all 1987 admissions were alcohol-related. Not only were such cases more expensive to treat, if only because alcoholics often come in for care at the end stage of illness, but they also required longer stays and more intensive care.[15] So, too, for the one-third of all patients who entered the VA system for psychiatric care.

The VA was often a godsend for such patients, a "third tier" of America's health-care delivery system, located somewhere between private hospitals for the insured and charity hospitals for the uninsured, a fact confirmed by the patients themselves. According to data drawn from a 1984 survey conducted for the VA, when faced with a need for care, 72 percent of veterans with private insurance said they would go to a private doctor first, compared to just 38 percent of those without private insurance. Conversely, only 15 percent with private insurance said they would go to a VA hospital or clinic, compared to 51 percent of veterans with no private insurance.[16] Rarely do data speak so clearly to the impact of having insurance on what patients decide. Given a choice, most veterans would opt for private care.

That the VA's urban hospitals provided a health-care safety net for needy veterans is evident from the VA's own statistics. Huge inner-city hospitals in the Bronx, Brooklyn, Chicago, Baltimore, New Orleans, Philadelphia, Los Angeles, and Boston drew the vast majority of their patients from the nonservice connected veterans population. (Readers in these cities need only drive to the hospitals for a visit to get a sense of the critical role the VA plays in providing care to low-income patients.) A study prepared by staff at the Baltimore Veterans Medical Center summarized the average VA patient:

> many many veterans presently being cared for by the VA will not be the most attractive patients for the private sector. . . . In addition to being medically and economically indigent, their higher incidence and prevalence rates of chronic and multiple health conditions, coupled with a sizeable proportion of veterans being unable to conform to society's norms, and being further hampered by disabling physical, psychological or substance abuse problems all combine to make many veterans unattractive to the private health industry, regardless of a guaranteed payment system. . . . The current private sector competitive system is already discharging veterans as soon as possible after their current financing erodes, and then the VA system becomes the veterans' and, in effect, society's safety net.[17]

Yet, by 1987 the GAO was at work on a study that would report that over 40 percent of the days patients spent in a sample of seven VA hospitals were medically unnecessary, leading to even further questions about cost and benefits.[18] Congress was also asking questions about the quality of care provided in VA hospitals and regional benefit offices. In April 1987, for example, the House Government Operations Committee released the report, *Patients at Risk: A Study of Deficiencies in the Veterans Administration Quality Assurance Program.*[19]

The title was the most favorable part of the report. Although the committee noted that its conclusions were "not always typical of care at VA hospitals," the text was amply illustrated with gruesome stories of medical negligence in VA hospitals. Consider the following example:

> Some of the incidents are reminders of how easy it can be to become lost in the massive medical bureaucracy

of the VA. In one case, a patient died after being literally lost at the Buffalo, New York, VAMC [Veterans Aministration Medical Center]. The patient was admitted to the hospital with congestive heart failure on January 10, 1985. The patient was disoriented and had removed his own catheters and intravenous attachments. For his protection, the staff restrained him in a wheelchair.

Eight days later, the nursing staff reported the patient missing. The patient was missing six days when his body was discovered lying face down in a hospital stairwell by a pharmacist jogging the stairs for exercise. The patient died of cardiac arrest. Despite an organized search of the building prior to the body's discovery, the patient could not be located.[20]

Six months earlier, the GAO had released an equally damning report on the VA's patient injury-control system. Such systems are based on immediate reporting of unexpected deaths during surgery, falls, suicides, transfusion errors, patient abuse, equipment failures, and so on, and are designed to help identify preventable incidents, thereby reducing future malpractice claims by alerting hospitals to recurring problems—surgeons who consistently lose patients on the operating table, for example.

Unfortunately, according to the GAO, only 16 percent of all patient injuries were reported through VA's quality assurance process. This report, titled *VA's Patient Injury Control Program Not Effective*, was also illustrated with horror stories about cases that should have been reported as unexplained but were never reported at all:

A 61-year-old patient released from a VA emergency room after complaining of shortness of breath was found unresponsive at the ambulance entrance 1½ hours later. The patient was admitted to the hospital, but died 1 hour later.

A 50-year-old patient was transferred by taxi about 300 miles from one VA center to another for radiation treatment. Upon arrival, the patient was found dead in the cab. No autopsy was performed and the cause of death was listed as lung cancer.

A 56-year-old veteran underwent five successive surgeries—four at a VA medical center and one at a private hospital—in an attempt to repair a colon perforation resulting from previous VA surgery. The perforation could not be repaired, and the veteran subsequently filed a malpractice claim.

Following bypass surgery, a 68-year-old patient lost considerable blood and was returned to the operating room. During the return, he suffered cardiac arrest and could not be resuscitated. His abdomen was quickly opened, and about 2,000 cc of blood and a tear in a vein was noted. The patient subsequently died.[21]

Remarkably, the VA's main response to the report consisted of the following statement from the administrator: "We cannot accept GAO's statement, as indicated by the report title, that the program is not effective. We suggest that a more accurate description of the program, and the title for the GAO's report, would be *Improvements Needed in the VA's Patient Injury Control Program*." But what better term for a system that failed to catch a remarkable 86 percent of patient injuries?

None of these reports argued that the VA's care was somehow worse than that of the private sector. On one hand, the VA argued that its malpractice rate, and therefore its quality, compared favorably with the private sector, and, indeed, it did. Patients sued VA physicians roughly half as often as private physicians, while average awards were one-third as large.[22]

On the other hand, the number of claims against the VA doubled from 1977 to 1987, and total payout in awards jumped from $16 million in 1983 to $34 million in 1987. The VA's typical patient seemed much less likely to sue for malpractice than the typical private-sector patient, thereby limiting the usefulness of comparisons with other health-care providers. The real question, of course, was whether there was cause to be concerned about the quality of VA medical care. The answer was a resounding "yes."

Ultimately, the burgeoning GAO reports and congressional investigations betrayed a weakening of legislative confidence in the VA. Congress was no longer willing to let the VA operate quite so freely. That the *Patients at Risk* report came from the House Government Operations Committee, not the Veterans Committee, was merely a symptom of the growing suspicion toward what was once an invulnerable agency.

More important, the problems in the VA's medical system were nothing compared to the emerging portrait of a Department of Veterans Benefits in complete disarray, a portrait that forms the basis for much of this book.

The Veterans Administration was hardly in danger of being closed, however. Despite the mounting criticism, Congress still cared deeply about veterans programs, and veterans still cared deeply about Congress. Members of Congress could still count on a special place in the Veterans Day parade, while the VA internal phone book still listed its hospitals and clinics by House district and member.

Nevertheless, by 1987 there was little doubt that defending the vast array of veterans programs had become more difficult. In 1981, Congress cut the burial benefit from $450 to $300, cut dental benefits, and eliminated some educational loans, for a total savings of $116 million.

In 1982, Congress cut the VA budget by $522 million, primarily by rounding all benefit checks down to the next dollar.

In 1983, Congress approved a cost-of-living (COLA) freeze on all veterans compensation and pensions.

In 1984, Congress gave veterans a lower COLA than Social Security beneficiaries, drawing a distinction between the needy elderly and the needy veteran.

In 1985, Congress overhauled the home-loan program,

cut the COLA again, and signaled its intent to restrict free health care for well-to-do, nonservice connected veterans.

In 1986, Congress imposed the first means test on the VA health-care system, forcing some veterans to pay for hospital and clinic visits. Much as the veterans group blamed many of these cuts on Reagan's Office of Management and Budget and its nonveteran director, David Stockman, Congress went along willingly.*

The veterans lobby was hardly dead, of course. Veterans still turned out in droves for congressional hearings, still wrote letters, still campaigned for their friends. Nevertheless, if not quite dead, the veterans lobby was hardly alive and kicking either. "If the iron triangle was so strong," one VFW lobbyist said, "all we'd have to do is write down $30 or $40 billion [and Congress would pass it], but we have to fight like dogs for an adequate budget."

The problem was that the veterans lobby no longer depended on moral persuasion for its legislative success. Size was the most important factor, an inevitable consequence of the strategic decisions made in the 1920s, culminating in the remarkable political success of 1930. Since wars create veterans, and since veterans create political strength, peace becomes just about the greatest enemy the veterans lobby has, driving the numbers of potential constituents ever downward, while eroding any moral obligation the nation might still feel toward those who risked life and limb in defense of God and country. "The further away we get from wars, the less people consider those who did the job," Democratic Rep. G. V. ("Sonny") Montgomery of Mississippi, chairman of the House Veterans Affairs Committee, argues. "They say, 'Let them just carry on the best they can.' "[23]

By 1987 the veterans lobby faced at least three demographic threats: shrinking, aging, and greening.

First, as the ten million World War II veterans, five mil-

* Many in the veterans lobby believed that Stockman had dodged the Vietnam war.

lions Korean veterans, and eight million Vietnam veterans steadily aged, the total number of veterans could only shrink. Looking beyond 1987 and assuming all new wars are fought with today's relatively small volunteer army, the veterans population would drop from twenty-eight million in 1987 to eighteen million by 2030. In 1987 441,000 veterans died, while only 237,000 were created.[24]

Second, again assuming no new call-ups, the number of veterans over age sixty-five can only increase—up from six million in 1987 to almost nine million by the year 2000—while the number over age seventy-five will quadruple—up from just one million in 1987 to 4.4 million by the turn of the century.[25] Thus, there will be fewer veterans overall and the remaining will be less able to lobby and in greater need of care.

Third, as the number of older veterans thins, a new generation of volunteer soldiers—soldiers recruited into service because "It's not a job, it's an adventure"—is taking their place. Few would doubt America's continuing commitment to these new veterans, particularly in the aftermath of the Persian Gulf War. However, it is not yet clear that this new generation of high-tech, well-paid, low-casualty, quick-war veterans will be as vocal in support of traditional VA health and benefit programs.

Clearly, these three demographic trends threaten the future political strength of the veterans "caucus" in Congress. "I'm very concerned about the composition of the next and succeeding Congresses," said one top DAV official in 1987. "We're getting more and more members who are not in touch with veterans, most of them not having served in the military. The further you get away from a war, the less desire there is to do much about veterans."[26] "It used to be a joke," a former House Veterans Committee staffer added, where veterans groups "would say, please give us nonveterans on the committee, because they'd give us the moon. They're sensitive to being nonveterans. How long that will last I don't know. Time could make a lot of difference."[27]

By 1987, it already had. Many younger members of Congress had barely been eligible for the Vietnam draft, and many, like former Indiana senator Dan Quayle, seemed to have done their utmost to find some way out of active service. Moreover, even the Vietnam veterans in line for key committee posts were not necessarily in favor of continued expansion of the veterans agenda.

Indeed, most Vietnam veterans seem to share little of the camaraderie of their older comrades in arms. "What would be the worst set of social, economical, and political, and psychological conditions you could create for the returnee?" one Vietnam veteran asked the U.S. Senate Veterans Affairs Committee in 1980.

> First, you would send a young man fresh out of high school to an unpopular, controversial guerrilla war far away from home. Expose him to intensely stressful events, some so horrible that it would be impossible to really talk about them later to anyone else except fellow "survivors." To ensure maximal stress, you would create a one-year tour of duty during which the combatant flies to and from the war zone singly, without a cohesive, intact, and emotionally supportive unit with high morale. You would also create the one-year rotation to instill a "survivor mentality" which would undercut the process of ideological commitment to winning the war and seeing it as a noble cause. Then at DEROS [Date of Expected Return for Overseas Service] you would rapidly remove the combatant and singly return him to his front porch without an opportunity to sort out the meaning of the experiences with the men in his unit. No homecoming welcome or victory parades. Ah, but yet, since you are demonic enough, you make sure that the veteran is stigmatized and portrayed to the public as a "drug-crazed psychopathic killer." By virtue of clever selection by the Selective Service [draft] system, the veteran would be unable to easily reenter the mainstream of society because he is undereducated and lacks marketable job skills. Further, since the war itself was difficult, you would want to make sure there were no supportive systems in society

for him, especially among health professionals at VA
hospitals who would find his nightmares and residual
war-related anxieties unintelligible. Finally, you would
want to establish a GI bill with inadequate systems to pay
for education and job training and unemployment. Last,
but not least, you would want him to feel exploited for
volunteering to serve his country. Tragically, of course,
this scenario is not fictitious: it was the homecoming for
most Vietnam veterans.

This homecoming still haunts many Vietnam veterans.
According to a recent study published in the *New England
Journal of Medicine*, that homecoming may even explain why
Vietnam vets face higher risks of drug and alcohol dependency, emotional depression, and divorce than their non-
veteran peers. The study found that, compared to non-
veteran peers, Vietnam vets are "65 percent and 49 percent
more likely to die from suicide and motor-vehicle accidents
respectively," odds attributable to military service during
the Vietnam War.[28]

In many respects, therefore, where veterans stand on
politics may depend on when they served. Not only were
the homecomings completely different (recall the pictures
of New York's Time Square on V-E Day), even the movie
heroes cut a different swath—John Wayne for World War
II, Willem Dafoe (*Platoon*) and Martin Sheen (*Apocalypse
Now*) for Vietnam. Rent *The Best Years of Our Lives* and *Coming Home* for a comparison.[29] Then review the homecoming
specials from the Gulf War.

Given the nature of the Vietnam War, it should not be
surprising that Vietnam veterans have been less likely to
join a traditional veterans organization. Nor should it come
as a surprise that Vietnam veterans are deeply suspicious
of the Veterans Administration. They are less likely to say
the VA is responsive to their needs and they have formed
several smaller, more radical veterans groups to represent
their needs. One in particular, the Vietnam Veterans of

America (VVA), quickly earned the ire of the traditional groups for its aggressive reform agenda.

"Unfortunately, the VVA is out there constantly trying to make things look bad for what they call the old-line veterans' organizations," a former executive secretary of the VFW once claimed. "They better try to keep the laws on the statute books that we have now, or someone else will try to take over the VA system."[30]

Veterans had ample cause for wondering about the future as Congress gaveled in its bicentennial session in 1987. As older allies retired from Congress, the prospects for continued success seemed poor at best. Ultimately, veterans had to ask whether it was time to move a bit closer to the president, to accept greater White House control in return for protection from an increasingly unfriendly Congress.

As I entered this world of separate systems, separate programs, and separate care, there was one separation that made no sense: veterans were not allowed to take the VA to court. As I was to find out, the VA's immunity from court review was one more way in which the veterans lobby and the VA protected the separate safety net. If protecting the safety net meant denying the right to go to court, so be it. The question, of course, was whether the veterans triangle was still strong enough to resist the pressure for reform. Fifty years after its greatest victories, there was about to be a test.

2

A Department of Fat
(Agenda Setting)

THE STORY OF the *Department of Veterans Affairs Act* begins on February 17, 1987, when the most senior Republican in the Senate, Strom Thurmond of South Carolina, introduced Senate Bill 533, "A Bill To establish the Veterans' Administration as an executive department." At virtually the same time, a companion, or identical, measure was introduced in the House. Thurmond, who had introduced the same bill every Congress for over thirty years with absolutely no response, was about to get lucky.

Strom Thurmond was a Senate classic. First elected to the Senate in 1954 in a write-in campaign, he was eighty-four years old when he introduced S. 533. He had been the "Dixiecrat," or States' Rights, candidate for president in 1948, bolting the Democratic Party when then-Minneapolis mayor Hubert Humphrey rallied the national convention to a strong civil rights stand. But what was most remarkable about Thurmond was his wind up and delivery on the Senate floor. He could trade fire with the best of the Senate, his arms always waving as if to pump more air into his lungs for the next blast.

As a retired army general and senior member of the

Senate Armed Services Committee, Thurmond was unabashedly pro-veteran. In 1987, his bill had four original cosponsors: Frank Murkowski (R-Alaska), ranking Republican on the Veterans Committee and a Coast Guard veteran; Chich Hecht (R-Nev.) a former counterintelligence officer; Alan Cranston (D-Calif.), Democratic chairman of the Veterans Committee and an army veteran; and Larry Pressler (R-S.D.), Vietnam army veteran. By the time the *Department of Veterans Affairs Act* reached the floor of the Senate eighteen months later, sixty-seven senators had joined the list. Throughout the debate, Thurmond wanted one thing and one thing only: a Department of Veterans Affairs. He would have done just about anything to get the bill passed.

As one of over 3,300 bills introduced in the one-hundredth session of the Senate, the bill itself was really quite simple, suggesting from the onset that Cabinet status was more symbol than substance.[1] Only six pages long, S. 533 started with the standard "enacting clause" that opens almost all bills, followed by two key sentences explaining its general purpose:

> "*Be it enacted by the Senate and House of Representatives of the United States of America in Congress assembled,* That (a) the independent establishment in the executive branch of the government known as the Veterans' Administration is hereby redesignated as the Department of Veterans Affairs and shall be an executive department in the executive branch of Government. (b) The positions of the Administrator of Veterans Affairs and the Deputy Administrator of Veterans Affairs are hereby redesignated as the Secretary of Veterans' Affairs and the Deputy Secretary of Veterans' Affairs, respectively."*

* The standard enacting clause exists almost entirely as a way to amend a House or Senate bill with the other chamber's measure, as in "strike after the enacting clause and replace with H.R. or S. whatever." Once the new measure exists under the old bill number, it can be returned to the other chamber for further action.

For those interested in political nomenclature, the political pecking order in a governmental department runs from secretary to deputy secretary, undersecretary, assistant secretary, and deputy assistant secretary.

Even a detailed reading of S. 533 required no more than five minutes. The bill had six simple sections, the bare minimum for establishing a Cabinet department: (1) a short title designating the bill as the Department of Veterans Affairs Act and appointing two principal officers, (2) a section establishing the Veterans Administration as an executive department by redesignating the VA as the Department of Veterans Affairs, (3) a standard technical provision reconciling the act with every statute contained in the U.S. Code, (4) a savings provision keeping all contracts, legal documents, etc., in effect in the new department, (5) a reference section defining any mention of the Veterans Administration in existing U.S. law to mean the Department of Veterans Affairs, and (6) an effective date giving the president the right to establish the new deparment by executive order as soon as he wanted, but no later than six months after enactment of the act. Figure 2 summarizes the revised VA wiring diagram under S. 533.

Thurmond's bill was the "floor jack" approach to executive branch reorganization. Under S. 533, the president would merely slip a floor jack under the existing agency, raise the agency up a notch to Cabinet level, and change its title. There would be no reorganization of the agency's internal structure, no new officers or political appointees, no greater coordination, just a new sign on the door and a seat at the Cabinet table. Indeed, S. 533 was little more than a series of "technical" or "conforming" amendments designed to reconcile the legislation with existing statutes where the words "Veterans Administration" would become "Department of Veterans Affairs."

Just to make sure every base was covered, S. 533 contained a "notwithstanding" clause: "Any reference to the Veterans Administration or to the Administrator of Vet-

Figure 2. The Department of Veterans Affairs, S. 533 and H.R. 1707 as Introduced

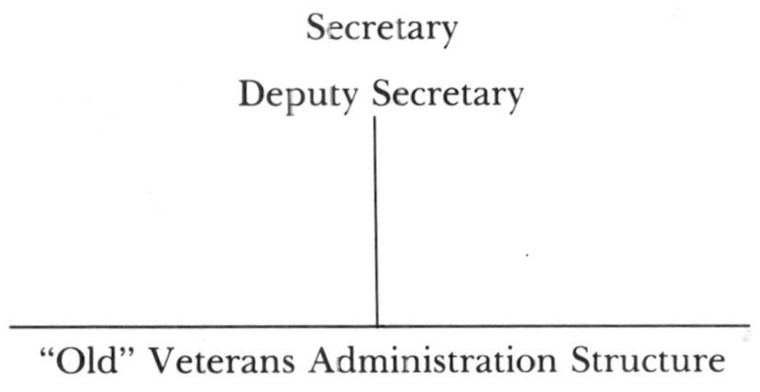

Secretary

Deputy Secretary

"Old" Veterans Administration Structure

erans' Affairs in any law, rule, regulation, certificate, directive, instruction, or other official paper in effect after the effective date of this Act shall be deemed to be a reference to the Department of Veterans' Affairs or to the Secretary of Veterans' Affairs, respectively." (Notwithstanding is actually one of my favorite words in the legislative dictionary, meaning "forget everything else I have ever said, this is what I really mean." It is a great word to insert in legislation now and then just to protect oneself.) Thus, notwithstanding the specific legislative language, S. 533 was more noticeable for what it did *not* contain: no reform, no new political appointees, no change in the internal structure of the VA. It was little more than a symbol.

This bill was in John Glenn's hands at the start of the one-hundredth Congress thanks to a series of small coincidences that ultimately led to the Ohio Democrat's elevation as chairman of the Senate Governmental Affairs Committee. The Democrats had won enough close races in the 1986 mid-term elections to recapture the Senate majority lost in the 1980 Reagan landslide. Suddenly, dozens of Republican chairmen and their staffers were out of work, as Democrats vacated the fluorescent-lit cubicles reserved for the minority and moved across the halls into the larger, freshly painted offices reserved for the majority.

Before Glenn could be named chairman of Governmental Affairs, the committee's more senior senators, Sam Nunn of Georgia and Lawton Chiles of Florida, had to decline. A senator may chair only one full committee. Thus, when Nunn and Chiles decided to chair other, more powerful committees—Armed Services and Budget, respectively—Glenn became first in line for Governmental Affairs.

For Glenn, his staff director Len Weiss, and the rest of the Governmental Affairs Committee staff, the difference between majority and minority status would be in the view from the windows: the majority got the parks, streets, and flowers surrounding the Dirksen Senate Office Building; the minority, the rooftop and heating ducts of the Dirksen auditorium, built where a courtyard once blossomed. There was no ceremony for turning over the keys, merely the endless packing and unpacking back and forth across the halls.

The only predictable element in those first weeks with Governmental Affairs was the fact that the Department of Veterans Affairs Act came to Glenn's committee in the first place. Every bill introduced has to be sent someplace, and Governmental Affairs is where Cabinet bills go. Although introduced by the former chairman of the Senate Veterans Committee, S. 533 was automatically referred to the Senate Committee on Governmental Affairs under Standing Rule XXV of the Senate. A bill involving organization and reorganization of the executive branch had to go to Glenn's committee, and, in turn, through Len Weiss to the staffer responsible for executive organization issues, me.

Rule XXV was more than a routing mechanism for the veterans bill, however. It also defined the Governmental Affairs territory. All bills pertaining to the Archives of the United States, budget process and accounting measures, census and collection of statistics, including economic and social statistics, congressional organization, federal civil service, government information, intergovernmental relations, the District of Columbia, organization and management of United States nuclear export policy, organization and reorganization of the executive branch of the government, the U.S. Postal Service, and government pay were ours.

Moreover, the Committee had standing responsibility for issues related to government economy and efficiency.* Translated into simple English, committee members could go pretty much anywhere and investigate anything. More

* The committee's formal responsibilities can be found in Committee on Governmental Affairs, *Legislative Calendar*, One-hundredth Congress (Washington, D.C.: U.S. Government Printing Office, December 31, 1988).

to the point, the committee had the staff to make the mandate stick. With 126 staffers, Governmental Affairs was the third largest committee in the Senate. Only Judiciary, and Labor and Human Resources had larger staffs. That Glenn intended to use his staff and mandate was clear in what quickly became a grueling hearing schedule that stretched the committee staff to its physical limits.

Despite the work load, Glenn was the perfect chairman. He was willing to let his staff take risks. If he had learned any lesson during a military career spanning twenty years—first as a fighter pilot in Korea, then as a test pilot in the 1950s, and finally as one of America's first astronauts—it was to trust his staff. It is hard to imagine Glenn strapped into his capsule awaiting lift-off asking if anyone had fueled the rocket.

Glenn was willing to invest time in his committee. He had more than his share of what he called MEGO hearings—**M**y **E**yes **G**laze **O**ver—during the One-hundredth Congress, but he worked hard as chairman. First elected to the Senate in 1974, and reelected by an overwhelming margin in 1986, Glenn also had the political freedom to let his staff run—with reelection six years away, he had a little more time to spend in Washington. He had also given up his ambition to be president.[2]

For many of us, Glenn was still a national hero. I never forgot that I was working for my boyhood idol, the first American to orbit the earth. I could still remember listening to my portable transistor radio as Friendship 7 rocketed into space. If ever I were to forget, all I had to do was glance around Glenn's office. He had very few pictures of himself on the walls and none from his astronaut days, but, oh, the models of spacecraft, aircraft, space stations, and rockets scattered around the room. The models were not so much advertisements of past success as reminders of Glenn's love affair with flight.

Glenn never made much of his astronaut days, however, and he never reminisced with us. He did have a pile of baseball bats in a corner of the office and he once told of the days when Ted Williams, the Boston Red Sox great, flew under his command in Korea. There were times in formation, Glenn remembered, when the fog was so thick that Williams had to bring his jet in under Glenn to avoid collision, William's canopy almost touching Glenn's belly tank. Hard to imagine a man who could see the stitches on a baseball as it left the pitcher's hand blinded so completely.

Perhaps those kind of experiences explain why Glenn was so at ease with himself. He had a good sense of humor, and never once tore down his staff in public the way so many politicians do. Having Ted Williams under your wing might teach that to a future senator.

That Glenn was committed to his job as chairman was clear in the hearing schedule. Hearings are rather formal affairs designed to ventilate issues or build a record of testimony in support or against legislation. Normally lasting a morning or afternoon, hearings generally consist of opening statements from the committee chair and members, followed by panels of witnesses who present formal statements and answer questions. The staff director sits directly behind the chair, with the rest of the professional staff arrayed around the dias. Alas, while committee members are always free to get a cup of coffee or a glass of ice water, staffers might as well be stranded in the middle of the Sahara Desert. No one dares get up to even visit the bathroom, lest the boss turn around.

In all, Glenn held sixty-seven days of hearings during the One-hundredth Congress, on topics ranging from the quixotic to the traditional—from reactor safety issues at Department of Energy facilities to civil service reform, from the causes and consequences of alcohol abuse to ways of improving presidential transitions—almost doubling the pace of the previous chairman. Glenn's goal as chairman was simple. He believed in improving government.

Ultimately, of course, the committee was in business to produce legislation. And produce it did, from the Nuclear

Protections and Safety Act of 1987, which failed on the Senate floor; the Whistleblower Protections Act of 1988, which was vetoed by Reagan, the Inspector General Act Amendments of 1988, which was signed into law; and the Presidential Transitions Effectiveness Act, also signed into law. Even the bills that didn't pass would not be total failures—they would be ready and waiting for the next president, perhaps a Democrat, to adopt as his own on January 21, 1989, just as John F. Kennedy had done in building his policy agenda almost thirty years before. In all, the Committee handled 207 bills during the One-hundredth Congress, reporting thirty-four for full Senate consideration. Of those, twenty-nine were passed by both chambers and signed into law, an 85 percent success ratio.*

One bill few in Washington expected to pass, however, was the Department of Veterans Affairs Act. It was hardly a new idea and had never had so much as a hearing in either chamber. Either the veterans groups had something more important on the agenda or Congress just wasn't interested.

Surely President Ronald Reagan would never allow this bill to move, not with all his rhetoric against big government, not with his promises to abolish the departments of Education and Energy. Surely the feisty, cigar-chomping Texas Democrat Jack Brooks would never permit a hearing on the companion House of Representatives bill 1707. As chairman of the House Government Operations Committee, he had impeded its passage for twenty years. From my perspective, this bill was going nowhere fast, an interesting example of gentle pandering to a special-interest group, but not to be taken seriously. As the staffer in charge of Cabinet bills, it was my initial call to make: Filed for Future Reference.

Within six months the bill had become a speeding freight

---

* Under the Republicans in the Ninety-ninth Congress, the Committee handled 242 bills, reporting thirty-nine for full Senate consideration. Of those, twenty-one were passed by both chambers and signed into law, a 54 percent ratio.

train. By October every staffer on Capitol Hill was digging feverishly through file drawers and waste baskets in search of a copy. Obviously, the signals had changed. Brooks was suddenly very serious about moving forward with H.R. 1707. Over a scant six months, H.R. 1707 had attracted 275 cosponsors (well over half the House), and seemed destined to pass with or without Brooks's support. The bill was gaining speed in the Senate, too, but was still far short of fifty cosponsors by October.

The House was the logical target for veterans pressure from the very beginning. First, every member of the House was up for reelection in 1988, compared to just one-third of the Senate. The fact that Cabinet status was a legislative priority for the national veterans groups meant that its passage would be an election priority for their state and local posts, and, hence, for their local member of Congress.

Second, the House had always been more responsive to veterans issues, having establishing its Veterans Affairs Committee almost fifty years before the Senate. The House prided itself on taking care of constituents back home—and veterans were very strong constituents indeed. The sweet attraction of VA elevation was that it cost virtually nothing in an era of tight, tight budgets, yet gave members a chance to vote for veterans. It was a classic "cake and eat it too" issue. And for the veterans groups, moving closer to the president might just protect the VA.

Moreover, it was not clear that Brooks could have stopped the bill even if he had wanted to. Committee chairs in both chambers long ago lost their authority to bottle up legislation forever, particularly if a given measure has a broad base of support. Gone are the "good old days" when House members and senators were to be work horses, not show horses, specializing in one of two issues over their entire careers. Gone, too, are the days when new members were to be seen and not heard, serving a suitable apprenticeship before rising for their first speech or amendment.

Remarkably, the House took less than a month to pass

the Department of Veterans Affairs Act once Brooks introduced his own version of the bill. At some point, Brooks had to either move or get out of the way—far better to be at the front of the parade than sweeping up afterwards.[3]

Brooks introduced his bill not so much to prevent passage of H.R. 1707 as to signal to his colleagues that Cabinet bills must come from his committtee. Although H.R. 1707 had more than enough cosponsors to pass on its own, it needed substantial revision to meet Brooks's standards.

Thus, late in October, Brooks dropped a new draft of the Department of Veterans Affairs Act in the hopper at the well of the House. Numbered H.R. 3417, it would be the only way veterans would get a Department. As chairman of the key authorizing committee, Brooks had declared his willingness to pursue Cabinet status, but only on his terms.

Like the two pending proposals, Thurmond's original S. 533 and its identical twin, H.R. 1707, Brooks's bill had the standard enacting clause. Unlike them, it ran eight pages longer with eight additional subsections, most dealing with name changes and nomenclature: (1) a section requiring that the Secretary of the Department "shall be appointed by the President by and with the advice and consent of the Senate," (2) a section establishing a deputy secretary, chief medical director, and chief benefits director, all also subject to Senate advice and consent, (3) a provision creating eight assistant secretary slots, relegating the mission of the old Department of Memorial Affairs to one of the eight, while leaving the designation of responsibilities for the other seven up to the new secretary, (4) a section creating the Veterans Health Services Administration to replace the existing Department of Medicine and Surgery—a *Department* of Medicine and Surgery within a *Department* of Veterans Affairs just doesn't work, (5) another creating a Veterans Benefits Administration to replace the existing Department of Veterans Benefits for the same reason, (6) a provision creating an office of General Counsel for the lawyers in the new department, (7) a section making a title change in the

Office of the Inspector General, chief watchdog of the new department, and (8) a provision requiring the newly appointed secretary to submit any additional legislation needed to smooth the transition. Figure 3 summarizes the more complex organizational structure implied in Brooks's bill.

In spite of the greater detail, this was still the floor-jack approach—albeit much more sophisticated. Aside from the rather unusual requirement that there be a regional veterans office in every state, Washington, D.C., and the Philippines (a requirement in Section 6 of the bill which preserved this one small piece of pork for every state in the event of continuing budget pressure), Brooks's bill merely added a new layer to the old structure of the VA. Political appointments would be subject to Senate confirmation and would be made "without regard to political affiliation and solely on the basis of professional integrity and demonstrated ability."

Under all three of the pending bills, Reagan would have the honor of appointing the first secretary of Veterans Affairs, since the bill would go into effect as soon as possible after passage.

That Brooks had put the energy into drafting a bill could mean only one thing: the House was going to pass a Cabinet department bill. Would Ronald Reagan stand in the way? This question was answered on November 10, 1987, one day before Veterans Day, but, more importantly, one day *after* the House Government Operations Committee passed its Cabinet bill.

Most assumed Reagan would say no, allowing the House to pass a Cabinet bill, while giving the Senate a reason to demur. Reagan, however, did what he had done so many times before in his administration: defy both his staff and conventional wisdom. Taking advantage of a photo opportunity, Reagan announced his support for Brooks's bill, H.R. 3417. "This is the first time you've ever tricked me," Rep. Gerald Solomon (R-N.Y.) reportedly told the president

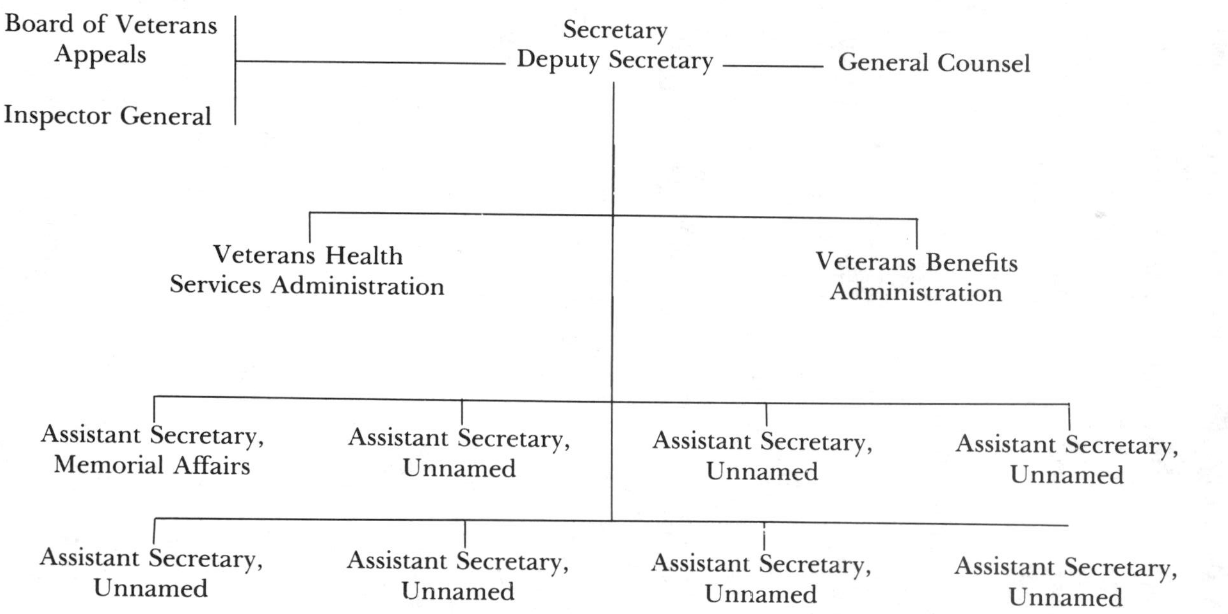

Figure 3. The Department of Veterans Affairs, H.R. 3471 as Introduced

after the meeting. "We came here to have to sell you a bill of goods, and you were already sold. Thank you." The five-minute press conference went as follows:

Remarks by the President
at Photo Opportunity with
Veteran Leaders

The Cabinet Room

11:53 A.M. EST

Q: Mr. President, are you going to have a Supreme Court Nominee today? You sort of hinted at it earlier. We wondered.

The President: Not that part of it, but right now I have an announcement to make, as—all of you that tomorrow our nation will pause and remember those veterans who've served in the armed forces—both at home and abroad. And we'll remember those who gave their last measure, fighting for what our country represents, freedom.

There's not a better time or better way to salute both that of men and women than to announce today my decision to support the creation of a Cabinet level Department of Veterans Affairs. [Applause.]

This is a personal decision that I've thought about for some time. There are six times as many veterans alive today as there were in 1930, when the agency was first created. And veterans have always had a strong voice in our government, but it's time to give them the recognition that they so rightly deserve. So, I'm joining with those here today in support of this effort.

Veteran: Thank you. [Applause.]

Q: Are you sure the Congress will go along with this? (Laughter.)

The President: Yes.

Veteran: You bet they will.

Veteran: You can count on it, you can count on it.

Q: Mr. President, a *Washington Post* columnist say [sic]

today that Ed Meese is an embarrassment to the administration and should resign. What are your feelings?

The President: I don't know where they get that idea. He's no embarrassment to me. I've known him for twenty years and I've found him of sound mind and great loyalty and capability in all that time.

The Press: Thank you.

End   11:56 A.M. EST[4]

No reporter asked the president to explain his endorsement in light of his earlier promise to abolish the departments of Energy and Education. Photo opportunities are not for asking questions anyway. Besides, it is not clear that Reagan himself could explain the decision. "It's something of a mystery to a great many folks here," one senior presidential aide told the *Washington Post*. "I don't think there was anyone here who thought he would sign off."[5]

Reagan's decision involved more than patriotic fervor, however. The only discernible motive in Reagan's endorsement was to make sure Cabinet status did not become a Democratic issue. Reagan was nothing if not a political realist. Recognizing that the House was about to pass H.R. 3417 by an overwhelming margin, he had the same choice as Brooks: jump on the bandwagon or risk getting steamrolled.

Elevation of the Veterans Administration may have been embarrassing to many as a blatant case of political pandering, but it was hardly likely to hurt any veterans, and, at an estimated cost of only $30,000 for new stationery and new building signs, elevation was a throwaway vote. As the Government Operations Committee explained its rationale in its legislative report accompanying the bill: "The veterans of this Nation have served their country well over the years. The country owes them and their families a debt of gratitude. Such a constituency should be represented in the highest councils of the land and the Committee believes it is fitting at this time to make the change."[6]

Ironically, at almost the same moment, the VA administrator was widely quoted as saying that elevation would not make an "iota of difference." What he meant, of course, was that the VA would continue delivering high quality services regardless. Nevertheless, his comment had an entirely different ring of truth.

That does not mean that everyone who voted for passage liked the idea. "It was an awful case of congressional pandering to special interest groups," said one of only seventeen House members who voted against the bill. "I can't begin to tell you how many colleagues have told me they wish they had the guts to vote against it." "It's nothing but weight lifting for the veterans lobby," said a senior House Democrat off the record. "It's a glandular thing," said Sen. Alan Simpson, the Wyoming Republican who would eventually become one of the heroes of the Cabinet fight.

This was hardly the first Cabinet seat created for a special-interest group, however. Teachers won their own Department of Education in 1978 and unions won their Department of Labor years before. Over the previous decade, ninety-nine bills had been introduced to create one department or another, including thirty-eight bills to create a Department of Peace by combining the Agency for International Development, the Peace Corps, the Arms Control and Disarmament Agency, and portions of the departments of State and Agriculture (none passed); thirty-six to create a Department of Trade by combining elements of Commerce, State, Agriculture, and Treasury (none passed); one to create the Department of Older Americans; two to create a Department of Health, one a Department of Science and Technology; one a Department of Environment and Natural Resources; and one a Department of Food, Agriculture, and Renewable Resources (none passed).[7]

Despite the rhetoric surrounding each proposal for a new department, public-administration scholars have long known that reorganization rarely accomplishes much in terms of long-term efficiency or better service. Unless cabinet reorganization is used as a vehicle for other reforms, it is primarily a symbolic gesture. When in doubt, reorganize. If a president wants to be seen as the "environmental" president, for example, far better to put more money or energy into the Environmental Protection Agency than to elevate it to Cabinet status. Likewise, if a president wants to be the "veterans" president, far better to insist on an effective agency than to throw a floor jack under the VA.

With H.R. 3417 now headed for the Senate, Glenn faced the same decision Brooks had faced only weeks before. Engrossed on special blue paper, H.R. 3417 would be referred to Governmental Affairs just like any other bill. Although Glenn would be under no obligation to take it up as formal committee business, it was clear that stopping Cabinet status for the VA would be difficult, if not impossible.

The veterans groups clearly sensed a strong chance for victory and turned their legislative steamroller toward the Senate. There was only one small committee now in the way. If Glenn didn't like H.R. 3417, he could always take up Thurmond's old S. 533 or draft his own bill. The fine print hardly mattered to the veterans groups. Just get it done.

Nevertheless, Glenn worried about moving forward. The Senate, which has to confirm every Cabinet officer, has always been reluctant to establish new departments. When establishing the Department of Energy in 1977, for example, the Governmental Affairs Committee held twelve days of hearings involving fifty different witnesses compared to just three days in the House. Just as the House has held a much stronger line on taxes, the Senate has traditionally held the line on reorganization.

Glenn, as a new committee chairman, rightly worried about being bullied into action without at least minimal thought. He did not want his committee to be seen as a pushover, nor did he take kindly to the notion that he had to step aside in deference to the House. As a national hero and life member of all the major veterans groups, Glenn had nothing to fear from the veterans lobby, or so he thought. After all, he had always been both a strong supporter of defense and veterans programs.

Also, Glenn worried about the precedents involved in establishing a Department of Veterans Affairs. How many other special-interest groups would line up to ask for their own department? Much as a Department of Veterans Affairs might help veterans win a bigger slice of the national budget, few of the cosponsors asked how it would help the president.

Even though H.R. 3417 was a better bill than S. 533, it had serious drawbacks, too. Thus, even if Glenn wanted to move forward with a Cabinet bill, he would need time to draft his own alternative. Not only did H.R. 3417 increase the number of political appointees at the VA, it created a confusing and possible unworkable organization chart consisting of eight assistant secretaries and two operating directors, one for Medicine and Surgery, the other for Benefits. And it had the early effective date that gave Reagan the honor of the first appointments.

Glenn was not the first Democrat in either the House or Senate to rebel against the effective date. The Democrats, having listened to Reagan attack big government for the better part of eight years and having repelled his efforts to abolish the Departments of Education and Energy, did not want him to reap any last-minute political benefits from creating more bureaucracy.

Even after House passage, the odds of final Senate passage were still somewhat less than 100 percent. By mid-November 1987, virtually every major newspaper had come down against a Department of Veterans Affairs as a Thanksgiving turkey that ought to be stuffed. It was not just the *New York Times* or *Washington Post* either, although the *Post* did run five, count 'em, five editorials against the bill over a three-month period. The following sample of headlines merely hints at the range of angry editorials:

"The Department of Fat"
The New Republic

"Reagan should forego this veterans parade"
Minneapolis Star Tribune

"Veterans Cabinet post not needed"
San Antonio Express

"No pork for vets"
Washington Times

"Cabinet-level spot for VA completely without merit"
Austin American Statesman (Texas)

"Ronald Reagan's Surrender"
Phoenix *Arizona Republic*

"Who Needs the Flattery"
Army Times

"Reagan Panders to Special Interests"
Detroit News

"Such a Bad Idea"
Washington Post

"No More Bureaucracy Needed"
Durham Herald (North Carolina)

"Shameless play to the veterans' gallery"
Atlanta Journal / Constitution

"Bill of Goods"
Richmond Times-Dispatch

"All symbol, no substance"
Danville Commercial-News (Illinois)

"Veterans hardly need cabinet level clout"
Milwaukee Journal

"No to a Veterans' Department"
New York Times

"No to a Veteran's Department"
Washington Post

"Cabinet-level unit for vets doesn't make real sense . . ."

" . . . But VA care inquiry needed"
Philadelphia Inquirer

"Veterans are doing fine, thank you, without an invitation to gluttony," said the Durham, N.C., *Herald*.

"Children don't vote. Veterans do. Perhaps that explains why a president who tried to abolish the Department of Education now supports legislation to make the Veterans Administration a Cabinet-level department," opined the *St. Petersburg Times*.

The best editorial of the lot came from the *Minneapolis Star Tribune*: "Two world leaders made news last week for seeking to change their national bureaucracies. One received attention for efforts to cut by half the number of bureaucrats in his national capital. The other attempts to create a new ministry. Which one was Mikhail Gorbachev, leader of that most statist nation, the Soviet Union, and which was Ronald Reagan, staunch foe of big government? Clue: this is a trick question."

Even the most favorable editorials were less than overwhelming. "VA Plan Acceptable," cried the Columbia, South Carolina *State*. "Veterans Need Representation," said the Longview, Texas, *News*. "Veterans Department Needed," declared the *Near North News* of Chicago, Illinois. In the meantime, the cartoonists had a field day.

Ultimately, the most damning attacks came from Reagan's closest friends. "If the effect of departmental status is to promote unreasonable benefits, we will regret it by and by," wrote conservative columnist James J. Kilpatrick.[8] "The end of the Affair" was the title of his equally conservative colleague William Safire's piece. "Does anyone imagine that the vast new clout given the professional veterans' lobby will not cost all taxpayers (including vets not seeking the public trough) billions in the future? This is Washington; a place

Copyright © 1988 by Herblock in the *Washington Post*

at the cabinet table cannot fail to put bread on the constituency's table."[9]

Much as the veterans lobby defended elevation as the very least of what America's heroes deserved, the newspapers, cartoonists, and columnists saw cabinet status as little more than a ruse to win a bigger slice of the budget pie.

Privately, many senators were asking whether there wasn't some way to stop the juggernaut or to make an "aye" more graceful. Thus, even as the veterans lobby demanded action with an onslaught of letters and phone calls just before Thanksgiving, Glenn opted for delay, giving us the green light to draft an alternative bill.

More important, Glenn signaled his interest in giving veterans the right to sue the VA in the federal courts as part of the deal for cabinet status. Under a 1933 statute called the Economy Act, every decision made by the administrator of the VA was absolutely final. Once veterans had exhausted their internal administrative appeals, they could not go to court to challenge their government. No matter that they may have fought to protect the right of judicial review for every other American—from shop owners to welfare recipients, defense contractors to labor unions, illegal aliens to criminals. The right to judicial review was a right they did not have.

I am still not sure why we suggested judicial review in our first briefing memo. "Do we want to address other organizational questions alongside this bill—for example, judicial review of VA benefit decisions, giving veterans the right to sue VA?" Nor am I sure why Glenn caught it. He had cosponsored judicial review legislation before and had always voted "aye," but had never been a fiery champion on the floor. That role had fallen to others, most notably former Veterans Committee chairman Alan Simpson (R-Wyo.), who had succeeded in winning Senate passage only to see the bill die repeatedly in the House Veterans Committee.

Nevertheless, the suggestion was there, Glenn paid attention to it, and the seeds of a year-long fight were sown. Perhaps Glenn felt that including judicial review was the right thing to do. Much as political scientists and pundits like to find hidden motives in the actions of politicians, Glenn never talked about judicial review as anything but a right veterans should have. Glenn, having laid his own life on the line so many times, just questioned why veterans were denied a right they fought to defend. Judicial review seemed like such a simple thing.

Before starting the drafting process, however, Glenn had to dilute some of the lobbying pressure. The VA bill had what former presidential candidate George Bush had once called "Big Mo," or momentum. One of the House sponsors had even promised a Cabinet bill on the president's desk by Christmas. Unless Glenn did something to mark the committee's territory quickly, the Senate might act with or without Governmental Affairs.

Unfortunately for me, Glenn decided to advance the first Cabinet hearing from February to early December, giving me two weeks to mount the hearing. As the following checklist suggests, a successful hearing is only slightly less intense than staging a successful Broadway show:

1. Audition the cast—since this was to be the "pro" hearing, we went to the list of "usual suspects": vets groups, past and current VA administrators, and the key Senate and House sponsors.
2. Write the chairman's soliloquy—although Glenn always did a fair amount of editing on these drafts, it was pretty much up to staff to shape the direction of his initial comments; in this case, Glenn's statement signaled a reluctance to move the bill by Christmas.
3. Rehearse the witnesses—it is perfectly appropriate to help a friendly witness prepare for a specific line of questions; what we wanted from the past administrators, for example, was an explanation of why their president hadn't recommended elevation.
4. Write the playbill—part of the challenge for any hearing is to get favorable press coverage; our primary message was that Glenn was opening the debate on Cabinet status, not merely waving at the train.
5. Write the chairman's script (questions and answers)—although Glenn often followed his own instincts in questioning a witness, staff must prepare

questions and likely answers just in case; for this hearing, we worked up a line on the possible problems with the number of political appointees in the new department.

6. Hold prehearing run-throughs for committee staff— up to this point in the process, other senators and their staffs only know that the hearing is scheduled and who will testify; this briefing is to telegraph any specific directions the chairman wants the other members to follow, giving other staff an opportunity to find a niche for their bosses.

7. Prepare the director's script—again, assembling all the speeches, testimony, lines of questions and answers is no big deal, unless, of course, the witnesses happen to be late with their testimony or you happen to be late with your questions and answers; just get every scrap of paper into an ordered black binder.

8. Brief the chairman—no big deal either, unless the senator happens to be tied up in negotiations on the floor or in another committee; for this particular hearing time we had to wait only until 7:30 P.M.

9. Rehearse any special witnesses again—it is perfectly appropriate to work through a line of questioning one last time with a special witness.

10. Hold hearing—opening night!

11. Review the notices—collecting the press clips and such is part of proving that the hearing went well.

12. Correct the transcripts—both the House and Senate are big on allowing their members to correct the record, including the deletion of particularly embarrassing or unflattering statements; Glenn's approach was to leave everything in except for typos, making our job a lot easier, but the transcripts perhaps somewhat less elegant.

13. Check final copy proofs prior to the publication of the hearing—the last step in the process and the most tedious.[10]

That this was to be a one-sided hearing was obvious in the list of lead-off witnesses: Strom Thurmond and Frank Murkowski, both from the Senate Veterans Affairs Committee, Jack Brooks, the prime sponsor in the House, and his key Veterans Committee sponsors, Montgomery Solomon. The four Veterans Committee members had asked Glenn if they could testify; we had invited Brooks as a courtesy to our companion committee and to remind the Veterans Committees in both chambers that this was still a government organization bill.[11]

The second panel consisted of the VA's administrator, Thomas Turnage, and two former administrators, Max Cleland (under President Jimmy Carter) and Harry Walters (under Reagan), followed by a third panel of representatives from the veterans lobby. Interestingly enough, we got into a fight with the veterans lobby over the order in which the five groups would testify. We had drawn the order at random, with the VVA to testify first. The big groups—the American Legion, the DAV, and the VFW—didn't think much of the VVA, partly because of its smaller size and partly because of its efforts to reform the VA. The fire fight needed to defend this trivial decision to the groups, while brief, was a harbinger of what we were to face later in the process.

That we were looking for alternatives to Cabinet elevation was obvious in Glenn's opening statement. That Glenn was already feeling the heat for delays was clear in his opening line: "I want to start out by saying at the very beginning that I certainly do not intend to delay this issue, but we also do want to look at it so that as we establish a new department, we do it in a proper way and one that is going to be most beneficial for the future."*

Facing an audience composed almost entirely of veterans group members, each wearing a corporal's cap with a post insignia, staring into the hot lights of live C-SPAN coverage,

---

* All of the hearing quotes are taken from Senate Committee on Governmental Affairs, *Proposals to Elevate the Veterans' Administration to Cabinet Status*, S.R. 100th Cong., 1st Sess., December 9, 1987, and March 15, 29, 1988. I have elected not to clutter the text with endless footnotes and page references in the hopes that the reader will trust my faithful reporting.

and knowing that thirty-nine senators were now cosponsors of S. 533, Glenn nevertheless promised at least one more hearing early in the very next session, "but I wanted to indicate that I am certainly not trying to delay this. We just want to do it right when we do it."

The rest of his statement consisted of one question after another. What are the pros and cons of elevation? How much will it really cost? Should we elevate Social Security at the same time? How many political appointees do we need? Should we put the benefits program and the medical program at the same level? What kinds of assistant secretaries should there be? "This was not meant to be a balanced hearing this morning," he concluded. "We will balance it off with other hearings later on that will take different viewpoints of this."

Former Governmental Affairs chairman William Roth (R-Del.) also addressed the "do it right" theme: "Should the legislation pass, the question then becomes one of what have we created? Are we simply making a hollow, symbolic gesture, or creating higher visibility and a full voice in shaping policy for our veterans? And while we construct the department for our nation's best, are we simply legislating new stationery or indeed providing an improved internal management and fully accountable benefit delivery system?" Roth's comments were echoed by committee members David Pryor (D-Ark.) and George Mitchell (D-Maine), as the hearing room fell quiet.

The veterans were starting to realize that a Cabinet bill was no longer possible by Christmas and that it might just be in jeopardy altogether. The committee clearly did not want to be rolled on cabinet status. Carl Levin (D-Mich.), of all the committee members, was the toughest, providing a good example of how a former city attorney can rattle a witness, in this case VA administrator Turnage. With his reading glasses perched precariously on his nose, Levin worked quickly, no pauses for effect, no visible anger, just plain old-fashioned hammering:

Senator Levin: My understanding is that the president can make the VA administrator a member of his Cabinet at any time he wants to. . . . Do you know why President Reagan has not invited you to sit in the Cabinet, since he supports the VA becoming a department now?

Mr. Turnage: No sir. My principal role in this entire affair has been to support within the administration, and I have tried to do it in a most delicate way without personal implications. . . . and I cannot tell you whether or not your first statement was true, that he has the authority to do that now. I have not even inquired.

Senator Levin: Well, assuming that it is true, do you know why he just simply does not—

Mr. Turnage: No, sir.

Senator Levin: Well, is that not a pretty critical issue for us, while we are working on this legislation which would make the VA a department? One of the effects of that is to make the head of VA a secretary of the department and have Cabinet status, but the head of the VA can have Cabinet status right now without us doing anything.

Mr. Turnage: It may be less delicate if you made that recommendation, as opposed to me.

Senator Levin: Well, sir, you have advocated the elevation to Cabinet status, have you not?

Mr. Turnage: Yes sir, he has and—

Senator Levin: No, you have.

Mr. Turnage: I have.

Senator Levin: So what is the delicacy? You have already advocated this.

Mr. Turnage: First of all, if this legislation passes, sir, and the department is elevated from an agency to a department, then it still is within the President's prerogative to make his choice of who that secretary will be. . . . So, I think because of the personal implications of that, that would be someone else's choice, not mine.

Senator Levin: Mr. Chariman, I think it would be useful for our Committee to ask the President why the VA Administrator has not been given Cabinet status since he supports the Veteran's Administration becoming a department. Could we make that inquiry of the White House?

Senator Glenn: I am sure we could.

Senator Levin: President Carter did do this, and one of the advantages to having the VA as a department is that the Administrator then becomes a Secretary and sits in the Cabinet. That again can be accomplished, I assure you, there are now members of the Cabinet who are not heads of departments.

Mr. Turnage: Yes, sir.

Senator Levin: And I assure you also that the VA Administrator under President Carter was a member of the Cabinet. I assure you of both those things. That being true, I think it would be useful for this Committee to ask the question which apparently you find too delicate for yourself to ask.

Mr. Turnage: I hope you appreciate my position.

Senator Levin: Not really, frankly, You have advocated this strongly, you say in your testimony. . . .

Mr. Turnage: Yes.

Senator Levin: It sounds to me like you have already strongly advocated within the administration the elevation to Cabinet status, so I do not understand the delicacy of your position, but, nonetheless we will find out the answer to this question.

Glenn and Levin eventually cosigned a letter to Reagan asking the question directly. However, Levin was wrong in at least one respect: the committee never got an answer. For the veterans groups, an Executive Order was not enough—it could always be overturned by the next president.

The most interesting comments of the day came from Brooks. As always, it was not so much what Brooks said, but how he said it. Here was a good old-fashioned Texas politician, one of the last of a fading breed, a man who clearly loved what he was doing. As chairman of his committee for roughly forever, Brooks had drafted most of the basic statutes on government organization and management. He was a walking encyclopedia of detail, a bulldog of a representative, a cigar always in his pocket, and a razor-edged wit at the ready. No wonder the House so often followed his lead. He had been around long enough to educate almost all of the members.

His testimony this day did not disappoint. After saluting Chairman Glenn—"I am not one of those who thinks you are still in orbit"—Brooks gave a short endorsement of the Cabinet bill. "This is a great bill and it is not going to do any harm to anybody." He then launched into a stinging attack on the VA. "I would just add that in my district we know all the facts and figures about the VA system," he said. "There is about $26 billion. They might even save money if they will just get their head in the game. I wish they would give me $26 billion to do [what they do]." Laughter. "I could do it for a little less." More laughter. "I think everybody can tighten up and do a little better and I would hope that the VA would do a little better with this Cabinet status. I think they are going to be under a lot more scrutiny by Congress and by the American people, so I expect them to shape up if they are going to be wearing those fancy suits."

Brooks then showed his tougher side, censuring the VA for mismanagement of the home loan program in his home district of southeast Texas. "Many of these homes could have been saved for the veterans who own them and who were trying to pay for them, and the cost of foreclosing and disposing could have been avoided if the VA had better used the resources and powers under the laws presently available. I hope that they will." All in all, it was hardly a ringing endorsement of the Cabinet bill. This was not an agency that had earned elevation through good performance. Although Brooks ended his brief statement by asking for speedy passage, his remarks may have toughened Glenn's resolve to do something more than floor jack the VA to the Cabinet table.

The only other excitement in the hearing came from the upstart VVA. With the other groups sitting side by side at the witness table, the VVA witness proceeded to dress down the Veterans Administration: "In our judgment, the VA has been free to abuse veterans' programs and the benefits adjudication processes because of wide-ranging unchecked discretionary authority. We know that the VA has resisted congressional intent in some instances. . . . The VA has even disregarded legal processes, and an example of that came last spring when the VA was fined $115,000 by a Federal judge for destroying documents critical to a discovery process in a case brought by the National Association of Radiation Survivors." Therein, of course, was our legislative redemption, for in offerning this list of reform, the VVA supported Glenn's growing interest in judicial review.

Despite our effort to frame the hearing as the opening salvo in the Cabinet fight, the newspaper editorials were unforgiving. The *Washington Post* attacked the witness list in a lead editorial titled "Department of the Month Club": "The witness list suggests what is already wrong with this agency. The veterans' groups, the present and two former veterans' administrators and senior members of the congressional veterans' committees were the ones to testify—all in favor, of course. No one came from the world outside."[12] The *New York Times* was even harsher in a piece titled "Veterans Stampede Congress": "Senator John Glenn, chairman of the Governmental Affairs Committee, accommodated the stampede by moving up to last Wednesday a hearing that originally had been scheduled for February. He now can give reason and responsibility their turn simply by holding off any further action until at least February. Perhaps after a few weeks of sober reflection, a majority of the Senate will appreciate the unwise precedent they would be setting."[13]

It was impossible to tell if the editorials had a sobering effect on the veterans lobby and the House. Perhaps they agreed with Rep. Montgomery's analysis of the editorializing: "Curiously, many of these editorials share an entirely too coincidental similarity in words, phrasing and clichés, that suggest a concerted effort to prevent this long-overdue action. I have to wonder why when such a move is in the best national interest, involves insignificant costs, does not expand government, and affords the Nation's defenders the deference they have earned. Why would editorial boards oppose it?"[14]

Moreover, even as the editorials chastised Glenn for moving too fast, the news pages were dutifully warning the veterans groups of delays. A *Washington Post* news story ran under the headline "Senators Fear Politicization of the VA: Plan for Cabinet-level Status Would Add Political Appointees." The *Columbus Post-Dispatch* story was titled "Glenn questions VA Strategy: Giving agency cabinet status may not help veterans." Even *U.S. Medicine*, a normally calm trade publication widely read inside the VA, seemed to overstate the hearing results with its headline "VA Cabinet Proposal Stalls." We were between a rock and a hard place, unable to move without angering the editorialists and pinned down by heavy fire from the veterans groups.

The key players in this evolving play are summarized in Table One.

It was increasingly apparent that the Cabinet bill was to be cast as a test of patriotic stamina, of love of country. Had Glenn not been a former Marine of unquestioned courage, we might have surrendered right then.

Table 1.
Dramatis Personae

JOHN GLENN	Democratic senator from Ohio, chairman of Senate Governmental Affairs, strong supporter of judicial review
ALAN SIMPSON	Republican Senator from Wyoming, conservative, strong opponent of Cabinet status, leader of judicial review
ALAN CRANSTON	Democratic senator from California, chairman of Senate Veterans Affairs, strong supporter of judicial review, strong opponent of linkage between Cabinet status and judicial review

STROM THURMOND	Republican senator from South Carolina, strongest supporter of Cabinet status
JACK BROOKS	Democratic representative from Texas, chairman of House Government Operations, general supporter of Cabinet status, no known position on judicial review
G. V. "SONNY" MONTGOMERY	Democratic representative from Mississippi, chairman of House Veterans Affairs, strong supporter of Cabinet status, strong opponent of judicial review, absolute opponent of linkage
RONALD REAGAN	Two-term president of the United States, strong conservative opposed to big government, supporter of Cabinet status, no clear position on judicial review or linkage
U.S. SENATE	Strong supporter of judicial review (four times), general supporter of Cabinet status, generally opposed to linkage
U.S. HOUSE	Strong supporter of Cabinet status for VA, growing supporter of judicial review, likely opponent of linkage, but not clear
VETERANS ADMINISTRATION	Absolute opponent of judicial review, strong supporter of Cabinet status, absolute opponent of linkage
EDITORIAL WRITERS	Strong opponents of Cabinet status, strong supporters of judicial review for veterans, strong supporters of linkage
BIG VETERANS GROUPS	Strong supporters of Cabinet status, traditional opponents of judicial review, absolute opponents of linkage
VIETNAM VETS OF AMERICA	Strong supporter of judicial review, general supporter of Cabinet status, strong supporter of linkage

Charge of the Very Light Brigade (Drafting)

EVERY DRAFTING PROCESS is haunted by the ghost of legislation past. So, too, was the Department of Veterans Affairs Act. Reading the veterans code was like stepping into a time warp going back through history, as one war and its benefits package flashed by with each turn of the page.

Located in the 619 finely printed pages of law that comprised the current veterans cumulative statute were references to the Spanish-American War, the Mexican border campaign, the Philippine Insurrection, the Boxer Rebellion, and hostilities in the Moro Province (look that one up in the history books). There is a reason why the statute carried all the old wars, of course. As of 1987, there were three living Spanish-American War veterans and sixty living veterans of the Mexican campaign.

The code also contained an obscure historical provision denying veterans the right of judicial review—a provision many senators felt had long outlived its purpose. Passed in 1933 as part of the Economy Act, the ban was designed to protect the Veterans Administration from thousands of suits by veterans who were about to lose benefits they had won just three years earlier in legislation passed under Herbert Hoover.[1]

What no one could have known at the time was that the Economy Act would become part of an intense legislative struggle over the question of VA Cabinet status fifty years later, for under Section 5 of H.R. 2820, passed March 20, 1933, "All decisions rendered by the Administrator of Veterans' Affairs under the provisions of this title, or the regulations issued pursuant thereto, shall be final and conclusive on all questions of law and fact, and no other official or court of the United States shall have jurisdiction to review by mandamus or otherwise any such decision."[2] Simply put, veterans who felt wronged by VA could not take their case to court for judicial reversal.*

To this day, the Economy Act stands as one of the most sweeping grants of judicial and legislative powers ever given to the executive, a testament to the legislative panic of Franklin Delano Roosevelt's first one hundred days in office.

At the time, neither Congress nor the veterans groups seemed to grasp the enormity of the Economy Act. Nor did they understand that Roosevelt would use his new-found powers to cut veterans benefits, even as the prohibition against judicial review protected the VA against court action by veterans who were about to lose their pensions. In fact,

---

* Over the years, this prohibition against judicial review was strengthened to read as follows: "the decisions of the Administrator on any question of law or fact under any law administered by the Veterans' Administration providing benefits for veterans and their dependents or survivors shall be final and conclusive and no other official or any court of the United States shall have power or jurisdiction to review any such decision by an action in the nature of mandamus or otherwise."

What a difference a preposition makes. Changing "*by* the Administrator" to "*of* the Administrator," for example, tightened the ban by making any and all decisions of the VA, not just those formally made at the Administrator's desk, final. Adding the term "under any law administered by the Veterans' Administration" broadened the prohibition to legislation not codified as part of the veterans code.

the only objection to be found in the legislative history of the Economy Act at the Franklin Delano Roosevelt Presidential Library came from the California chapters of the American Legion, VFW, and United Spanish War Veterans (a group no longer in existence) in a joint telegram to the national commander of the VFW:

```
SPEAKING FOR ONE HUNDRED THOUSAND
OF VETERANS OF CALIFORNIA WE ARE
MILITANT AND ORGANIZED  STOP  WE
HAVE IMPLICIT FAITH IN THE PRESI-
DENT OF THE UNITEDSTATES IN THIS
HOUR OF EMERGENCY IN OUR COUNTRY
STOP  WE ARE UNALTERABLY OPPOSED
TO AND VIGOROUSLY DENOUNCE ANY
CONTEMPLATED ACTION ON THE PART
OF OUR REPRESENTATIVES IN THE
UNITEDSTATES SENATE TO ANY DELE-
GATION OF CONSTITUTIONAL POWERS
OF OUR LEGISLATIVE REPRESENTA-
TIVE PERTAINING TO ANY MATTER
INVOLVING VETERAN BENEFITS AND
IT IS BECAUSE OF OUR BELIEF IN
AND OUR FORMER SUPPORT TO THOSE
WHO AND IN THOSE WHO NOW EXECUTE
ALL POWER OF GOVERNMENT THAT WE
ASK YOU AS ONE REPRESENTATIVE TO
A MAJOR VETERANS ORGANIZATION TO
PRESENT TO THE HONORABLE FRANKLIN
D ROOSEVELT THIS MSG  STOP  WE
BELIEVE IN ECONOMY  STOP  TAKING
FROM THOSE WHO HAVE NOT AND
GIVING TO THOSE WHO HAVE IS NOT
ACCORDING TO OUR LIGHTS GOOD SOUND
ECONOMY FOR THE MASSES OF CITIZENS
IN THESE UNITEDSTATES  STOP  WE
BESEECH YOU TO PERSONALLY LAY BE-
FORE THE PRESIDENT OF THE UNITED-
STATES OUR URGENT PLEA  STOP [3]
```

Even after Roosevelt slashed veterans benefits under the twelve Executive Orders authorized by the Economy Act, the national veterans organizations remained quiet. What the veterans had won in 1930, they quietly surrendered in 1933.

By the time Congress finally figured out what it had done, it was too late to stop the cuts. Senator Robinson of Indiana called the legislation "misrepresentation of the worst hue. . . . trickery and nothing less than that, because it had a sound with its weasel words that might somehow or other be attractive to the American people. . . . deceit, pure and simple," while Senator Cutting of New Mexico described the Economy Act as "the most infamous act ever passed by the Congress of the United States." Their rhetoric was tame compared to that of Louisiana's Senator Huey Long, the populist who would later be assassinated in his home state:

> How long are we going to sit here and see people turned out of hospitals and starved to death by these little 2-by-4, squinteyed experts, fumbling around under their desks and issuing pronunciamentos, and exercising more authority than the 96 members of the United States Senate. It is one of the most disgraceful things that have ever occurred in the history of our country. . . . Instead of being men, standing up on 2 legs and 2 feet, and running this Government for the people of the United States, we are authorizing some little 2-by-4, two-bit job-hunting politician to prescribe limits and rules under which he will work, and then he goes off and does what he pleases. That is the trouble with the whole "plague-and-take-it" outfit, and that is the reason why the veterans are in the fix in which they find themselves today.[4]

Remarkably, however, the veterans lobby eventually came to support the Economy Act. As the veterans lobby built an agency virtually brick by brick, it became as much a part of the VA as the bureaucrats themselves. Criticism of the VA increasingly became criticism of the veterans groups.

By 1987, it was almost impossible to tell where the VA ended and the veterans lobby began. The top jobs at the VA were either reserved for the veterans groups or subject to their veto.[5] The veterans groups still had free office space in virtually every hospital, clinic, and benefit office across the country—space that they used as beachhead for five thousand bureaucratic commandos called "veterans service representatives" who provided free help to any veteran who asked.

Although the VA benefits process was designed to be "user friendly," most veterans found the free help offered by the veterans groups irresistible, particularly if they had to appeal a negative decision to the next bureaucratic level. For one thing, veterans had almost no alternative if they wanted help. Under a Civil War law still in effect in 1987, attorneys were not allowed to charge a veteran more than ten dollars to represent a claim—not ten dollars an hour or ten dollars a day, but ten dollars total, start to finish.

For another, the service reps had earned a reputation for acheiving success. After all, they had become the institutional grease of the VA, acting as informal administrative gatekeepers. They screened the applicants, filed the paperwork, haggled with VA adjudicators, and usually provided the first word on the final decision. In many ways, the veterans groups service reps did work for their clients that the VA should have been doing for everyone, whether represented or not.

Little wonder then that of the 3.8 million initial claims filed in 1987, over half were represented by the veterans groups, and, of the nearly 40,000 cases appealed upward after denial, only 14 percent were *not* represented by the veterans groups.[6]

Unfortunately, the VA hardly viewed the office space as "free" at all, but as one possible lever *against* the veterans groups. In 1985, for example, the VA warned the groups of the dire consequences that would result should the Economy Act be repealed under then-pending legislation: "many special considerations currently extended to veterans service organizations may have to be curtailed. The providing of VA space and facilities, informal access to adjudicatory personnel, etc., could be affected by judicial oversight and increased representation by private attorneys."[7] The implication was that rent of some nature, although impossible to quantify, would be charged to the vets groups.

More troubling was that several of the veterans groups used the free space and the increased access as a way to recruit new members. None of the veterans groups required a membership card before providing representation per se. Indeed, the Vietnam Veterans of America (VVA), for example, explicitly instructed its representatives that "in no circumstances should a VVA Service Representative suggest to a potential client that (s)he should join VVA in order to have his/her case accepted for representation."[8]

Rather, individual veterans sometimes got the not so subtle message that joining the vets group might increase their chance of winning a claim. Take the following form letter used by a branch of the Disabled American Veterans (DAV) to inform clients of decisions pending inside the VA. Note that the DAV office announces the benefit decision long before the veteran gets a letter from the VA. Note also the membership pitch in paragraph five and the mailing address at the top of the letter:

Disabled American Veterans
VA Regional Office
VA Center Bldg 6, Room C-231
Wood, Wisconsin 53193

August 19,1985

Dear——— :

This is regarding your claim for service-connection of Post-Traumatic Stress Disorder.

I personally presented your case to the Rating Board today. I am pleased to inform you that based on the evidence of record, including your recent Veterans Administration examination, the VA has granted your claim. You have been awarded a 10% evaluation for the above disability.

You will receive an official letter from the VA concerning this matter. The VA will inform you of the amount of compensation payable, and the effective date of your award. Shortly after you receive the VA letter, you will receive a check for all benefits due.

Due to the establishment of a new service-connected disability, you may be entitled to life insurance through the VA. The VA Insurance Office will notify you of the procedure to follow to apply for this insurance. If you need assistance in this, please contact us.

A review of our State membership file indicates that you are not currently a member of our organization. The representation provided by this office is wholly supported by the Disabled American Veterans and we must rely on membership to continue our work. I am enclosing a Membership Application for your consideration. . . .

Please return your application for membership to this office.

Not too subtle at all. No wonder it was hard to tell where the VA ended and the veterans groups began.

This tight relationship between the VA and the veterans lobby hardly constituted a case for judicial review, however. There was certainly nothing wrong with service representatives as long as veterans understood the cost. Would that all clients of government had such effective guardians. Moreover, as many senators and House members argued, what was so wrong with keeping lawyers out anyway? To some, judicial review legislation might as well have been titled the Lawyers Full-Employment Act.

To appreciate the case for judicial review, however, I had

to learn much more about how the benefits process worked, which was another trip into a long-lost world, a maze of internal regulations and endless paperwork. Although the following bureaucratic "map" oversimplifies what was a very complicated journey, it does provide a feel for what individual veterans faced when they applied for help in 1987.

Step One: Apply

Like many public programs created in the 1930s, veterans benefits were available only to those who applied. It was a "seek and ye shall find" system. Simply put, veterans needed enough information and interest to find the program, for the program would almost certainly not find them.

It was logical, therefore, that the benefits process would begin only when a veteran submitted an application at one of the VA's fifty-eight regional benefit offices, which were located in every state and Puerto Rico. Again, veterans injured in service were eligible for service-connected *compensation*; those injured after discharge were eligible for nonservice-connected *pensions*, provided they could prove their income did not exceed certain income levels under a so-called means test.

Filling out the application form was not always as easy as it sounded in the VA's advertisements about its informal system, however. For the most part, it was up to the applicants to obtain their old service records from the Department of Defense, and assemble any and all other materials required to complete the claim, including birth certificates for dependents, marriage certificates, employment histories, physicians' statements, and corroborating evidence. If essential evidence was missing, the regional office was required to give the veteran at least sixty days to respond before closing the file. (As I was to find out, some of the regional offices sometimes "forgot" to tell the veteran about the missing information, failing to notify the veteran of the problem, but eventually denying the claim for a "failure to prosecute" nonetheless.)

This process was complicated by the continuing effects of a 1973 fire at the Defense Department records center in St. Louis. In all, the fire destroyed eighteen million records, including the files of all army personnel discharged during World War II, the Korean War, and the 1950s, and air force personnel with last names beginning with the letters I–Z discharged during the Korean War and the 1950s. Those who were affected had to reconstruct their records as best they could.[9]

Step Two: Develop the Claim

Once a veteran submitted an application, the VA was required by regulation to help develop the claim—that is, to seek any additional information needed and prepare the file for a decision. Oftentimes, the VA's role in developing a claim involved nothing more than sending the applicant a letter asking for additional materials. But, when an application indicated a reasonable probability of a valid claim, the office was also required to schedule a physical exam at a local VA hospital or clinic.

It is impossible to overestimate the importance of this second step, for the factual record contained in the claim file, and in that file only, determined the final decision. The VA claims process was both informal and "ex parte" in nature. Indeed, VA regulations clearly specified that the benefit of the doubt would always go to the veteran—that is, every one was to take the side of the veteran; there was no other side.[10]

These regulations notwithstanding, the veteran still bore the "de facto," or actual, burden of proof. It was entirely up to the veteran to "submit evidence sufficient to justify a belief in a fair and impartial mind that the claim is well grounded."[11] This burden became particularly difficult in the more complex cases where the scientific evidence was murky and the automatic "presumption" of a service-connected disability nonexistent.

Step Three: Initial Decision

Once the file was complete, with every piece of paper in the proper order, a rating board composed of a medical specialist (not necessarily an M.D.), a legal specialist (not necessarily a lawyer), and an occupational specialist made the first of several "final" decisions.

The board, using a forty-year-old disability schedule to guide its decisions, asked two basic questions about each claim: (1) was the veteran's injury received in service, and (2) how disabling was the injury today? If the answer to the first question was "no," compensation was denied, leaving the veteran to apply for a means-tested pension. If the answer was "yes," the veteran was automatically entitled to priority medical care, even if the disability was rated zero percent disabling.

The problem with using such an old rating schedule is that rates of recovery and disability change over time with medical advances. The heart attack that would have crippled its victim in the 1950s could be prevented with a bypass surgery operation and six weeks of recovering in the 1980s.

Step Four: Notification

Whatever the rating board's decision, the veteran was to be notified immediately, although the VA's was often the second word. The service reps usually gave the news, sometimes with a membership appeal, to their clients long before the letter came from the VA. Technically, however, the claim was not resolved until the VA sent the veteran a "notice of decision" that explained both the basis for the denial and the veteran's rights of appeal.

To be fair, most of the VA's three million claims were handled with little or no disagreement—the system was informal, the representation more than adequate. Even though the benefits process had been troubled by increasing delays, veterans were mostly willing to give the VA the benefit of the doubt.

Step Five: First Disagreement

But for veterans who felt wronged, the system could become a quagmire of endless appeals even though the process started innocently enough. To challenge a decision, all a veteran had to do was submit a "notice of disagreement" within a year. All the notice needed to say was that he or she disagreed with the VA. A handwritten note would clearly do, though many service reps preferred a certified letter just to make sure, the VA logged the disagreement immediately. Given that many VA offices were overworked and understaffed, merely opening the mail in a timely fashion took effort.

Step Six: Statement of the Case

Once the VA received the veteran's appeal, it was required to develop a "statement of the case" summarizing all of the facts, arguments, and conclusions that led to the denial. In theory, this statement would help veterans perfect their claims on the way through the appeals process informing them of weaknesses in evidence and specific findings of fact. In reality, most statements were a jumble of legalese, filled with code words referring to the VA's internal regulations and schedules.

Nevertheless, the findings of fact were a key to eventual appeal, for the findings told the veterans what the VA did and did not believe about a specific claim, conclusions that had clear consequences for each applicant. If the VA concluded, for example, that a veteran was not injured in service, that veteran would not be eligible for service-connected compensation. If the VA concluded that a specific atomic test was not a cause of a veteran's cancer, that veteran would not be eligible for VA health care. Alas, even if the VA made a mistake in a finding of fact, the Economy Act prohibited any challenge in court.

Step Seven: Second Disagreement

After a veteran received the statement of the case, he or she had sixty days to (1) ask for a personal hearing before the rating board that denied the initial claim, (2) appeal the decision to the Board of Veterans Appeals (BVA) in Washington, or (3) accept the denial.

An appearance before the local rating board was generally useless. It was rare indeed that a rating board reversed itself. Acquiescence was simple: the veteran could merely let the sixty-day clock run out and the case would be automatically closed. Appeal was hardly more complicated: the veteran had to fill out a one-page document that stated, according to the instructions, "in specific detail the benefits sought on appeal and your reasons for believing that the action appealed from is erroneous."

A veteran who took this step had now disagreed with the VA at least twice: once with the notice of disagreement, and again following the statement of the case. By this time, the claim could have been in the system for at least six months, if not much longer. It should be easy to understand why some veterans just gave up. Some just did not have the energy to pursue their claims. "Applying for benefits should not be another Bataan Death March," one veteran lobbyist remarked. Following up an appeal often took more time than the veteran had spent in the military.

Step Eight: Final Appeal

The Board of Veterans Appeals was theoretically the final arbiter of all disagreements. Even in the court of last resort, however, the veteran was hardly finished. After reviewing a given claim for anywhere from three months to five years, the BVA might grant the appeal, deny the appeal outright, or remand the appeal to the regional office from whence it came for further "perfecting"—perhaps a new medical examination or more paperwork for the veteran.

For the one appeal in five that was granted, the process was now over: the veteran had won. For the one in four remanded, the process could linger on indefinitely: a claim could disappear for years as the regional office and the BVA bantered about the need for additional information. Finally, for the three in five actually denied, there was always the option of a request for "reconsideration" based on new evidence or an allegation of an obvious error of fact or law, which meant starting the process all over again at the regional-office level.

Whatever the BVA's decision, veterans who happened to live in certain congressional districts or states, namely those of the chairmen and ranking members of the House and Senate Veterans Affairs Committees, always received a personally signed decision from the chairman of the Board of Veterans Appeals. Small solace for those who lost.

There was no doubt that this system was designed to be friendly. For most veterans, it most certainly was. They applied for benefits and won. But for veterans who felt wronged by the system, this was anything but a friendly, informal process. There was no option but to slug it out within the system.[12]

Unfortunately, by 1987 the VA benefit process was reeling from a decade of budget and staff cuts. Delays in processing claims were increasing, administrative fairness was in jeopardy, veterans were prohibited from hiring private attorneys to help sort out the problems, and the final arbiter of disputes, the Board of Veterans Appeals, was on the verge of complete collapse.

The VA's antiquated computer tracking system was a prime example of the breakdown. Working with a tiny computer budget, the VA could not keep track of its workload. But if the agency did not know where a claim was in its own process, it could not know whether the claim was being handled properly or quickly.

Moreover, the VA could not even know many claims it had pending at any given moment in the day, week, month, or year.* In fact, the VA's computer system was so outdated that every office had to hand count its files every Monday morning to know how many claims were pending. Even with a hand count, the VA couldn't be sure of the number, for Monday mornings are notorious for high employee absenteeism. Employees who were out could not count the files on their desks.

For the veteran waiting for a decision and the benefit check that might follow, the VA's tracking system promised far more than it could possibly deliver. As one General Accounting Office (GAO) investigator told me in my early visits, "This system defies audit and understanding. The cases selected for quality-review are easy to manipulate to show the best possible error rates, and local office directors are in charge of evaluating their own performance one way or the other. It is impossible to know what the real error rates are." Consider, for example, two cases that illustrate the delays:

Veteran A

Application: 8/84
First denial notice: 10/85
Notice of disagreement: 10/86
Statement of the case: 12/86
Appeal filed to BVA: 1/87
BVA hearing: 11/87
BVA remands case to regional office: 12/87

Total time pending as of 3/88: 3 years, 7 months
Time for regional office to make initial denial: 1 year, 2 months

* When pressed by Glenn in 1988 to merely count the total number of claims in the system, the VA could not account for January 1, 1980, through March 31, 1984; July 1984; September and October 1985; and November 1986. Nor did the VA know how many claims were pending on January 1, 1988.

Time for BVA to hold hearing after appeal made:
10 months
Time pending at BVA since appeal: 1 year, 2 months

Veteran B

Application: 11/83
First denial notice: 10/84
Notice of disagreement: 10/84
Statement of the case: 11/84
Appeal filed to BVA: 2/85
BVA hearing: 11/86
BVA denies benefits: 10/87

Total time pending: 3 years, 11 months
Time for regional office to make initial denial: 11 months
Time for BVA to hold hearing after appeal made: 1 year,
9 months
Time pending at BVA before final decision: 2 years,
8 months

According to the private attorney representing the two
veterans, "Such delays are outrageous, particularly when
compared to the deadlines imposed by federal law in other
programs. In the AFDC [Aid to Families with Dependent
Children] program, for example, an applicant must receive
an initial decision on eligibility within 45 days of application.
. . . There is no reason why welfare applicants should have
the right to decisions in a matter of weeks while a veteran's
application can remain pending for four years or more."[13]

Scattered internal documents buried within the VA confirmed similar problems across the case load. That we had
access to the documents was entirely due to a VA "whistleblower" who leaked the material to the Governmental Affairs Committee in early January. The documents came to
us in a simple brown envelope. (Congressional committees
thrive on whistleblowers, those people within agencies who
identify internal problems even at the risk of losing their
own jobs. Given the channels of political review at the top
of an agency, it is often impossible for Congress to ever get

at the real story far below. Without an occasional leak, Congress would be far less able to do its job.)

Just about every document we received told the same story: The VA was making many more mistakes than it was counting in its official statistics. One of the reports showed "a 26.6 percent chance of a case, picked at random having a substantive or judgmental error. There was a 3.5 percent chance that the VA will err in favor of the claimant. There was a 13.7 percent chance that the VA will make an error that would work against the claimant." Another noted "a national pattern of failure to take action, improper development [of cases], inadequate notification and premature denial. There is also a pattern of errors involving a complete absence of notification."

Still another suggested that "it is in the best interest of our managers to have their people do, as quickly as they can, as many cases as possible" and that procedural fairness, such as "control of claims, supervisory review of old claims, thorough development, recognition of all issues, providing adequate notice, documenting that notice was given, and careful quality review, to adversely affect gross productivity and timeliness." If a claim folder got lost in the struggle to meet productivity targets, so be it.

On top of what would have been a daunting process for a simple case, veterans with more complicated claims faced an almost never-ending process: they could expect to go through the claim process for each shred of scientific evidence suggesting that radiation or Agent Orange might be linked to a disability such as cancer.

Perhaps the system could have worked with enough staff and resources. In the 1970s, when each of the fifty-eight regional offices had the money, there were more than enough people to write the letters, maintain the files, move the paper, schedule the hearings, and assure the due process needed to run a separate system. By 1987, however, those staff and resources had been stretched way beyond the breaking point.[14]

The lack of budget or staff did not consitute a prima facie case for judicial review, however.[15] At most, it constituted a case for more budget and staff. Yet, when it came time to divvy up scarce resources inside the VA, the benefits program had few friends. Not only was the chief benefits director paid at a lower rate than the chief medical director, the veterans code contained a provision requiring the VA to operate *no fewer* than 90,000 hospital and nursing-home beds and employ *no fewer* than 194,140 health care employees.*

With the Department of Medicine and Surgery protected by these bed and employment "floors," it should come as no surprise that the benefits program suffered first and suffered the most when the budget crunch hit in the early 1980s. Between 1976 and 1988, DVB lost nearly 40 percent of its staff, dropping by 700 or so a year from a high of just over 20,000 employees to a low of 12,600 by 1988.[16] During the same period, the work load dropped only half as fast.

The 40 percent personnel cut meant that the VA could guarantee neither due process nor fair treatment. "We have noticed not only a pattern of inadequate notification letters, but a pattern involving claims where there is no evidence that the claimant was notified at all," one of the leaked documents concluded. "There is also a pattern of claims being delayed. Part of the reason this is being done is to present a better statistical picture of the local adjudication division."

In theory, for example, the VA's rules gave every veteran the right to a hearing at any time along the way, whether to find out the status of their claim or to argue on their own behalf before the Rating Board itself. Since such hearings improve the chances of success in almost all administrative settings—in large measure because it is more difficult

---

* Constitutionally, the president cannot be required to submit any specific budget number, whether for 90,000 beds or 194,140 employees. Politically, however, the president is wise to read these congressional signals closely.

to deny a claim from a person you know than one you don't—one might have expected a very large number of hearings in the VA.

In practice, however, some veterans were denied that right by regional office personnel who saw hearings as a waste of time and bureaucratic energy. Consider the following paragraphs taken from a 1985 letter addressed to a California veteran as but one example of the antipathy toward hearings among the VA adjudicatory staff:

> We have your substantive appeal wherein you indicated you wanted a personal hearing.
>
> You are, of course, entitled to a personal hearing. It is, however, our responsibility to advise you of certain facts. First, due to the backlog of scheduled hearings, it would be most likely several months before a personal hearing could be held, and with the time allowed for typing the transcript of the hearing, could result in a substantial delay in submission of your appeal to the Board of Veterans Appeals in Washington. Secondly, a personal hearing in the Veterans Administration Regional Office, San Francisco, would be before the local rating board which has evaluated your case previously, not the Board of Veterans Appeals personnel. Thirdly, certified statements carry as much weight as in-person testimony. Fourthly, if you do not have new and material evidence, preferably medical, but would be merely restating previously furnished information, no change could be made based on the personal hearing alone.
>
> If you still wish to have a personal hearing, please advise us within 30 days, and we will be happy to schedule one for you.

These threats to due process might have been tolerated but for the fact that veterans who wanted to hire an attorney ran straight into the ten-dollar-fee limit. If a veteran discovered that the VA was being unfair, there was almost nothing to do except wait.

This is not to argue that every veteran needed an attorney. Indeed, most clearly did not, if only because their claims were simple. For example, a veteran walks in with an old shrapnel wound causing some muscle stiffness, has the records to prove the injury occurred during service, and a medical exam to confirm the disability. Claim awarded.

But there *were* times when a veteran needed extra help, largely because his or her claim was too complex for the average service representative. For example, a Vietnam veteran develops a cancer usually linked to dioxin—the main chemical agent in Agent Orange, the herbicide widely used in Vietnam—but does not have the maps and spraying records to prove exposure, and cannot prove for certain that Agent Orange caused the cancer anyway. Thus, no medical exam can confirm the linkage. Claim denied.

(What I found puzzling was that the VA fought these cases, while routinely approving service-connected benefits for diseases such as lung cancer, which was clearly related to smoking, not war, and arthritis, which was clearly linked to aging, not combat. It was as if the VA had decided to give the benefit of the doubt to World War II and Korean veterans, while always second-guessing Vietnam veterans and the "atomic" veterans of the bomb tests.)

The most powerful case for letting attorneys into the process was made by Gordon Erspamer, a San Francisco attorney with the law firm of Morrison and Foerster, who filed suit in 1983 against the fee limitation as an abridgement of the First and Fifth Amendments (freedom of speech and right of due process). According to Erspamer, attorneys simply knew more about how to win medically complex claims, particularly cases involving ionizing radiation.

Erspamer's involvement in the case was deeply personal. His father was a navy metallurgical engineer involved in the atomic bomb tests at the Bikini Atoll in the late 1940s, and later died in 1980 of chronic myelogenous leukemia, a disease believed to be linked to radiation exposure. After fighting for years to force the VA to provide benefits to his mother under the Disability and Indemnity Compensation

(DIC) program, Erspamer eventually filed a class-action suit on her behalf, and on behalf of several other individual veterans and the National Association of Radiation Survivors (NARS), a group of atomic veterans who had all experienced some sort of radiation-induced sickness or cancer.[17] His brief to the court was disarmingly direct:

> (1) The VA adjudication system is procedurally and substantively complex, particularly the rules and regulations concerning ionizing radiation claims; (2) the development and presentation of facts and documentation in ionizing radiation claims is difficult; the medical and scientific issues associated with these claims are complex; (3) the ability to retain counsel is necessary given the actual practices of the VA and the Defense Nuclear Agency [which estimates how much exposure each soldier might have received at a given test]; (4) the internal controls in the VA adjudication system are inadequate to insure adherence to applicable statutes, rules and regulations; and (5) service organizations do not provide adequate representation to ionizing radiation claimants."[18]

Translated point by point into lay terms, (1) not only was the VA system confusing to start with, (2) but radiation claims were especially complex, (3) particularly given the VA's reluctance to pursue evidence from the Defense Nuclear Agency, (4) the VA's problems following its own rules, and (5) the lack of legal training among the service representatives who normally handled veterans claims.

Thus, without the help of a skilled attorney, help unavailable given the ten-dollar-fee limitation, most veterans would lose the complex cases. As Erspamer summarized his case, "the rights of veterans who have served our country are far more circumscribed than those of welfare recipients, social security claimants, and, ironically, those of criminals, who are often provided legal counsel at Government expense."[19]

Few people have taken a bigger swing at the system or done more to open the process for veterans, though the big veterans groups would never agree. In one fell swoop, Erspamer had challenged the entire system—the VA bureaucrats who ran the system, the scientists who had participated in the nuclear tests of the 1950s, the Defense Department and the bomb makers, and the veterans groups.

According to his own estimate, while working entirely "pro bono," or for free, Erspamer spent thousands of hours and $2.5 million of his firm's money searching for ways to prove his case. Had he been a political insider in Washington, perhaps he would have taken a different route, working his connections to win a fee increase for attorneys. But, as an individual attorney, he chose the courts, knowing that the Senate had tried in vain to change the fee limitation in four straight Congresses.

Not that Erspamer had never tried. He had testified before the House Veterans Affairs Committee several times, never mincing words. In 1986, for example, he testified that "by any objective standard, the VA adjudication system is primitive. In the age of computerized file-control methods, the VA still maintains files in hard copy with a primitive control system. As a result, veterans' files are frequently lost or misplaced, and the VA cannot compute the success rate for claims in regional offices or even the number of extant claims."[20]

In reading through Erspamer's testimony, I was struck by how often the committee members asked him about his military service, as if being a veteran had something to do with one's ability to discern truth. No wonder Erspamer felt on more solid ground in court. No one impunged his case because he was not a veteran.*

* Indeed, I was subject to the very same treatment by the then-General Counsel of the VA, who popped the question, "Have you ever served in the military?" in the middle of a briefing about judicial review. My response was that I was eligible for the draft lottery, but my number came up high.

In order to prove his case in court, however, Erspamer needed raw data showing that the veterans he represented would have a higher probability of success with an attorney than without. And that meant getting into the VA's files and checking the numbers.

Using a legal device called "discovery" in which the court orders an agency to open itself to inspection, Erspamer had received a million pages of internal memos, notes, studies, even phone logs from the VA. These documents told a sobering story of declining quality, increasing delays, frustrating and complex rules, and a disregard for the basic rights of all veterans to be treated fairly whatever their claim.

Erspamer even found one memo written by a "devil's advocate" inside the VA showing top agency officials how Erspamer could win his case. According to the memo, "Mr. Erspamer can show that a managers' bonus and merit pay evaluation is based in part on the adjudication divisions productivity. He will state that our system encourages some adjudication managers to report incorrect quality levels because they know that their failure to do this part of their job will not be held against them. If Mr. Erspamer can show that our system pits the financial interest of adjudication officers against the fair and resonable treatment of our claimants, he would be well on his way to proving the VA does have an unfair, adversarial claims adjudication system."[21]

The discovery process was not without travail, however, for Erspamer eventually discovered that the VA had been destroying the very evidence he needed. Erspamer learned about the document shredding in an anonymous letter dated July 11, 1986. According to the letter, authored by someone inside the VA whom Erspamer called his "deep throat," "your interrogatories recently sent to the Veterans Administration have been received. You are heading in the right direction. However, there is a conspiracy by the supervisors of the Field Operations Staff in the Compensation and Pension Service [of the Department of Veterans Benefits] to deny you the information requested." Apparently, key officials inside the VA had ordered a "purge" of derogatory information that might prove Erspamer's case.

Moving as fast as possible, Erspamer went to court to stop the VA shredders. After hearing the arguments, a federal judge in San Francisco fined the VA $120,000 and placed a "special master" in charge of all future discovery. It was an unprecedented slap at the agency. (Interestingly enough, one of the key agency officials who participated in the events was eventually promoted in 1988 to head the compensation and pension program, an unusually clear statement of the VA's unyielding commitment to maintaining the old system.)

Even with these obstacles removed, Erspamer's case was still far from resolution in 1987. In fact, the suit was moving at sub-glacial speed. At best, Erspamer could hope for a lower court decision by 1990, a decision that the VA would likely appeal directly to the Supreme Court. Although he certainly wanted to win his case, Erspamer also wanted to establish the right of judicial review for veterans. Thus, when I called in late January 1988, to ask if he would share some of his information, Erspamer readily agreed. Whatever happened in National Association of Radiation Survivors v. Turnage, Erspamer might yet help judicial review pass.[22]

By 1987, as if the delays, due-process violations, and lack of attorneys were not enough, the Board of Veterans Appeals, the ultimate guarantor of a veteran's right to a fair review, was an emerging fiasco. The BVA was beset by internal dissension and driven by a productivity system gone mad in which BVA members had to decide a certain number of cases per week in order to win end-of-the-year salary bonuses. Clearly, the BVA was afflicted by the same productivity pressure facing the regional benefit offices. The following exchange in 1987 between the BVA chairman,

Kenneth Eaton, and Rep. Douglas Applegate (D-Ohio), a Veterans Affairs subcommittee chairman, illustrates the point. Eaton's answers were obviously somewhat of a surprise:

> Mr. Applegate. There have been allegations, also, that there is too much emphasis on productivity that has been made, and that year-end bonuses are tied to the number of cases decided. What do you say to that?
> Mr. Eaton. Well, that's true.
> Mr. Applegate. That's true.
> Mr. Eaton. We do that. It's a relatively small amount of money, but it is money, and all money counts, as you know. We use that as an incentive for high production. We need high production in order to get all the cases done. The fact that we've always done it is not a good reason, I understand that. But we have always had high production, and we encourage that through this bonus situation.[23]

There were only two problems with the production bonuses. First, they were clearly a violation of presidential orders exempting the BVA from any kind of performance pay. The whole point of the exemptions, which were actually requested by the VA administrator on the BVA's behalf in 1985, was to protect the board from just the kind of productivity pressures implied in Eaton's statement.

Second, and more important, the productivity pressure created an incentive for the BVA *not* to decide. Indeed, perhaps the easiest way to dispose of a case on appeal is to return it to the regional office for futher development, which takes less paperwork and less time. In 1978, for example, 13 percent of all cases forwarded to the BVA were subsequently remanded to the regional offices. By 1987 that number had grown to 21 percent. This rising remand rate was cause for a special task force in 1988, which found that approximately one-third of the remands were unnecessary.[24]

In the final analysis, these growing cracks reflected a simple choice within the VA to either keep its hospitals running at full steam or cut the benefits system. The VA had little choice—it is far easier to tolerate the delay of a benefits decision than of a heart-bypass surgery.

Paging through document after document in January 1988, it became clear that the VA believed a fair benefits process might drive up the overall cost of its benefits program. Not only would the VA have to spend more on personnel and staff, more veterans might find their claims awarded. According to one of the leaked internal memos, "WARNING: Be careful about slowing increased benefit costs because of judicial review. That would be a tacit admission that current procedures don't pay the claimant what he/she is entitled to." In short, judicial review might just force the VA to do the right thing.

Much of this fact-finding occurred in January 1988, during the long Christmas recess. Recess is a wonderful thing. Staff get to come in late (9:00 A.M.) and go home early (5:00 P.M.). Unfortunately, the more we mused about judicial review during the short days of December and early January, the more we members of the committee staff strayed outside the traditional boundaries of Rule XXV which set the committee agenda. If our questions had been about personnel or procurement, we would have been free to legislate to our hearts' content, but the closer we drifted toward judicial review, the more we strayed into the veterans triangle and the direct jurisdiction of the congressional veterans committees.

Given the strength of the doctors inside the VA, however, judicial review seemed to be the only way to force Congress and the president to give the benefits program the funding it needed, including the dollars for a new computer system, staff, and training. Judicial review was a very big stick to use, but increasingly seemed like the only option. Instead of just pushing on a floor jack or playing with the VA wiring diagram, elevation to Cabinet status now presented an opportunity to make a difference.

Interestingly, the only groups that took an interest in the guts of the Cabinet bill were the Paralyzed Veterans of America and the Vietnam Veterans of America, organizations whose credibility depended on expertise, not sheer numbers. As a result of their smaller size and clarity of mission, both could speak with certainty about what they did and did not favor. They did not have to poll an endless number of state and local chapters to make a decision.

In contrast, if the VFW, American Legion, and DAV had a preference on Glenn's emerging bill, they never expressed it, perhaps because they represented such large numbers of veterans. While sheer size alone made them formidable adversaries, it also required an artful smudging of their agendas—ambiguity is one way to keep the four million or so VFW members, Legionnaires, and disabled American veterans from fighting within their respective councils. Like a huge aircraft carrier in battle, they had ample firepower, backed up by thousands of local posts and Legion halls, but they were mighty hard to turn. An occasional submarine, like the PVA or VVA, or the Governmental Affairs Committee for that matter, could wreak a great deal of damage with a single torpedo.

Nevertheless, an aircraft carrier is no small threat in a firefight. The big groups began to mobilize as we continued researching for an alternative bill. Having been denied a bill for Christmas, they now demanded a bill-signing ceremony on Memorial Day. That would mean fast action at the start of the second session of Congress in late January, something neither Glenn nor his staff were prepared to do. If judicial review was to be part of the package, Glenn needed some way to stall the veteran's groups. He eventually chose two of Washington's most traditional steam valves.

The first was to commission a study, which can act rather like the heat shield on a space capsule. Short of a national commission named after known Washington newsmakers like the Greenspan (social security), Scowcroft (MX missile-basing), Kissinger (Central America), or Packard (defense procurement) commissions, a study provides the best political cover for either developing new ideas or delaying action.

Needing a bit of both cover and delay, Glenn asked the National Academy of Public Administration (NAPA), for a study of the pros and cons of Cabinet status. As a nonpartisan, congressionally chartered cousin to the prestigious National Academy of Sciences, NAPA just might give us some protection from the increasing pressure to move. If the scholars and practitioners at NAPA also weighed in against Cabinet status, so be it. They'd be the first group in Washington to stand in front of the train.

The second steam valve was the Christmas recess. Out of sight, out of lobbying mind. Unfortunately for me, while my friends went to far-off places like China, Japan, or the Middle East, I took a detour from a Florida vacation for a couple of trips to see what a VA hospital and benefits office looked like. Some people go to Disneyworld; I went to VA offices in Tampa, St. Petersburg, and Daytona Beach, hardly the way to get a good tan.*

The St. Petersburg benefits office, for example, was a *DUMP*—leaky roof, asbestos in the ceilings, and hundreds of cardboard boxes containing the records of one of the busiest benefits offices in America. No wonder timeliness had declined. The Tampa Bay VA hospital was no Taj Mahal either, but that didn't seem to matter one bit. Every patient I talked to (and I picked them all at random) was grateful for the care. From the alcoholic I spoke with in

* Lest readers think otherwise, this wasn't a junket, although the VA did offer to finance the trip with special funds set aside for congressional staff.

intensive care to the amputee in vocational rehabilitation, every one said the very same thing: VA had saved their lives. Some were patients who would have gotten care elsewhere, others had been denied until the VA opened its doors, but they all swore by their hospital.

Yet, no one I talked to in Florida gave one whit about VA Cabinet status—not the doctors, nurses, or patients. "Do you think it will make a difference?" I asked one of the intensive-care nurses who had just spent almost thirty minutes berating me for her staff shortage. "Are you kidding?" she answered. "The pinheads in Washington will just get better cars."

Despite Glenn's success in buying a month or so of extra time, there was no way this bill was going to be detoured any longer. The only question was whether we could find any way to redeem the cause as we drafted Glenn's bill.

Legislative drafting is not a difficult process. First, one can always steal from existing law, since there is no copyright protection on legislation. Once one figures out what the basic recipe is, for example, anyone can bake a Cabinet bill. The Brooks bill in the House had been drafted in large measure by copying from the statutes that created the departments of Education and Energy.

Second, one can always sit down at a computer screen and start drafting. Legislation is often little more than writing exactly what one means, albeit always organized in very specific outline form: roman numerals followed by capital letters followed by arabic numbers followed by lower-case letters. Although legislative "baking from scratch" is celebrated in civics texts, it is rare on Capitol Hill, if only because it takes so much time and energy.

Third, one can always work with a bill right off the shelf. The "ready-mix" approach is particularly attractive for beleaguered congressional staffers, and it involves merely expanding and refining the best version of a given bill available. In this case, the House version, H.R. 3417, provided the basic flavor for Glenn's bill. Not only would the bill seem familiar to the House, the added Senate "spices" might go down more easily. In truth, however, the Senate amendments were rather like adding a cup of cayenne pepper to a can of chili.

Whichever approach one chooses—plagiarism, baking from scratch, or ready-mix—drafting starts with a list of ideas, and holding down the number of new political jobs in the department was clearly Glenn's first priority. An increase from the VA's three current Senate advise-and-consent appointees to the fourteen in Brooks's H.R. 3417 was just too much, especially since each would bring a complement of lower-level political appointees not subject to confirmation.[25]

Alongside a cap on political appointees, Glenn wanted some consolidation and streamlining of headquarters, too. The VA was an agency that had been wound and rewound more times than a videocassette, as one administrator and Congress after another imposed their vision on the agency. The constant chaos at the top of the VA meant the administrator was almost entirely dependent on the line departments for information about what they were doing, putting the administrator, Congress, and the president at the mercy of the line departments, whose natural bureaucratic instincts were to look good. Little wonder that Reagan's first adminstrator, Robert P. Nimmo, once told the *National Journal*, "It is not uncommon for Congress to ask about a project I haven't heard about."[26]

The Governmental Affairs Committee did not have a secret template or cookbook for organizing a new department, however. No one does. Rather, it was clear that the medicine and benefits programs had long since broken free of headquarters, taking advantage of the confusion and infighting at VA headquarters to create their own separate fiefdoms in hundreds of field units outside of Washington. The fact that none of the top leadership in the VA stayed very long—four administrators in ten years, constant vacancies in the deputy administrator and associate administrator posts—and the fact that the organization charts kept changing allowed the decentralization of the VA to continue long after the decentralization provided any return.

Beyond slowing the growth of "politicals" and streamlining the organization chart, Glenn wanted to give the first secretary of Veterans Affairs some maneuvering room to manage the department. The problem was that the VA could not reorganize itself without first informing Congress under a report-and-wait provision—that is, the VA would report its intention to, say, transfer an audiovisual office from one unit of headquarters to another, then give Congress up to a year to say yes or no. In theory, the proviso prevented the kind of sweeping hospital and benefit office closures proposed early in the Reagan administration. In practice, the fine print actually required that Congress be notified of any reorganization plan involving 2.5 or more full-time employees!* As far as Glenn was concerned, if the VA deserved to be at the Cabinet table, it deserved a little more decison-making flexibility.

Glenn also wanted a stronger Office of Inspector General. Created in twelve departments and agencies of government under the 1978 Inspector General Act, the inspectors general, or IGs, were to be the chief watchdogs of the bureaucracy, responsible for digging out fraud, waste, and abuse in their agencies. Unfortunately, pound for pound, the VA's inspector general was one of the weakest in government, being understaffed and underfunded. It was time to give

* Since all of this paperwork had to flow up the agency and over to the Office of Management and Budget Legislative Clearance Division for proper clearance—all executive branch communications must be approved by the OMB, including testimony, budgets, legislative requests, and reports—even before entering the vast maze of congressional review, most VA administrators and their staffs quickly learned not to waste the bureaucratic energy on internal reorganizations.

the office a little more help—if there was an employment floor under the doctors, why not create one under the inspector general?

Glenn also agreed to give the chief benefits director a little more status within the VA. It just made no sense to have the medicine and benefits directors at different salary levels. Although the Department of Medicine and Surgery had more employees to supervise (194,000 versus 13,000), the Department of Benefits had a larger budget ($15 billion versus $10 billion), and probably a more complicated mission, dealing with education, home loans, life insurance, burial allowances, compensation, pensions, survivors payments.

Finally, Glenn did not want Ronald Reagan to make the first appointments to the new department. This was not a partisan swipe at Ronald Reagan, although I must admit it was hard to imagine giving this honor to the president who had once promised to abolish the departments of Energy and Education. Rather, with less than a year remaining in the president's term, it would be very difficult for Reagan to find and appoint the first officers, nearly impossible for the Senate to hold nomination hearings and confirm those appointees, and senseless for those officers to take charge of an agency they would serve only for a brief period. From a management standpoint, it would make sense to wail for the next president, whether Democrat or Republican.

With the basic outline of a Cabinet bill almost finished by late February 1988, all that remained was deciding on whether or not to include judicial reveiw. Here, Glenn faced his most important drafting decision: accept a package of incremental solutions to improve the process, or go for something big.

On the one hand, the incremental solutions, such as tinkering with the current benefits process, promised less conflict with the veterans groups. There was even an internal

VA memo in Erspamer's files outlining the agency's own list of incremental options for defusing judicial review: allow a slight increase in attorney's fees, permit veterans to go to court over Constitutional questions, separate the Board of Veterans Appeals from the VA, make the internal rules governing administrative due process part of the veterans statute, authorize a study, set legislative targets for timeliness and quality inside the VA, outlaw productivity pressure, or create some kind of internal legal-aid program to provide VA attorneys to veterans with complicated cases.

All good ideas, no doubt, but timid responses to what was a desperate problem. Moreover, it already seemed clear under case precedents that veterans could go to court on Constitutional questions, for example, but not on the all important findings of fact.

More important, the Senate Veterans Committe would never permit Glenn to muck about with the veterans code without a fight. Although somewhat more liberal than its House counterpart, having passed judicial review four times only to see it die in the House, the Senate Veterans Committee was hardly likely to permit another Senate committee to wander so widely in its legislative pasture.

On the other hand, Glenn could go for something big, something nonincremental. After all, the problem with tinkering is that it is just tinkering. If Glenn was going to have a fight with the Senate Veterans Committee, why not fight over something big?

Among all the big-ticket options, judicial review was the most attractive, carrying great political risks but equally great policy benefits. Not that anyone expected judicial review alone to make a difference inside the VA—only a small number of veterans would ever appeal their cases to the courts. Rather, judicial review would clearly put the fear of court review into the VA, thereby encouraging the agency and its supporters to own up to serious reform. Judicial review just might balance the internal scales, giving the chief benefits director a needed lever in the fight for staff and resources.[27] By early March, it seemed clear that Glenn would push for judicial review as part of the package.

In doing so, Glenn could bake from scratch or go with a ready-mix. After all, there was a judicial review bill (S. 11) pending in the Senate, one that had passed four times.[28] The advantages of adopting that bill as his own were obvious. Starting with just six cosponsors in the Ninety-fourth Congress, the bill had become increasingly popular, and already had thirty-eight cosponsors in the 1987 version, including Glenn, Jeff Bingaman (D-N.M.), Lawton Chiles (D-Fla.), William Cohen (R-Mass.), John Heinz (R-Pa.), Levin, Mitchell, and James Sasser (D-Tenn.). What those eight names meant, of course, was that eight of the fourteen members of the Governmental Affairs Committee were cosponsors, a significant reason in itself for sticking with S. 11.

Yet the problems with the ready-mix bill were also clear. It just wouldn't taste as good. Originally authored by Sen. Gary Hart (D-Colo.), the bill was simple enough. Not only did it give veterans the right to proceed directly into the federal courts after denial by the BVA, it also gave veterans the option of paying an attorney up to five hundred dollars, and codified many of the rules and regulations that the VA should have been following, such as giving the benefit of the doubt to the veteran.

But, in dictating to the courts a new standard of review—how much they could ask about a given case and how to weigh the evidence—S. 11 gave the benefit of the doubt to the VA. Although the courts would have the right to look at the facts of a case—medical and service records, hearing testimony, even X rays—they would be able to reverse a VA decision only when a finding from the facts was "so utterly lacking in a rational basis in the evidence that a manifest and grievous injustice would result if such a finding were not set aside."

What a standard! Instead of using the traditional standard of review that allows the courts to set aside a finding of fact if it is arbitrary, capricious, an abuse of discretion, or otherwise not in accordance with the law, the Senate Veterans Committee had crafted its own separate mumbo jumbo. "We didn't want to flood the courts," one veterans committee staffer explained, "so we created a standard that wasn't likely to be met too often." No doubt. It would take years, decades perhaps, for the courts merely to define the standard. What does "so utterly lacking in a rational basis" mean? What is a "manifest and grievous injustice"? The consensus among our legal counsel was that the standard would actually *prevent*, not facilitate, court challenges.

Nevertheless, the advantages of taking the ready-mixed S. 11 were clear. It was a done deal, ready to go, tested four times on the floor, familiar to the Senate, and it came complete with a hearing record containing the testimony and legislative history generally required for final passage.

More to the point, if Glenn didn't like S. 11, he would have to draft his own judicial review amendment from scratch, a daunting task at best. Although he certainly had the legal talent to write such a bill, the problems were obvious. He would have to develop his own hearing record, and there was no question whatsoever that the veterans committees would want a sequential referral. Glenn could be tied up for months negotiating over the two versions of judicial review, wasting needless time and energy. With the House Veterans Affairs Committee sure to oppose judicial review of any kind, there was no point in making enemies in the Senate. Every floor fight has a cost—stealing S. 11 from Senate Veterans Affairs would be tough enough.

Equally important, if Glenn wanted to add other reforms to the Cabinet bill—a stronger organizational structure, fewer political appointees—he would need all the Senate support he could get, including that of the Veterans Affairs Committee. The best decision was to just swallow the com-

plaints about S. 11 and proceed with what the Veterans
Committee had already done.

That Glenn was moving forward on judicial review was
increasingly apparent, particularly as we scurried for additional evidence to make the case for linkage with Glenn's
nearly finished Cabinet bill. Much as we hoped to keep
Glenn's interest quiet, there was only so much we could do
without additional information from the VA.

Although we had our own whistleblowers deep in the
VA, as does every congressional committee, there were certain documents that we just couldn't get. Therefore, on
February 18, Glenn sent the VA administrator a three-page
letter I had drafted asking for detailed information on errors in the benefits process. To those who understood the
issue, the letter had judicial review written all over it.

Within hours, the veterans groups had their own copies
of the letter. It was a game of leak and counter-leak. "Once
we get that kind of letter on our computer system," one of
the VA legislative liaison officers later said, "who knows who
will see it? And with that kind of list, what other conclusion
could they reach?" As a result, by five o'clock the very day
Glenn signed the document request, the veterans groups
were on full alert, mobilizing against any linkage between
their prized Cabinet bill and judicial review. Any hopes that
Glenn might be able to drop judicial review into the bill as
a surprise at the very last moment were dashed.

Even if the letter hadn't leaked, the vets could have read
about judicial review in the papers. Although the House
Government Operations Committee had never even de-
bated judicial review as part of the Cabinet bill in October,
several members were now pushing the idea, privately lobbying the Senate to take a step they had been too timid to
take on their own. This private pressure to link S. 11 and
S. 533 became public in a Government Operations subcommittee hearing in February, a hearing that would eventually
lead to a damning committee report. Imagine how the vet-

erans groups reacted to the lead paragraphs of the *Washington Post* story the next morning:

Vets' Right to Sue for Benefits Pressed

Senate to Be Urged to Add Provision
To Bill on Restructuring VA

Supporters of legislation that would give veterans the right to sue over denied benefits said yesterday that they will urge the Senate to add the controversial provision to legislation elevating the Veterans Administration to a Cabinet-level department.

The provision, which proponents say would give veterans "their day in court" and extend a right granted most federal welfare recipients, has been passed four times by the Senate, but has died each time in the House Veterans Affairs Committee.

Rep. G. V. (Sonny) Montgomery (D-Miss.), the committee chairman and a champion of the bill making the VA a department, said last night that if the Senate adds the judicial review provision to the House-passed departmental bill, it could end the decade-long effort to create a Department of Veterans Affairs.

"I can't speak for the administration, but I know they are violently opposed to judicial review," Montgomery said in an interview. He said it was likely that President Reagan, who announced his support for the department bill in November, would veto legislation that includes judical review.[29]

Then imagine how they felt after reading the *Post* editorial on judicial review two days later.

The Vets: Having It All

Supporters of the bill to raise the Veterans Administration to a Cabinet-level department say not to worry, the legislation is not the power play it seems. Their soothing and not entirely implausible argument is that the bill would increase the agency's visibility more than its power, thereby making it more accountable rather than less.

Now they are being given a chance to demonstrate their devotion to this principle of accountability. Opponents of the bill, and some who are not opposed, want to add a codicil subjecting the agency's benefits decision to judicial reveiw. Unlike the comparable decisions of, say, the Social Security Administration, the benefits determinations of the VA are not subject to such review now. A post-Civil War statute limiting the legal fees that can be paid basically bars disappointed veterans from hiring lawyers, and a Depression-era cost-cutting statute forbids most appeals to the courts anyway. The result is that the veterans' organizations provide most of the representation in veterans' benefits cases, and the agency's own appeals board provides the final level of review.

As you might expect, the organizations and the agency both like this arrangement. They say the all-in-the-family system works to the veteran's benefit and that lawyers, by turning it adversarial, would rip it both up and off. But some veterans' advocates feel otherwise. They note that if the system does work so well, the agency had nothing to fear. In fact, they say the system can be arbitrary and ask: What can possibly be more American than to allow a citizen to take his government to court?

In the past three Congresses the Senate has several times provided for judicial review, always with an eye to preserving the best features of the present system. The House Veterans' Affairs Committee has been the burial ground. Now the issue has returned in the context of the bill to make the VA a department. The House-passed bill, which lacks the judicial review, is awaiting action in the Senate Governmental Affairs Committee, where some members may propose the provision. Some veterans' groups and veterans stalwarts on the Hill say they would rather have no bill than one with this provision. They want the clout of Cabinet status without the restraint. Who wouldn't?[30]

This wasn't a staff conspiracy to sneak judicial review past the veterans lobby per se. Yes, we had known about the

House hearing. Yes, we were moving toward linkage. But no, we did not orchestrate these events. Quite the contrary, we would have preferred a sneak attack at markup, the stage of the process where a committee or subcommittee takes a formal bill and "marks it up" for final passage to the floor. Now we would have to fight it out.

The remarkable part of this growing conflict between those who favored linkage and those adamantly opposed was not its intensity—although I must admit I was surprised by the level of hostility on both sides of the issue—but the emerging alliance between those of us who had protested the Vietnam War and those at the PVA and VVA who had fought in it. We all knew that veterans reform was a cause worth fighting for. Perhaps we were all looking for some kind of redemption, and hardly recognized at the time that at least part of it would be found in working side by side.

4

Not with a Bang
(Building a Record)

ALAN SIMPSON WAS either the funniest United States senator or the most honest. He was one of the few senators publicly opposed to Cabinet status for the VA and he was willing to call the veterans groups on the carpet for opposing judicial review.

This tall, lanky Wyoming Republican could launch a blistering floor attack without the slightest change in tone and, without so much as raising an eyebrow, could swear a blue streak that could peel paint. He talked as if he were sitting in a barber's chair back home in Wyoming. His position on veterans was always unmistakably clear.

Simpson on Congress and veterans: "When they put out the word in the Capitol Hall of Congress about a veterans issue on the floor, you better step back into the cloak room because the velocity of those rushing in to cast an 'aye' vote will suck all the air out of the chamber."

Simpson on Cabinet status as a way to recognize America's twenty-eight million veterans: "If we were to follow that reasoning, there should almost certainly be a Cabinet-level department of women's affairs, and surely there should be a department of aging, without question. We are all

Americans; we are not constituencies. Who's next?" Simpson on the Cabinet bill itself: "It is neither a necessary nor a prudent move, although I realize my voice is one of the very few in Congress that is raised in opposition. . . . they are going to have a ceremony on the parade ground and rip my epaulets off some dark night."

Simpson on the veterans groups: "If there are twenty-eight million veterans and only four million belong to the various veterans' organizations, what does that say?" Simpson on the "professional fund-raising veterans" who work at the groups: "I refer to those who are paid handsomely (check the books) by veterans organizations to lobby Congress day and night, and whose existence and exorbitant salaries are justified by fund-raising efforts poured out to unsuspecting citizens, trying to represent to the American people that Congress is ever and always on the verge of lopping off all funding for veterans programs." Simpson on the groups that opposed judicial review: "They have flunked the saliva test on this issue."

To say the veterans groups disagree with Alan Simpson would be the understatement of the century. Not only had he impugned the groups by calling them "professional fund-raising veterans," his primary goal was to add judicial review into the Cabinet bill. If he could not stop Cabinet status, he absolutely intended to improve it. As one of my colleagues said at the time, "to the vets groups, adding judicial review to the Cabinet bill is like carrying Alpo in the Holy Grail."

No group was more opposed to linkage than the Disabled American Veterans. As the largest single provider of representation for individual veterans inside the VA, the DAV had plenty to worry about. Given that the DAV handled almost 40 percent of all cases appealed upward to the Board of Veterans Appeals, some cynics argued that the DAV simply could not survive the loss in business—and membership—that might come with judicial review, particularly given the DAV's penchant for soliciting its clients.[1]

But the DAV was not fighting judicial review because of its need for members. None of the big veterans groups understood the VA's benefit process as well as the DAV, which had the largest number of service representatives in the field. Those representatives knew that judicial review might be the final straw in an already sluggish system.

Out in the field, where the service representatives had daily experience with the increasing delays, Cabinet status was seen as a way to address the continuing staffing shortages and judicial review as an attack on an already weakened process. As one DAV service representative testified before Glenn in the final hearing in March, "I do not fully understand the workings of the Federal Government here in Washington, D.C., but I do feel that [if] the elevation of the VA to a cabinet level enhances management efficiency and helps alleviate conditions which place extreme pressures on VA personnel to produce more with less resources, then it will be worthwhile. It is time to place the emphasis on quality and timely VA benefit determinations. The system must serve the veterans, not the system." It was the most honest an endorsement of Cabinet status I heard.

Back in Washington, however, Cabinet status was seen as a way of honoring America's veterans and judicial review as nothing more than a delaying device. The DAV's case against linkage between the two issues was made in a March 11, 1988, mailing to every Ohio DAV member.

One: "The full House of Representatives has *already* overwhelmingly *approved* the VA/Cabinet level status bill."

Two: "*Before* S. 533 can be considered by the full Senate and sent to the White House for Presidential signature, it *must first* be reported out of the *Senate Govermental Affairs Committee*, chaired by *Senator John Glenn* (D-Ohio)."

Three: "The DAV has learned that during consideration by the Governmental Affairs Committee, a possible attempt may be made to *amend* S. 533 to include a provision relating to *judicial review* of VA benefit determinations in the Federal District Court System."

Four: "Regardless of whether or not you support the issue of judicial review, such an amendment would virtually *kill the entire bill*. Both Chairman and Ranking Minority Members of the House and Senate Veterans Affairs Committees agree, stating that if judicial review is attached to the Cabinet bill, *the entire measure is doomed*."

Five: "Nevertheless, the proponents of judicial review *are willing to sacrifice* Cabinet level status for the VA in pursuit of their objective."

Therefore: "The DAV believes that both these important issues—judicial review and VA/Cabinet level status—should be considered *separately* on their own merits. *Neither* should ride the coattails of the other into the statute books, and *neither* should be responsible for the *legislative death* of the other."

As if Glenn needed more letters from home, just two days later, on March 13, the *Washington Post* ran a story titled "Dispute Threatens VA Cabinet Bill: Efforts to Revamp Appeals Process Could Trigger Presidential Veto." The first three paragraphs would have given any right-thinking veteran pause:

> A dispute over the way the Veterans Administration handles claims from the nation's 27 million veterans is threatening to kill legislation that would elevate the agency to a Cabinet-level department.
>
> Until recently, the measure—endorsed again this month by President Regean and approved by the House by a wide margin Nov. 17—seemed certain to clear the Senate. It was expected on the President's desk before the summer's political conventions.
>
> But VA critics recently seized the legislation as a vehicle for allowing veterans to press their claims for benefits in the federal courts—one of the most explosive issues that has confronted the VA in the past decade. If attached to the bill creating the department, its supporters predict it almost certainly would provoke a presidential veto, killing the legislative prize that veterans' groups have sought for years.[2]

"Seized the legislation as a vehicle." "Threatening to kill the legislation." Talk about waking the neighborhood! If the *Washington Post* was trying to create momentum for judicial review or slow the Cabinet bill, as the *Post*'s own ombudsman later claimed, it didn't work.[3] The following VFW letter to Glenn is but a sample of the mail that poured in over the next days:

Veterans of Foreign Wars of the United States
The Executive Director
Washington Office
March 15, 1988

The Honorable John Glenn
United States Senate
Washington, D.C. 20510

Dear Senator Glenn:

The Veterans of Foreign Wars of the United States is solidly behind elevating the Veterans Administration to a Cabinet level department. This is undoubtedly the single most important veteran's issue now facing the United States Congress.

Hearings have already been conducted in both Houses of Congress and most everyone agrees that our country would benefit from adding the Veterans Administration to the President's Cabinet.

Support has been voted by 87 percent of our elected national leaders, the United States House of Representatives voted 399-17 in support, President Reagan has openly declared his support and 65 of your fellow Senators have overwhelmingly declared their support. Faced with these facts it is obvious that you, as Chairman of the Senate Government Affairs Committee, are making every effort to delay full Senate action on this important veteran's legislation.

Cabinet level status for the Veterans Administration is not considered a controversial measure. However, after reviewing the agenda for your upcoming hearing, it becomes abundantly clear that you are encouraging the introduction of nongermane amendments to S. 533, thus diluting and possibly destroying an otherwise excellent piece of legislation. We ask that you and your advisors re-evaluate your position on the bill and join us in supporting legislation whose sole intent is elevating the VA to Cabinet level.

The veterans of this nation and the vast majority of their elected representatives want this bill passed. Any amendments, not directly related to Cabinet level status, should be introduced as separate legislation and given the full scrutiny of the Congress, to do less would defeat the intent of S. 533.

There are 2.9 million men and women in the Veterans of Foreign Wars of the United States and its Ladies Auxiliary, which includes 150,000 members of Ohio, all eyes are focused on this most important issue. Will S. 533 survive on its own merit or will S. 533 become a vehicle for less worthy issues? You have our attention.

Sincerely,

Cooper T. Holt
Executive Director

With the veterans groups on full alert, the second hearing on Cabinet status began promptly at 9:00 A.M., Tuesday March the 15th. This hearing was the flip side of the December opening, consisting of the "con" side of the issue.

The tension over linkage of the two bills was obvious as Glenn gavelled in the hearing. In contrast to the Christmas glee of December, the hearing room how had an angry glow. The murmurs among the audience seemed to focus almost exclusively on judicial review, while every veteran in sight seemed to be wearing a big campaign button reading "A Department of Veterans Affairs Has My Vote!"

The first panel represented the National Academy of Public Administration. The NAPA witnesses did nothing more than offer a list of criteria for judging the merits of Cabinet status for VA, but, oh, how those criteria cut. Even though the witnesses had their backs to the audience, they must have felt the heat from the veterans seated just behind them.

The NAPA report was direct. Asked by Glenn *whether* VA should be elevated and, if so, *how*, the three NAPA witnesses presented their list of fourteen criteria that could be used in elevating almost any proposal for Cabinet status. The criteria, presented as questions, led to one inescapable conclusion: VA should *not* be elvated.

> 1. Does the agency or set of programs serve a broad national public goal or purpose not exclusively identified with a single class, occupation, discipline, region or sector of society?

Obviously, the answer was "no." Veterans programs were created for veterans only. "No other set of programs serving a single service-related group has been elevated to Cabinet rank," the report argued. "Other federal departments meet major functional needs and serve all citizens across mulitple professional backgrounds, occupations and sectors of society." In short, you don't create a department to serve one group.

> 2. Is there evidence that there is a significant need of the veterans population that is not now adequately recognized or addressed by the Veterans Administration, the president, or the Congress which would be better assessed or met by elevating the agency to a Cabinet department?

Much as supporters of VA Cabinet status argued that the agency needed more money, the facts were clear: the VA's budget had grown 31 percent during the 1980s, clearly not as fast as the vets lobby wanted, but larger than both Energy and Education, the two most recently created Cabinet departments.

3. Is there evidence of impending changes in the needs
of, or the circumstances surrounding, the veteran population which would be better addressed if the VA were
made a Cabinet department? Are such changes expected
to continue into the future?

Although the veterans population was surely changing
(growing older and more chronically ill), the VA had shown
itself to be a proven fundraiser on Capitol Hill and an especially effective lobbyist for new programs. Despite a series
of budgetary defeats under Reagan, the VA had managed
to build a new inventory of programs that would exert unyielding pressure in the competition of future budget
dollars.

4. Would a Cabinet department increase the "visibility"
and thereby substantially strengthen the active political
and public support for programs assisting veterans, including the volunteer service and donated cash assistance
currently being provided through veteran service organizations and the non-organized citizenry?

Again, the answer was "no." How could a Cabinet Department of Veterans Affairs be any more visible than the
VA? According to the NAPA report, "while a Cabinet department would clearly provide some additional visibility
and political support, in view of the extraordinarily broad
level of public recognition and active support which are
already in place, the impact would be marginal."

5. Is there evidence that becoming a Cabinet department
would provide better analysis, expression and advocacy
of the needs and programs which constitute the agency's
responsibilities?

One of the most frequent arguments for elevation was
the need for access to the president. Yet the VA administrator had already testified in December that he met with

the president on veterans' affairs matters "every time I had the need to do so." In fact, the VA was represented on practically every forum, council, advisory body, commission, task force, and working group in government.

> 6. Is there evidence that elevation to a Cabinet department would improve the effectiveness of service delivery to veterans and their beneficiaries?

This was one of the most important questions in the report for, according to NAPA, "effectiveness of VA's programs is not likely to be improved materially by the legislation presently before the Committee." The implication was clear. About the only reason for elevating the VA would be serious reform, and neither S. 533 nor H.R. 3471 offered any substantive change.

> 7. Is a Cabinet department required to better coordinate or consolidate programs and functions which are now scattered throughout other agencies in the executive branch of government?

Although NAPA answered "no," the increasing proportion of aging Americans meant that all agencies of government would have to work more closely together. This was one question on which the Governmental Affairs Committee disagree with NAPA's position. Anything that would increase the probability, however slight, of interagency cooperation was worth a try.

> 8. Is there evidence that a Cabinet department with its increase in the centralized political authority would result in a more effective balance, within the agency, between integrated strategic planning and resource allocation, and the direct participation in management decisions by the line officers who are responsible for directing and managing service delivery? Would the staff officer-line officer interaction be improved?

Translating NAPA's bureaucratese into plain language, would the VA be better managed at the top as a result of elevation? The answer was "maybe," depending upon the final legislation. If we stayed with the original S. 533 or H.R. 3471, however, the answer was clearly "no," for both bills employed the floor-jack approach.

> 9. Is there evidence that there are significant structural, management or operational weaknesses within the VA that could be more easily corrected by elevation to a Cabinet department?

Again, the answer depended upon action in the Governmental Affairs Committee. "An organic act establishing a Cabinet department does provide the opportunity to realign critical internal management functions and strategies," NAPA argued. "However, neither bill before the Committee proposed to do this." Another implied boost for serious reform.

> 10. Is there evidence that there are external barriers and impediments to timely decision making and executive action that could be detrimental to improving the efficiency of VA programs? And would these impediments be removed or mitigated by elevation to a Cabinet department?

Reading between the lines, the NAPA report clearly gave encouragement to the reform movement. If the VA was to be elevated whatever the reason, Congress ought to use the opportunity to remove some of the micromanagement devices that would limit the secretary's ability to govern the vast veterans bureaucracy.

> 11. Would elevation to a Cabinet department help recruit and retain better qualified leadership within the agency?

Great question. According to the report, the answer was probably "yes." Basically, more presidential appointees might actually strengthen the VA: "a Cabinet secretary position is customarily more attractive to senior executive talent with a broader base of expertise. Since more prestige is attached to presidential appointments, this may also be true for the VA sub-cabinet line officers who have the day-to-day operational responsibilities."

12. Is there evidence that a Cabinet department would facilitate more uniform achievement of broad, cross-cutting national policy goals such as: better integration of biomedical research; a national AIDS program; drug prevention and treatment programs; health care cost containment; equitable needs tests in areas beyond disability compensation benefits; government-wide personnel and budgetary controls; more efficient management and disposition of federal real property assets; and the comprehensive coordination of health care, income maintenance, education and training and other service delivery strategies?

Again, NAPA's answer was "no": the two bills pending before the Governmental Affairs Committee were floor jacks, not major reforms. Although NAPA acknowledged the potential for "stronger policy alignment because of the natural pressure for equitable and uniform execution across all Cabinet departments," there was no evidence that such coordination would occur.

13. Would elevation to a Cabinet department for the VA weaken or strengthen the Cabinet and the Executive Office of the President as policy and management aids to the president?

Ultimately, this was the only question that mattered. Would the president be better served by the VA's elevation? After all, the Cabinet exists solely to support the president under the "Take Care" clause of the Constitution, which instructs the president to take care, or make sure, all laws are faithfully executed. On this score, however, there was little reason to argue the president would be either helped or hindered. One more Cabinet department would mean fourteen chairs at the table instead of thirteen, hardly much of a difference at all. Hence, another "no" answer.

14. Would the elvation to a Cabinet department have a beneficial or detrimental effect upon the oversight and accountability of the agency to the president and the Congress?

Whether Congress and the president paid so little attention to the VA had virtually nothing to do with Cabinet rank and everything to do with fifty years of not rocking the boat. Merely elevating the VA would not guarantee greater congressional oversight or presidential accountability. Just because the VA was at the Cabinet table did not mean the president would look that way.

Adding up the score for the two pending bills, Cabinet status failed the test, with twelve "nos" and two "yeses." More significantly, the report did not mince words in its general conclusion: "The Panel finds little evidence that the vital mission of providing for the present and future needs of our veterans would be materially improved by elevating the Veterans Administration to a Cabinet department. The Panel does not believe that such an elevation would significantly improve either access to the president, the adequacy of necessary resources, or the organization, management and delivery of high-quality services and benefits."[4]

In short, any gain from Cabinet status would be at "the margin." As dozens of scholars and public administrators had done before, NAPA conclusively demonstrated that reorganization is not the best instrument to use for implementing serious change. Despite the harsh conclusion, there were at least five questions on the list that depended on what the committee would do with its own legislation. With a strong bill, we might just tie on NAPA's criteria, seven to seven.

That the report said absolutely nothing about judicial review did not prevent Glenn and Levin from asking NAPA's opinion on linkage. Two of the three NAPA witnesses artfully ducked the question. After all, judicial review was not part of the study mandate, plain and simple.

Unfortunately for the vets groups, the third NAPA witness, a former DAV national officer, could not resist the chance to voice the party lines:

> DAV Witness. I think it is wrong for the veteran, very clearly wrong for the veteran, it is not in his best interest to pay a percentage of his compensation to a lawyer to have it done. That is what some of the proposals would result in. . . . I think it should be kept totally separate and apart because it does not help the veteran. . . .

Out came Levin's scalpel. With a little help from Glenn, he cut the witness to ribbons simply by asking the same question over and over: would veterans be more likely to win their claims with or without judicial review?

> DAV Witness. Clearly, judicial review would effect the service. None of us—
>
> Chairman Glenn. Well, wait. Stop right there. Why do you assume it would affect service?
>
> DAV Witness. Because none of us that have any conscience at all as an individual doing their job wants to be a loser. And if I am an adjudication officer at that regional office and I think that some lawyer is going to haul me off to court in the end, then I am going to be very, very careful about the award that I make to that individual.
>
> Senator Levin. Are you going to be more likely or less likely, if I can interrupt—
>
> DAV Witness. Oh, I am going to be very careful that I do not lose in court.
>
> Senator Levin. Are you going to be more likely or less likely to find for the veteran?

DAV Witness. Well, in this case? Less likely because—

Chairman Glenn. Wait a minute. If you know you are going to get hauled off to court eventually, you said that is what you were afraid of.

DAV Witness. That is right.

Chairman Glenn. What he is saying is, isn't that more likely to tilt you in favor of the veteran?

DAV Witness. No, why would it?

Chairman Glenn. How would it be the opposite?

DAV Witness. Because I do not want to lose a case. There are cases—

Senator Levin. Who is going to take you to court. The veteran is not.

Chairman Glenn. If you are judging in favor of the veteran, you are not going to court.

DAV Witness. Not necessarily. Not necessarily because we are talking about 99 percent of the cases now get satisfactorily resolved under the current system. So you are saying for that less than 1 percent that has been treated unfairly that we should have a legal process evolve.

Senator Levin. Who is going to haul you to court? That is my question.

DAV Witness. The veteran will. You only gave him 40 percent, and he will tell you he ought to have 60 percent.

Senator Levin. Aren't you more likely to tilt toward him to avoid being hauled to court by him?

DAV Witness. It depends on the issue. The ones that fight the problems now, as you would expect, are ones who want increases. A lot of the cases that are before the VA right now are adjudicating increases. In other words, their appeals have been—

Senator Levin. My question . . . is: Wouldn't you be more likely to find for him now if you know he may haul you to court later?

DAV Witness. Not necessarily.

Senator Levin. It is pure logic. I do not see how you can say no.

DAV Witness. Because it becomes an adversarial role.

Senator Levin. No, it does not. You keep the current role. You keep the current role of being an advocate.

(This is where the witness made his big mistake, ac-
knowledging that one reason he opposed judicial review
was the potential for higher awards.)

DAV Witness. You cannot. Because if it goes up for
judicial review, you have the possibility of losing. So,
therefore, you are going to dot every "i" and cross every
"t" to make sure that whatever the outcome of that case
is—and I am talking now about increases. The majority
of the denials come from increases in compensation, not
from an original case on compensation, if you look at the
record.

The only other point that I will make is that you all
talked about austerity and budgets and you may have to
change some services down the line. I would love to have
six million dollars of whatever the civil loss is for the loss
of the use of a limb should that occur. And I do not think
that this country, given the situation now, can have those
kinds of awards. That is just a by-product.

But then you start bringing out—

Senator Levin. Do you think the awards may be larger
to veterans?

DAV Witness. No. What I am saying is, the argument
that I am making in this regard deals with a cost, the cost
of doing that to the—because then you are going to
have—and I will be right there in line with all the rest
of them to get those millions of dollars that I forego
because I was a soldier for this country and I went into
an adversary—in other words, I went into a civil court
to get similar awards that you get in a civilian court. And
I do not think that is why I went to serve my country
was to do that. I knew the sacrifices that I may have to
make at the time that I did it.

Senator Levin. You think the awards may be larger if
there is judicial review, or there may be a greater number
of decisions in favor of veterans, and therefore, it may
cost the Government more? Isn't that what you are saying?

DAV Witness. Well, yes. That is right. That is exactly
right.

Senator Levin. That is exactly our point. You are more

likely to tilt to the veterans during the administrative process because you know that at the end of the line that court process is possibly going to help the veteran whom you turned down.

Game, set, and match, Levin. If only all of America's veterans could have heard the exchange, there would have been an outcry in favor of judicial review. Unfortunately, we could not educate twenty-eight million veterans in two weeks' time.

Alas, like so many committee hearings, there was hardly anyone listening. Aside from Glenn and Levin, the twelve other committee members left after inserting a statement for the record or they never came in the first place. Seven senators had been present at our first hearing in December, five at our second, and only four at our third.

By the end of this hearing, for example, only Glenn remained. Most of the veterans had already left, and the other committee members were long gone to other hearings, speeches, or to the Senate floor.

That is why staffers worked so hard to interest the press. The hearing itself was publicized *live* on C-SPAN, the cable network, and the *Washington Post* and *New York Times* both sent their senior veterans correspondents. For particularly controversial issues such as judicial review, the media become critical mediators, shaping congressional opinion and interest-group positions through their "spin" and choice of headlines.

The hearing sold itself, however, largely on the strength of the NAPA testimony. Just read the opening paragraphs of the two key stories that ran the following morning. In a story titled "Elevating the VA: Are There Benefits?" Bill McAllister of the *Washington Post* clearly signaled a problem: "A proposal to elevate the Veterans Administration into the federal government's 14th major department encountered strong skepticism during a Senate hearing yesterday, renewing doubts that the legislation will become law."

In a more mildly headlined piece titled "Cabinet Role for V.A. Called No Cure," Ben Franklin of the *New York Times* sounded a warning, too: "Experts on Government administration told Senators today that elevating the Veterans Administration to Cabinet status, as proposed by President Reagan and approved by the House, would not necessarily help the troubled agency."

More important perhaps, the news and editorial pages were in sync. The *Post* carried an editorial titled "Cabinet-Making 101" the very same day. The first and last paragraphs convey the strength of the piece:

> When the Senate Governmental Affairs Committee was confronted last winter with the bill to raise the Veterans Administration to Cabinet status, it asked the National Academy of Public Administration for its views. That was a serious act. The House had waved the bill along with scarcely a thought for its merits. The powerful veterans' groups wanted their agency made into a department; the president had surprised his advisers, who were about to urge him to resist, by endorsing the bill. Which congressman wants to throw his body in front of a speeding freight train like that. . . .
>
> If Congress decides to elevate the VA anyway, the panel urged that certain existing tethers on the agency's discretion be dropped; these keep the VA under the thumb of the congressional veterans' affairs committees by requiring that even some routine administrative decisions be clear. Others, if the agency is elevated, want to impose on its benefits decisions the same standards of judicial review that now prevail for other units of government—from which it is currently exempt. The message is that if the agency is going to grow up, it ought to grow up all the way. Maybe the veterans' groups will decide they're better off where they are.[5]

The message was unmistakable: if Congress wanted its cake and to eat it, too, it could elevate VA with judicial review attached.

Predictably, the vets groups responded with a flurry of

letters, phone calls, and visits. The halls of Congress resembled the beach at Normandy, clogged with vets in full legislative gear. My computer screen beamed with dozens of messages forwarded from irate veterans across the nation—"Stop this nonsense," "No to judicial review," "Let our Cabinet bill go." I seemed to be on every veteran's Rolodex in America.

Not that I didn't enjoy the company. Most of the veterans lobbyists were easy-going professionals, a little out of their element having to deal with a non-veterans committee, but always respectful toward Glenn. Besides the VFW, which could not resist the occasional shot at Glenn for "making every effort to delay full Senate action on this important veterans' legislation," the national groups never questioned Glenn's basic commitment to veterans.

Unfortunately, some of their state and local comrades took the campaign much more seriously. The following letter, written by an American Legion district commander in Ohio, is one example:

March 9, 1988

Fellow Legionnaire:

Going through the membership at Canton Post 44, this week, I noted that your 1988 dues are not yet paid. May be that I read the report wrong—if I did, please excuse me for bothering you.

If you have overlooked paying your dues, I have an important message for you: YOUR RIGHTS AND BENEFITS AS A VETERAN ARE IN DANGER. In danger from politicians who 1. are not veterans, 2. don't care at ALL about you as a veteran, or about the rights and benefits that you earned when you served your country.

How about this one: There is a bill in the Senate that will make the Head of the Veterans Administration a CABINET MEMBER. This will give the V.A. the strongest clout it has EVER HAD. A lot of Senators support the bill.

Except one; Ohio's John Glenn (himself a veteran). He has added a rider to the bill that means if the bill passes with this rider as part of it, you'll no longer be able to process any claim you have as a veteran, for medical help, hospitalization, insurance, or pension, through the normal V.A. channels. You will have to hire a lawyer and go through the courts. You know how long that will take. And think about this; if that law passes that way, the first time a judge throws out a veterans claim, it will establish a precedent to throw out all similiar claims. That's how the law works.

What we're trying to do, nationally, is get every last 1987 Legion member who has not yet paid his dues to do so, right now. Why? So we can show John Glenn, and people like him, that the American Legion is a strong, growing, tough organization, and that if he insists on punishing the veterans with lawyer fees and on dragging everything through the courts, our three million members and the one hundred and fifty thousand of us in Ohio, and our wives and friends, will show him who is boss in the only way he understands; with votes. . . .

And remember, your Free $1,500.00 accident insurance policy becomes effective the day we process your 1988 membership card.

The main opponent of judicial review was not in Ohio, however, nor in the big veterans groups in Washington, nor even at the VA. And although Glenn had already been warned by Alan Cranston, chairman of the Senate Veterans Committee, not to attach judicial review, the main opponent was not in the Senate either. After all, the Senate had passed judicial review four times. Cranston's warning was not to be taken lightly, if only because he might ask for a sequential referral on Glenn's bill. Under a sequential, the bill would take a detour to the Veterans Affairs Committee before moving to the floor. If the second committee changed any part of the bill during its perfectly legitimate review, Glenn could face a showdown on the floor just to reestablish his original bill as the first order of business. Nevertheless, if Cranston's motive was to protect his committee's legislative territory, just as Glenn and Brooks had earlier protected their's, perhaps some accommodation could be reached.

Thus, the main opponent of judicial review had to be in the House Veterans Committee, where the chairman, Mississippi Democrat G. V. "Sonny" Montgomery, had already let Cabinet status die four times before, three times without so much as a committee vote. Although the Senate Veterans Committee clearly played a role in veterans policy, its House counterpart held the pivot point. The Senate had not created a full Veterans Committee until the 1970s, and most of its staff members were nonveterans. The 1987–88 staff director was a non-veteran and a former Peace Corps official! As one former House Veterans Committee chairman once remarked, "Uh, it is, uh, a minor committee over there, compared to the function we perform over here."[6]

Montgomery's motives for opposing judicial review were not always clear. On the one hand, as a Southern conservative Democrat and non-lawyer, he had a natural distrust of the courts as a bastion of liberalism. More to the point, Montgomery may have felt insulted that any veteran would even want to go to court. "If a veteran has a problem," he was reputed to have argued, "he should come to me. I'll take care of him." He had always taken good care of "his GIs" as committee chairman, having pushed through major benefit increases, and he did not intend to turn over his responsibilities to unaccountable federal judges. On the other hand, as chairman of the House Veterans Committee, he had ample cause to protect his turf. Just as Glenn balked at rubber-stamping Cabinet status, Montgomery did not want to be backed into endorsing judicial review under threat of linkage.

Not surprisingly, supporters of judicial review believed otherwise, urging Glenn and others on the committee to call Montgomery's bluff. Under House rules, Montgomery would have only one chance to stop the linkage: he could rise to declare the judicial review portion of the Cabinet bill "nongermane," or unrelated, and call the question for a single up-or-down floor vote on a motion to strike the provision, a vote supporters of judicial review felt he would surely lose.

Nevertheless, even the optimists knew Montgomery would not yield gently. Facing a similiar test in 1986 when his committee threatened to pass judicial review over his opposition, Montgomery had turned to the veterans groups for help, asking groups then on record in favor of judicial review to change their position. AMVETS, the fourth largest group, quickly complied, as all but the Vietnam Veterans of America rallied round the chairman.[7] One only needs to compare the before and after positions of AMVETS to gauge Montgomery's persuasiveness:

Before	*After*
Veterans are full-fledged citizens and are entitled to the same rights and privileges as other citizens. The idea that they must be protected from the harsh realities of the real world by an insulted adjudicative system is an *insult*, not only to their intelligence but to the sacrifices they have made to preserve the very system of justice from which they are excluded. (July 1983)	AMVETS recognizes the current VA appellate system as being a unique example of objectivity, honesty, compassion and fairness among all other government administration agencies. AMVETS believes that to subject the VA adjudication system to the frustrations, prohibitive expense and precedential chaos of the federal court system would destroy the best administrative adjudication system in the government. (June, 1986)[8]

It is almost impossible to attribute AMVETS' change to anything but Montgomery's request. To call the VA the "best adminstrative adjudication system in the government" stretched even the most ardent case against judicial review.

Notwithstanding Glenn's effort to turn the judicial review issue into a debate over the right to go to court, the lobbying against linkage was withering. This was a political struggle of the first order.

Preparing for the third and final committee hearing, a hearing that would make the case for linking judicial review to Cabinet status, we were exhausted, running out of ammo, fighting hand to hand against a horde of battle-hardened opponents. Just returning the phone calls became a nightmare, with endless conversations spent trying to clear up the misinformation about judicial review. Would veterans need to have a lawyer? Would they have to pay high fees? Would they have to go the court to get benefits?

Unfortunately, public opinion on both Cabinet status and judicial review was either nonexistent or uninformed. There were no polls by Gallup or Harris, no national surveys of a steaming electorate. This was a nonissue outside the interstate beltway surrounding Washington.

The case for judicial review seemed to rest on the documents the VA had dumped on us in response to Glenn's February request—recall the letter leaked to the veterans groups. Lacking any public opinion to counter the interest groups, Glenn opted for a more rational process, strengthening the case for linkage as best he could through hard evidence of problems inside the VA. Alas, there was no dynamite to be found in the documents, nothing that would create the needed momentum for linkage. The stack of materials was interesting enough to a political scientist, but not to a national reporter in search of scandal.

Take the first document as an example. In response to Glenn's request for "a 1984 study or studies of productivity pressures inside VA," the agency instead provided a one-paragraph summary, claiming that the original report was lost somewhere in the system. As we were to find out in still another leak from inside the VA, however, even the one-paragraph summary was not the original summary. According to our source, the original contained three additional paragraphs:

> The review disclosed serious improprieties. Offices were apparently prematurely disposing of the end product control and within a few days re-establishing it. Multiple end-product credit was being taken for a single issue when obviously only one end-product credit was warranted. These actions would have the effect of distorting the timeliness and productivity calculated monthly for the adjudication division.
>
> I disclosed these findings to concerned supervisory personnel, including the Assistant Director, Field Operations. Members of the field operations staff utilized my data during field review visits. During the (3) visits, I recall my findings were substantiated at one office (San Francisco) which was intentionally manipulating end products and at another station (Pittsburgh) it was found that the personnel were not properly applying the procedures for end product control. The findings at the third office (New Orleans) were inconclusive.
>
> I also contacted a unit chief, at one office (Boston), who had previously been assigned to the Projects staff, and informed him of my review and that it appeared that 3 of the 4 unit chiefs were routinely taking additional end-product credit. He confirmed my findings and stated that they didn't care since no one in Central Office would do anything to stop their improper actions.

There was no reason for the VA to censor the answer. Merely explaining the concept of "end products" and why they were important as an indicator of abuse would have taken an entire hearing on its own. In fact, from a political standpoint, both sides on judicial review were totally wrapped up in statistics about error rates and technical jargon, when the more profound question was why veterans were denied a right to court review that most other Americans had.

Setting this first document aside as interesting, but unusable, next came something called the "Fact-Pattern Study," an ingenious piece of analysis by the VA's Office of Program Planning and Evaluation (OPPE). (Unfortunately, OPPE was also a victim of both political pressure and personnel cutbacks within the VA. As of 1989 it no longer existed.)

Designed to test consistency across the VA's highly decentralized system, OPPE took sixteen actual claims for VA benefits and erased all identifying marks—names, serial numbers, addresses—and sent identical copies of the claims to fifty-two of the fifty-eight regional offices, asking each to rate the claims using the VA's disability schedule. Recall that this process estimates disability in ten-point increments from zero all the way to 100 percent. Also recall that the higher the rating, the higher the benefit.

What is important to remember is that benefit decisions involve a great deal of subjective judgment. Although every conceivable illness is supposed to be listed in the VA's rating schedule—a "cookbook" that gives the rating boards a range of options for making their decisions—there is plenty of discretion. As explained in the OPPE report, "Diabetes mellitus, for example, as described in the rating schedule, can be severe, moderately severe, or moderate, and requires from large to moderate dosages of insulin, carrying 60, 40, and 20 percent disability ratings." This qualitative language relies on the judgment of the rating board members to define terms like 'large' and 'moderate,' used by examining physicians."[9]

By sending each office the same packet of claims, OPPE could gauge the degree of consistency across the entire agency. Unfortunately for the average veteran, the rating boards were anything but consistent, particularly on complex injuries. Even though the boards were dealing with identical information, their judgments on several cases varied widely. Because those variations mean real dollars one way or the other, some veterans win and some lose.

Take three examples from the study. On the same fracture of the left wrist, eleven rating boards assigned a zero percent rating, thirty-one gave a 10 percent, nine gave a 20 percent, and two gave a 30 percent rating. The difference between the high and low ratings in 1987 would have been $3,192 a year in benefits. On the same hypertensive heart-disease case, three rating boards assigned a 10 percent, two gave a 20 percent, twenty-five gave a 30 percent, twenty-one gave a 60 percent, and two gave a 100 percent rating. The difference between the high and low ratings would have been $15,540. On the same post-traumatic stress disorder, two offices gave a zero percent rating, sixteen gave a 10 percent, nineteen gave a 30 percent, thirteen gave a 50 percent, and one gave a 70 percent. The difference between the high and low ratings would have been $6,176.

My point isn't to suggest that every office must make exactly the same decision on every *similar* case. The rating schedule leaves room for judgments. Rather, it makes sense to ask that every office make exactly the same decision on every *identical* case. This "horizontal consistency" is a key component of basic fairness in an administrative setting.

There were several explanations for the study results, including the simple fact that the VA was, and still is, using an ancient rating schedule. However, OPPE could find no evidence of "liberal" or "conservative" rating boards. The variation was more or less random. What a veteran was awarded seemed to depend on what the rating board had had for lunch that day. As OPPE concluded, "no advantage is to be gained by shopping around geographically to obtain a higher percent of disability rating."[10] Rather, it appears that every veteran had a roughly equal chance of being either penalized or enriched by the inconsistencies.

The report clearly strengthened the case for judicial review as a check against inconsistency within the agency.

First, despite this indictment of the process, the VA had done little to improve the consistency of its decisions, ignoring OPPE's recommendations for improving a vague, outdated rating schedule. Judicial review just might force the VA to devote the resources and political muscle to a needed revision.

Second, if veterans with the same case could not get the same decision from every one of the fifty-eight benefit offices, they needed the right to advance to a higher forum. If that forum had a bias in favor of the original rating board, as the first step in the VA's appeals process clearly did, they needed the right to advance again.[11] If the next forum had a bias, too, as the Board of Veterans Appeals clearly did, they needed the right to advance again, even if that meant entering the federal courts.

Although the fact-pattern report was highly technical, there was no doubt Glenn could use it in the hearing, if only to illustrate the potential inconsistency in the benefits process. The problem was that the report was four years old. The VA could easily argue that the inconsistency had been corrected—indeed, when Glenn asked about the report at the hearing, the VA witness replied simply, "The first thing I would say is that that is a 1984 study and this is 1988."

Thus, still no dynamite, with but one more chance of finding it in the two-foot stack of reports on every regional office inspected by the VA's own internal auditors over the previous five years. Like any decentralized system, the VA had a mix of the good, the bad, and the inefficient.

The good news was that many of the VA regional offices were working well. Some were downright excellent. Offices such as Buffalo, New York; Cheyenne, Wyoming; Denver, Colorado; Indianapolis, Indiana; Little Rock, Arkansas; Muskogee, Oklahoma; Salt Lake City, Utah; Sioux Falls, South Dakota; and Waco, Texas, came across in good or excellent shape. What the offices seemed to share was a relatively small work load and low staff turnover, largely because federal pay in each city was relatively high vis-à-vis comparable jobs in the local private sector.

The bad news was that some of the VA offices were barely working at all. Several were horrifying. Offices in Baltimore, Boston, Houston, Jackson, Lincoln, Los Angeles, Newark, New Orleans, New York City, Phoenix, Pittsburgh, and Washington were either getting into trouble, coming out of trouble, or just plain bad. What these offices seemed to share was a very heavy workload and high staff turnover, largely because federal pay was relatively low compared to similar jobs in the private sector. Good people paid a high price for staying at the VA.

The report on Houston listed one problem after another, not the least of which was the discovery that "one of the more common occurrences was the failure to act on a claim until the medical evidence was so old that a new examination was justified."[12] Yet Houston was just the beginning. The report on New York City told of several problems characteristic of the large urban regional offices: "New York experiences constant and significant personnel turnover at all levels. Most other stations experience less turnover, and it is generally at the lower levels so that they are able to maintain a stable core of trained personnel at the higher levels. Since this is not the case at New York, the station is at an immediate disadvantage in all important areas—timeliness, quality and productivity—even before an analysis of the operation is made."[13]

Amazingly, this one paragraph was copied almost word for word in reports on New Orleans, San Francisco, and Balitmore, although it was not clear whether the same wording appeared because the paragraph always applied or because the inspectors were just too lazy to write something new.

But the productivity problems were not confined to big-city operations. Indeed, the report on Lincoln, Nebraska, was the worst. "This could be an excellent operation," the concluding section began. "It is not. In many ways this division is doing a disservice to all the veterans which it serves. . . . There is a general feeling in the Division that there is no real need to push hard to get work out. This feeling is caused by the fact that no one pushes them to get things out. The general feeling is that I am meeting my performance standard requirements, why should I break my back?"[14]

However troubling these reports, no dynamite. There was only the inefficiency, endless delays, and bureaucratic malaise that most Americans already expected of government.

The best we could do at this late date was to include the damning information in Glenn's opening statement, and hope again that the newspaper reporters were paying attention. We were simply out of time. With the final hearing approaching on March 28 and markup of Glenn's bill on April 14, we had to go with what little we had.

Still, the third hearing was one very hot ticket. We even had a surprise witness who was ready to testify that the VA lost roughly 20 percent of veterans' claims at one point or another in the benefits system, and we had cooked up a strong line of questions and answers for the chief benefits director. This was the hearing for making the case for linkage S. 11 and S. 533, with Simpson set as the first witness.

Alas, that linkage was not to be. From the moment the *Post*'s March 13 story had hit the newsstands, the veterans lobby was on fire. Virtually every Democrat on the committee reported a deluge of letters and phone calls from Legionnaires and members sof the DAV. Moreover, Legion commanders from each of the fourteen states represented on the Governmental Affairs Committee were to be flown in for the hearing. Even the strongest supporters of judicial review were wavering. As we worked down the list of swing votes on the committee—Levin, Mitchell, Chiles, Heinz,

Stevens—we simply could not find the votes for linkage.

Judicial-review supporters outside the committee were also under siege. Cranston remained dead set against linkage, promising the Senate that S. 11 would move forward on its own as soon as possible.

Although Simpson was unrelenting in his calvary charge, it was increasingly obvious that the Veterans Committee could enforce its threatened sequential referral, thereby opening every line of Glenn's bill to review. The fact was that Glenn didn't want the Veterans Committee mucking about with his handiwork on organizational structure any more than they wanted Glenn taking credit for judicial review.

Nevertheless, Glenn might still have crossed the line but for the lack of measurable support among veterans. He simply could not counter the intense lobbying campaign against linkage. The hundreds of handwritten letters we received did not always make sense—we even got two letters from the same vet, one in favor of linkage, one against, and both in the same envelope! There were enormous misunderstandings about the impact of judicial review, misunderstandings sometimes spread by the veterans lobby itself.

But, in the absence of an overwhelming tide in favor of judicial review, it was almost impossible to deny the respectful, handwritten pleas for action. The letters ran the gamut from the heartfelt to the respectful to the outraged.

"I've never penned a letter to anyone in Washington, D.C.," one of the letters began. "I guess there is a first time for all. I am a devoted wife of a Disabled Veteran. I'm pleading with you Mr. Glenn to consider reporting to the floor of the Senate S. 533 *without* any non-related amendments. My voice is of a Mother and a wife, but it is a sincere voice that needs to be heard."

"Please won't you and the Senate Governmental Affairs Committee report S. 533 to the floor of the Senate without further ado," read another. "Surely you will agree that our veterans of wars deserve cabinet level status. Allowing this important bill to be hung up and probably killed because of the attaching of non related amendments is shameful."

"I know that you must have a tremendous workload, however I hope that you will find the time to schedule this bill through your committee so that the full Senate can take action to approve S. 533 in a similar fashion to that of the House of Representatives so that the President can sign this legislation," argued a third. "I hear that attempts are being made to have a judicial review which I believe will doom this bill."

"Isn't it about time you people who are supposed to be our leaders did something good for our own people with no strings attached?????" read a fourth.

Most of the letter writers didn't know the first thing about the Economy Act, the VA's internal system, the "Fact-Pattern Study," nor any of the technical arguments we had made. Nor did most know what S. 533 was or what "non-related amendments" were. They didn't have to. All they needed to do was express their right to be heard with a pen and paper. Absent other letters, senators tend to listen.

After digging through the mail, counting the committee votes, and debating the issue back and forth for a week, Glenn finally made the only decision he could: linkage between Cabinet status and judicial review would be tabled for the time being. This was one of the most difficult announcements Glenn ever made as chairman. Ironically, Glenn made the announcement at the tail end of his otherwise blistering opening statement at the third and final hearing on cabinet status. "Veterans are not to me second-class citizens," he said, "I can guarantee that, being a veteran myself. And they should not be treated in a second-class manner. I do not believe, however, that the provision of judicial review should be in the elevation bill . . . Judicial review is in the jurisdiction of another committee, and the two issues should be considered separately on their own merits."

Before he could even finish the announcement, the veterans in the audience broke into applause, pushing Glenn into another rare display of anger: "I would urge the veterans organizations, of which I'm a member of almost every organization myself, to look at this thing—please look at it again, see if you don't believe that veterans are going to get a fair shake at the end of the VA process, if we go that route."

Although the committee staffers knew the announcement was coming, it was dispiriting nonetheless. Judicial review had been the centerpiece of our search for a way to redeem the Cabinet bill and Glenn's decision, however difficult, left us wondering whether we could salvage anything from the past six months. If not an explicit link to judicial review, then what?

Although it seemed like very small consolation at the time, the American Legion did promise Glenn that it would at least reconsider its position on judicial review. Within weeks, the Legion would become the first of the big groups to endorse the *case*, if not the Senate bill, for judicial review.

The hearing was not without its moments, however, particularly Simpson's opening statement. Whatever the Democrats thought of his stands on defense spending or Reaganomics, Simpson was right on target on veterans and funny to boot. "We do very nicely by veterans in this country, Mr. Chairman," he concluded, "always will. What is the gripe? What is the gripe? I guess it's simply that all good soldiers and sailors and marines do that—but it doesn't mean they always mean it. I think it's a real mistake, an overreaction to a non-problem. And I respectfully submit those views, knowing full well what awaits me in the next monthly publication of every damned one of [their] magazines."

There were occasional hot points in the hearing, too.

Both Glenn and Levin continued to pester the White House over Reagan's support for Cabinet status, taking their frustrations out of Office of Management and Budget (OMB) deputy director Joseph Wright. The OMB exists to give the president advice on both budget and management, and we know from inside sources that the advice on VA Cabinet status has not been in favor. Like any staffer, however, Wright was not about to criticize his boss. At best, all the Committee could do was make Wright a bit uncomfortable:

> Chairman Glenn. Mr. Wright, as I understand it, the original recommendation from OMB to the President was to oppose the elevation of VA to cabinet status, is that correct?
>
> Mr. Wright. Mr. Chairman, while I am reluctant to state exactly what our internal recommendations are—and I hope you appreciate that—with the president, you have to recall that OMB gives a careful review of most expansions and elevations. This is part of our job. We tend to be very conservative in the nature of our recommendations. And that's one of the reasons why we provide an offset in terms of the recommendations that come into the President. So if you don't mind, I would like to hedge that question a little bit, because that is Presidential Communication.
>
> Chairman Glenn. Well, OK, I understand that. I guess my next question, though, would be what caused you to change your mind?
>
> Mr. Wright. Well, that's very easy—it's called good career planning, Senator Glenn.

Despite an occasional breath of life, the hearing was hardly the high point of the year for us. Our secret witness who had promised to blow the whistle on the system got a case of stage fright and mumbled through a confusing discussion that eventually led Glenn to throw up his hands in frustration. Glenn simply could not understand how the veterans groups could oppose judicial review. He had never believed that the VA was abusing unsuspecting veterans or that the agency was making too many mistakes. Quite the contrary. He just felt going to court was a basic right that veterans had earned. His simple commitment was evident in his final bite on the veterans groups at the very end of the hearing. "I would think that just with what you gentlemen have heard here this morning," Glenn concluded, "the veterans organizations would be in here clamoring to get judicial review, not to stop it."

Even before the hearing was over, we all knew that Governmental Affairs was in for a licking on the editorial pages. The press table was packed the moment before Glenn's announcement, stark empty the next. Much as I braced myself, nothing prepared me for the *Washington Post* editorial the next morning. The painful truth was that the Senate and House got the editorial the old-fashioned way— they earned it:

> John Glenn let it be known early on that the Senate wouldn't be stampeded into raising the Veterans Administration to Cabinet status the way those weather vanes in the House had done. No sir. Senators are serious people, heavyweights, statesmen even. They'd do it right. "As I said at our first meeting on elevation last Dec. 9, if we are going to elevate this agency to the front lines of the executive branch, we must do it right."
>
> And the chairman of the Governmental Affairs Committee made it clear on several occasions that by "right" he meant, among other things, subjecting VA benefits decisions to judicial review. They aren't subject to such scrutiny now, which distinguishes the VA from the ordinary agencies of government. The law is such that dissatisfied seekers after VA benefits can neither hire lawyers nor go to court. The veterans' group represent them, their only appeal is to the VA's own appeals board—and the veterans' groups and agency like it that way. Now the Senate would use the Cabinet-status bill to change the system, open it up. "The rights of a few is what we're talking about," Sen. Glenn said. "I don't want to wax poetic, but that's what America is all about."
>
> Or was all about: he spoke before the veterans' groups

had gotten to him. They applied all the pressure for which they are justly famous over the past several weeks, and the other day the senator ignominiously caved. "I don't plan to clutter things up in this committee," he announced to applause. "Judicial review is in the jurisdiction of another committee, and the two issues should be considered separately."

The steamrolling of John Glenn is proof of how redundant this capitulative bill is. Its stated purpose is to see that the interests of veterans are not somehow neglected at the highest levels of the executive branch. Fat chance. The veterans have their own subgovernment— their own agency, their own committees of Congress— that already works so efficiently that they may regret the increased visibility and scrutiny that are likely to accompany Cabinet status. The veterans budget of $27 billion a year supports a double standard. No one disputes that the country has an obligation to those it sends to war— to support the wounded, to help other returnees make up for lost time. The veterans' programs go beyond these service-connected programs, and the advocates would extend them further still.

Having rolled a willing president and House, the subculture now appears about to have its way with a willing Senate as well. The only difference is that the Senate likes to look a little thoughtful as it folds. Remember that the next time you hear them talking about the world's greatest deliberating body. They talk big, but they're featherweights too.[15]

The headline of the editorial? "Featherweights."

Unfortunately, in a moment of despair right after the hearing, I talked to a reporter from the *New York Times* about judicial review, noting with some chagrin that Senator Mitchell, of future majority leader fame, had withdrawn his support for linkage, "leaving Senator Glenn hanging out there all alone, taking a terrible pounding from Ohio." The next morning, the *Times* faithfully reported the quote as being from an anonymous source, but my name might as well have been in bold face. No one involved had any trouble at all figuring it out, including Glenn and Mitchell. Two days in the cooler. That incident taught me one of the many rules staff must learn to live by when working on Capitol Hill: always assume that everything you say might end up in the paper, and therefore, never say anything you might regret.

5

Rules to Live By
(Markup and Committee Passage)

FIVE RULES TO live by as a Senate staffer.

Rule One: Never take the "Senators Only" elevator when Congress is in session. There is nothing worse than to get caught sneaking a ride on these exclusive elevators when a "senator only" happens to be waiting at your stop.

Rule Two: Never get caught without a tie. Even in the dog days of August, with everything baking in the Washington heat and humidity, there is always a chance that a senior White House official will call for a meeting or that the Senator just might be in town. It is definitely *not* okay to staple your shirt closed because you lost a button, or to wear blue jeans and a Toronto Blue-Jays T-shirt to a meeting between the senator and the director of the Office of Management and Budget.

Rule Three: Never swing at the first pitch in a Senate softball game. Odds are you'll just pound the ball into the dirt for an easy out or, worse yet, hit a weak pop-up to third base. Students who aspire to rewarding careers in public affairs ought to take softball and tennis as advanced coursework.

Rule Four: Never tell a U.S. senator "it can't be done." I once made the mistake of telling Sen. Wendell Ford (D-Ky.) that I simply did not have the time to work on his biennial budget bill, at which point he said, "There is night after day, Son."

Rule Five: Never, ever handle more than one bill at a markup. It is the quickest way to go crazy and inevitably leads to repeated violations of the first four rules. Alas, that is exactly what I was scheduled to do at our April markup, for I had more than one bill in my portfolio.

Like most committee staff, I was responsible for more than just the Department of Veterans Affairs Act. Despite those who say Congress is overstaffed, a better case can be made that Congress is over-billed. Not only was I the designated hitter on budget reform and all other executive organization bills, I was also hard at work on the Presidential Transitions Effectiveness Act, a bill we had developed at Glenn's behest.

The transitions bill moved forward in a very different way from the VA bill. While the VA bill had been initiated from the outside, driven forward by highly motivated lobbying groups, the transitions bill was initiated from the inside, pushed forward by the staff and a single senator. The VA bill reflected raw power politics; the transitions bill involved the influence of ideas. Simply put, the transitions bill was an inside job from start to finish, garnering very little publicity, yet making a substantial change in the way presidents come into office.

The purpose of the transitions bill was to smooth the transfer of power across administrations. Number one, we knew that there would be a new president in 1989. There was no question about it. Under the Twenty-second Amendment to the Constitution, Ronald Reagan faced a two-term limit, and his second term was just about up.

Number two, the next president-elect would have several thousand top jobs to fill, including at least ten to fifteen brand-new jobs at the Department of Veterans Affairs. Providing support for some advance planning just might help the president-elect pick better people.

Number three, the new president would have thousands of campaign workers, long-lost friends, financial backers, and hangers-on either looking for work or pushing their own pet projects. Limiting the amount of private cash raised during the transition might help the president-elect just say "no."

Number four, the incoming president would have but three months, and $2 million in federal funding, to prepare for office, making one decision after another on people and policy, setting an agenda that would determine the future of the administration. Upping the amount of federal funding for the transition might improve the prospects of success in getting it all done on time.

Given these pressures, it is little wonder that a transition is one of the most important and exciting moments in a presidential term. The risks are great, but so, too, are the opportunities. Although every presidential campaign must focus on winning the election as the first priority—transition planning hardly matters for candidates who know they are about to get slaughtered, such as George McGovern in 1972 or Walter Mondale in 1984—a little advance planning can spell the difference between hitting the ground running or merely hitting the ground flat.

Despite the case for a little advance planning, practically every incentive is to focus solely on the campaign. Not only are top political staff reluctant to spend scarce time and resources on the transition in the midst of a battle for political survival, the Federal Election Commission ruled in 1978 that transition planning is not a "qualified campaign expense" and cannot be funded out of the public money given to the two presidential candidates.[1] In short, there is no readily available money for a transition-planning operation before election day.

Unfortunately, if either candidate wanted to do some transition planning during the 1988 general election campaign, he or she would have to raise private funds to do so. Despite alloting $200 million in public financing for the presidential candidates, the federal government gave absolutely nothing for transition planning. Indeed, the federal government gave more money to the two natural parties to run their national conventions—to pay for balloons, receptions, platform committees—and to the outgoing president to move back home than it would allow a presidential candidate to spend on transition planning:

Amount given to each of the two party candidates in 1988 for the general election campaigns	$44,000,000
Amount given to the Democratic and Republican national committees each for their nominating conventions	$9,000,000
Amount given to the *incoming* president for transition expenses between election day and inauguration only	$2,000,000
Amount given to the *outgoing* president for moving expenses back home	$1,000,000
Total amount given to former presidents Jimmy Carter, Gerald Ford, and Richard Nixon for annual expenses (Secret Service protection, offices) in fiscal year 1989	$1,300,000
Total amount *given* to the two party candidates for preelection transition planning	0
Total amount *allowable* for transition planning by the two party candidates or the two party organizations out of any public funds	0

Admittedly, the lack of transition planning is not the worst scandal of all time. So what if presidents don't think ahead? So what if presidents are late filling the key jobs? So what if presidents have to raise private cash to make up the shortfall? The answer, of course, is that it matters very much. What happens in the first days of an administration has a profound effect on its ultimate success. Again, the risks are great, the opportunities greater.

Indeed, the more Glenn looked at the problem, the more it seemed worth fixing, especially the little problem with the growing amount of private cash given to the president-elect for the transition. After holding hearings to make the case, Glenn introduced the Presidential Transitions Effectiveness Act on February 4, 1988. It was the 2037th bill in the 1987–88 list—hence, S. 2037.

Glenn's primary interest in the Presidential Transitions Effectiveness Act was to limit the amount of private cash and in-kind contributions flooding the presidential campaign and transition under the label of transition planning. Unlike campaign funds, which have to be accounted for down to the penny, presidential candidates prior to 1988 were free to raise as much private cash as they wanted as long as it was *not* used to pay election costs—for expenses like television commercials, voter registration, phone banks.

Also unlike campaign funds, which must be reported publicly in amounts down to $200, including in-kind contributions like the $1,825 in chocolate cookies Famous Amos gave to the Democratic National Convention in 1984, past presidential candidates were not required to report any of the contributions for transition planning—not who gave the money, not how much, not what the money was used for. Basically, the lack of regulation created two kinds of campaign dollars: one tightly regulated and one completely unfettered.

The lack of reporting requirements during the campaign was paralleled in the transition. During the brief three months between election and inauguration, there were no accounting or reporting regulations on private cash at all, for the president-elect was neither a candidate for election nor a public official. As Glenn described the transition, "you can't spend a jillion dollars to get elected unless you report it, then we reach election day and all bets are off." (I never did find out what a "jillion" was.)

For Glenn, the problem with private cash was not so much that Nixon, Carter, and Reagan had raised private funds to cover some of their transition costs—Carter spent roughly $200,000 in 1976; Reagan spent about $1.1 million; and no one is quite sure how much Nixon spent. Rather, the problem was that none of the money was reported—no one knew who gave it or where it went. "We have passed, through the years, all sorts of things that the Federal Election Commission applies in the election process," Glenn explained at the first transition hearing in September 1987. "It has to be very carefully reported down to the penny and believe me I know from experience that if it is not right down to the penny, they get on your back and you have to account for it."

Glenn had had more than his share of Federal Election Commission squabbles over his 1984 presidential campaign. "I have been through that routine in spades so I am aware of the difficulty," he explained. "But then we get to the election and the transition period and all at once we say, now you can go out and accept the half a million dollars if you want to for whatever purpose you want and no ac-countability whatsoever. Talk about influence in govern-ment and conflict-of-interest potential."

The notion that the president-elect should be excused from any accounting just because the cash is for the tran-sition made no sense to Glenn. Whether the cash came in the campaign or the transition, it was all theoretically in-tended to purchase something. By making the cash visible in the campaign, at least the public could guard against influence peddling. As long as the cash was invisible in the transition, the potential for buying and selling remained.

The potential for scandal was heightened in 1980 when president-elect Reagan and his top staff raised $1.1 million in private funds to support the administration's transition.

According to available records, there were at least two Reagan transition bank accounts—the first called the "Presidential Transition Trust" and the second the "Presidential Transition Foundation, Inc."

Tax records on the Transition Foundation, Inc., showed contributions of just over $1.1 million, all of it raised in amounts of $5,000 or less, and most of it spent in three large categories of expenses: roughly $140,000 on salaries; $390,000 on travel, presumably for potential presidential appointees and transition staff; and $241,849 for something called "other professional service," whatever that means.[2] One of the biggest tickets was $86,047.83 to cover a bill from Califano, Ross & Heineman, the Washington law firm that helped prepare Alexander Haig for his confirmation hearings to become secretary of state.[3] No one ever found out how much the Transition Trust raised or spent—those figures were completely secret.

Although these amounts were trivial compared to the millions spent in the general campaign, the fact that future attorney general Edwin Meese and future CIA director William Casey were the key officials of Transitions, Inc., was troubling at best. By 1988, both had been linked to scandals involving money, favors, and influence peddling. Although the other officers of the Transition Foundation had impeccable credentials, the combination of Meese, Casey, and $1 million in private money made even the most trusting staffer gasp.

This is not to say that there was corruption at the Reagan transition headquarters on M Street in Washington, D.C. Indeed, all the evidence suggests that the money went for limousines, penthouses, luxury suites, black-tie dinners, caviar, first-class plane tickets, and such. Those kinds of expenditures for some may have set the wrong tone for a presidential administration, but they are not illegal.

Nevertheless, Glenn wanted those dollars regulated and any appearance of scandal eliminated. What made the overall bill particularly appealing, however, was that it was clearly in the Governmental Affairs Committee jurisdiction, was relatively simple and noncontroversial, and might actually make a small difference in the quality of government. As such, it stood in some contrast to the VA bill, which if left untouched, would hardly make a difference at all.

By this point in the process, both the Presidential Transitions Effectiveness Act and the Department of Veterans Affairs Act were ready for final committee action. Both had been through hearings to establish a reason for passage; both had been drafted and reviewed by Glenn, staff director Weiss, and a host of other players; both had parallel measures moving forward in the House, though this is by no means necessary for Senate action.

A parallel transitions bill meant that prospects for final House-Senate passage were good. The House had passed its version of Glenn's transitions bill, H.R. 3932, several weeks earlier, and was ready to appoint a conference committee to iron out the differences as soon as the Senate moved a parallel measure. A conference committee's sole purpose is to provide a forum for members of the House and Senate to reach a compromise. Instead of passing two bills back and forth until one is finally accepted, often with amendments, a conference committee short-cuts the process by forging a single bill from the two original versions.

The only remaining hurdle in the way of Senate floor action was the markup. A markup was an unavoidable part of the Governmental Affairs Committee procedures and an important signal to the Senate that these bills had the jurisdictional seal of approval.

On the surface, a markup looks like a very simple event. Get the fourteen Governmental Affairs Committee members together in one place, whether the hearing room or just off the Senate floor.* Discuss the given bill. Debate any

---

* Eight Democrats and six Republicans. The number and ratio of members is set by the final agreement of the Senate. In the House, the number is set by the majority party leadership only.

amendments. "Markup" the bill with the changes. Pass it with a committee majority and move on to the next item—bang, bang, bang. (The same process was used to approve presidential nominees.) In reality, a markup is sheer chaos, or at least that's the way it is in most congressional committees, including Governmental Affairs.

For one thing, markup may be of little interest to the members, especially with competing hearings, markups, and floor debate elsewhere. Thus, merely getting the requisite number of senators—or quorum—into the room may be next to impossible. Governmental Affairs, for example, could vote out a bill only with a quorum of eight members present. Those eight members had to be in the room for a brief instant, but they had to be there for that one single moment together. A "rolling quorum," in which eight members might come and go over an hour, is simply not allowed by committee rules for passing legislation. In fact, the absence of a quorum does not necessarily mean disinterest on the part of the absent members. Sometimes the best way to kill a bill is to deny a quorum, thereby avoiding an unpleasant public vote one way or the other.

Clearly, markup does not occur in a vacuum, and cannot be viewed as just another step in the legislative process. Decisions made on a bill today can and do reflect decisions made on bills past, as well as decisions on bills future, even if the bills are entirely unrelated. Members of Congress may have the longest memories of any living being. The fact that amendment X is important to Senator Y may trigger an instinctive wave of intense opposition, albeit disguised in courteous terms. Contrary to textbook notions, Congress does *not* consider every bill as a separate issue or in proper sequence—bills have a way of getting tangled up together.

Thus, markup is best viewed as the staging ground for future floor action in both chambers, as well as success in the final conference committee. For example, Glenn's decision to use Thurmond's original Cabinet bill, S. 533, as a vehicle for the committee alternative, meant he could keep all sixty-five cosponsors, clearly strengthening the committee's hand in conference, even though the bill number and list of cosponsors were just about the only thing that would survive intact. Instead of introducing his own bill, Glenn would offer an amendment in the nature of a substitute, striking every paragraph, sentence, word, and punctuation mark after the enacting clause of Thurmond's original measure, canceling the original bill in everything but name only.

The decision involved much more than simple deference toward Thurmond, however, Thurmond, the most senior veterans spokesman in either chamber, had first attempted to elevate the VA two decades before Brooks took up the cause in the House in 1987. Keeping Thurmond at the top of the Senate bill would, we hoped, dilute what little advantage the House had gained by passing the VA elevation bill first—because the House had *acted* first, the final legislation would carry a House bill number (H.R. 3471).

What goes into a bill at markup can determine what comes out at the final conference between the House and Senate. In the final legislative negotiation between two bills, the key is to figure out what each side really wants, and what each is willing to trade. Conferences become rather like a high stakes game of "Go Fish." As committees plan their conference strategies, they may add items as simple fodder for future trades. Political scientists Lawrence Longley and Walter Oleszek offer the following list as a partial sampling of markup tactics:

> Keeping something out of a bill that the other chamber favors so leverage can be obtained with the other body; or, alternatively, putting proposals in the bill that the other body wants in order to encourage that chamber reaching the conference stage;
>
> Adding politically palatable provisions that can be used as bargaining chips with conferees from the other body;

Weakening or otherwise changing a bill in committee so that it stands a better chance of winning majority support on the floor. Supporters can then try to persuade conferences to strengthen the measure in conference;

Providing guidelines or directives for decision making in conference; or

Crafting a bill that includes the priority proposals of targeted leaders and factions in the other body.[4]

Ultimately, a successful markup represents a rather unique combination of the mundane and spectacular. Not only must the staff make sure a quorum is present, they must write the opening statements, anticipate any hostile amendments, gather proxy votes allowing absent senators to vote, develop counterstrategies, and secure political support. This is the mundane.

Despite the endless list of phone calls to secretaries and lobbyists, markup is also one of the few times when staff ever have a speaking role in committees. For lack of time, most members simply cannot explain, let alone defend, all the fine points of their own bills. Therefore, key staff are always front and center, walking the committee through each bill and amendment, and sometimes finally getting just a bit of credit for all the work that goes into a bill. Even though it rarely happens, this is the spectacular.

Our April 14 markup of the Cabinet bill is a good case in point. Because it was the committee's first markup in almost six months, there was a veritable pileup of legislation and nominations at the Governmental Affairs Committee. The March 15 markup had been canceled for the lack of a quorum, leaving the following items for April, each one demanding a summary from the chairman, a separate discussion, and a final vote one way or the other. Given that we couldn't hold a quorum for more than two hours, if that, it was a staggering load:

Governmental Affairs Committee
Markup
Tuesday, April 14, 1988
9:30 A.M.
Room 342 of the Dirksen Senate Office Building

Agenda

Nominations

Frank Schwelb, to be an Associate Judge of the District of Columbia Court of Appeals

Cheryl Long, to be an Associate Judge of the District of Columbia Superior Court

Frank DeGeorge to be Inspector General, Department of Commerce

Legislation

S. 533, to elevate the Veterans' Administration to Cabinet status, with an amendment in the nature of a substitute

S. 1081, to establish a national nutrition monitoring and related research program, with amendments

S. 1381, to improve Federal cash management and ensure equity in funding Federal programs administered by the States, with an amendment

S. 1856, to authorize funds for programs of the National Historical Publications and Records Commission, with an amendment

S. 2037, to eliminate the use of private resources in the transition process and to provide for the orderly transfer of power between administrations, with an amendment in the nature of a substitute

S. 2215, to amend the Office of Federal Procurement Policy to authorize appropriations for an additional four years

Obviously, the first step toward success is to make sure the basic bill is ready, a step that involves negotiating with the boss, the staff director, and committee staffers. It is always possible to fix a bill once it has passed the committee by using "perfecting" or "techincal" amendments on the floor—amendments designed to fix typos and other mistakes. Every subsequent change has a cost, however, whether in the round of phone calls needed to explain the mistakes or in a growing reptuation for sloppy draftsmanship that will haunt future markups. We went through eight drafts of the bill before the Department of Veterans Affairs Act was ready for markup, each draft a little more precise, each one containing another small compromise to garner support from the Veterans Affairs Committee or some other corner of the Senate.

Each draft was also a little longer. By the markup in April, Glenn's Cabinet bill had grown from Thurmond's original six-page, six-section bill to thirty-seven pages and twenty sections! We had added sections to set limits on the number of political appointees in the new department and to change the rules governing internal reorganizations (remember that the VA could not reorganize an office of 2.5 employees or more without first notifying Congress), and even a section creating a National Commission on Executive Organization to study the basic structure of the president's Cabinet. We hoped the commission might forestall a rush of other proposals for elevation of other agencies. The extra length was the product of negotiation along the way, some between Glenn and Thurmond, some between the two key Senate committees, some in anticipation of troubles in the House.

One way to illustrate the bargaining that went into the VA bill is to look at the evolution of Glenn's provision on the appointment of the chief medical director, one of the top jobs in the new VA. Much to our surprise, the Senate Veterans Affairs Committee was absolutely opposed to any change in the existing nonpolitical status of the position. Keeping the job nonpolitical would give the Veterans Committee the greatest influence over its occupant. Why bring the president into it?

It was not that Glenn wanted a phalanx of political appointees running the new department. Quite the contrary. He had always favored tight controls on the numbers of political jobs. Nevertheless, Glenn also believed that the President should have a role in selecting the third most-important job in the department.

This is where a staff director comes in particularly handy, for Len Weiss was just as tough in defending our turf as the staff director of the Vets Committee, Jonathan Steinberg, was in asserting his. Steinberg's alias was "Senator Cranberg," a name coined to capture his prominent role as Cranston's alter ego on veterans policy. Weiss, going toe-to-toe against Steinberg through a series of excruciating negotiations, would not yield, making compromise at my staff level more likely. Both staffs knew that Glenn and Cranston would not want a floor fight over something as small as who would appoint the chief medical director.

The best way to appreciate the art of legislative negotiations, as well as the minutia, is to work through the compromise on the chief medical director appointment mechanism as a simple illustration of how a bill evolves, word by often boring word. (I'll skip the fine print here.) Version *one* of the bill, introduced by Thurmond, actually contained no provision whatsoever regarding a medical director. Version *two* of the bill, drafted by the House Government Operations Committee, contained one subparagraph:

(b) Chief Medical Director.—There shall be in the Department of Chief Medical Director, who shall be a doctor of medicine and shall, subject to subsection (e), be appointed by the President, by and with the advice and consent of the Senate, without regard to political affiliation and solely on the basis of integrity and demonstrated ability in the medical profession. The chief Medical Director shall be appointed for a period of four years, with reappointment permissible for successive like periods. If the President removes the Chief Medical Director before the expiration of that four-year term of office, the President shall communicate the reasons for such removal to both Houses of Congress.

A provisions go, this appointment mechanism was relatively straightforward. The medical director was to be a presidential appointee, heading the old Department of Medicine and Surgery under the new name of Veterans Health Services Administration, and would serve for four years unless the president decided otherwise.

Version *three*, drafted by the Senate Governmental Affairs Committee, tightened the rules significantly, balancing the Veterans Committee concerns about an infusion of partisan politics into the operation of the VA—no one wanted a political hack running the VA hospitals—with our demand for accountability to the president at the top of this huge health-care delivery system. This was the first of our several attemps to calm the Veterans Committee. The language was located at Section 3(b) of our bill:[5]

(b) Chief Medical Director.—(1) There shall be in the Department a Chief Medical Director, who shall be a doctor of medicine and shall, subject to subsection (f), be appointed by the President, by and with the advice and consent of the Senate, without regard to political affiliation *and solely on the basis of integrity and demonstrated ability in the medical profession*. The Chief Medical Director shall be the head of, and shall be directly responsible to the Secretary for the operation of, the Veterans Health Services Administration.

(2) *(A) When a vacancy occurs in the position of Chief Medical Director, the Secretary of Veterans Affairs shall establish a commission to recommend individuals to the President for appointment to the position.*

(B) The commission shall be composed of the following members appointed by the Secretary:

(i) Three representatives of medical education affected by the Veterans Health Services Administration.

(ii) Six representatives of veterans served by the Veterans Health Services Administration.

> *(iii) The Deputy Secretary of the Department of Veterans Affairs.*
>
> *(iv) Two representatives from departments and agencies of the Federal Government affected by the Veterans Health Services Administration.*
>
> *(C) The commission shall recommend at least three individuals for appointment to the position of Chief Medical Director. The Commission, after submitting its recommendations to the President shall provide additional individuals recommended for appointment to the position if the President requests the additional recommendations.*
>
> (3) If the President removes the Chief Medical Director, the President shall communicate the reasons for such removal to both Houses of Congress.

As far as compromises go, this was much more symbolic than substantial. Integrity and demonstrated ability in the medical profession is entirely subjective, while the search commission was entirely advisory. Turns out that the head of the General Accounting Office, the Comptroller General of the United States, was appointed under a similiar mechanism, setting a precedent for the VA. The beauty of the approach was that the president would receive three names, could ask for more, but would not be forced to appoint anyone. Any provision forcing the president to appoint someone from the search commission's list would be unconstitutional—the president, not Congress, was responsible for nominations under the appointments clause.

Advisory though it was, the Senate committees resolved their disagreements and agreed on a search commission, even though it later became the focus of intense bargaining between the House and Senate over both the number of search commission members and their qualifications. By adopting the search commission, we met the Veterans Committee's concern about presidential appointees, while addressing our own demand that the top jobs be subject to the president's authority.

The agreement notwithstanding, we still had several versions to go before finding the "right" combination of elements of the compromise, but with something called the Veterans Health Services *and Research* Administration in place of the old department of medicine and surgery. The name change had been requested, again, by the Senate Vets Committee, as a way to communicate an even broader mission for the health system:

(B) The commission shall be composed of the following members appointed by the Secretary:

(i) Three representatives of medical *research* and education affected by the Veterans Health Services *and Research* Administration.

(ii) *Two representatives of health care professionals employed by the Veterans Health Services and Research Administration.*

(iii) *Four* representatives of veterans served by the Veterans Health Services *and Research* Administration.

(iv) The Deputy Secretary of the Department of Veterans Affairs.

(v) *Any person who had held the position of Chief Medical Director, but only if the Secretary determines that it is desirable for such a person to be a member of the Commission.*

(vi) *Two experts in the management of veterans health services and research programs or similiar programs in the public or private sector.*

We are now engaged in an exasperating and time-consuming debate over the mix of representatives on the commission, the qualifications of the chief medical director, and the name of the new Veterans Health Services Administration. By the time we reached version *eight*, presented to the Governmental Affairs Committee at markup, on April 14, the level of detail had become stunning:

(b) CHIEF MEDICAL DIRECTOR.—(1) There shall be in the Department a Chief Medical Director, who shall be a doctor of medicine and shall, subject to subsection (e), be appointed by the President, by and with the advice and consent of the Senate, without regard to political affiliation or political qualification and solely on the basis of integrity and demonstrated ability in the medical profession, *in health-care administration and policy formulation, and in health-care fiscal management, and on the basis of substantial experience in connection with the activities of the Veterans Health Services and Research Administration. The Chief Medical Director shall be appointed for a period of 4 years, with reappointment permissible for successive like periods.* The Chief Medical Director shall be the head of, and shall be directly responsible to the Secretary for the operation of, the Veterans Health Services and Research Administration.

(2) (A) Whenever a vacancy in the position of Chief Medical Director occurs *or is anticipated*, the secretary of Veterans Affairs shall establish a commission to recommend individuals to the President for appointment to the position.

(B) The Commission shall be composed of the following members appointed by the Secretary:

(i) Three representatives of *clinical care and* medical research and education *activities affected by* the Veterans Health Services and Research Administration.

(ii) *One* representative of *physicians and one representative of nurses* employed by the Veterans Health Services and Research Administration.

(iii) Four representatives of veterans served by the Veterans Health Services and Research Administration.

(iv) *Not more than two persons* who have held the position of Chief Medical Director, but only if the Secretary determines that it is desirable for each person appointed under this clause to be a member of the Commission.

(v) Two persons who have experience in the management of veterans health services and research programs, *or programs similar in content or scope, in the public or private sector.*

(vi) The Deputy Secretary of Veterans Affairs.

(C) *At least two members of the Commission shall be veterans receiving compensation for service-connected disability under laws administered by the Secretary of Veterans Affairs.*

The Commission had grown from twelve members to fourteen, and the categories of appointment had changed dramatically, reflecting demands for representation from within the VA health system. This bill was very important to a small but intensely committed set of players from the iron triangle, which meant that we would argue over virtually every sentence, word, and punctuation mark in the bill.[6] Seeing a new opportunity for influencing veterans policy, the triangle wanted its piece of the action.

Indeed, the debate over the search commission confirmed two general rules about legislative drafting. First, because small words make big differences, be prepared to defend any and every point. Second, because symbols are every bit as important as substance, be prepared to fight over the structure of the bill, the order of names, and the titles of commissions.

That is not to say the final compromise was without its admirers. In fact, it actually became a model for subsequent proposals to elevate other agencies to Cabinet status—a group of moderate Republicans led by Sen. David Durenberger (R-Minn.) picked up our final version of S. 533, changed "Veterans Affairs" to "Environmental Protection" whenever it appeared, pulled one or two other items out, and introduced it as the Department of Environmental Protection Act. It wasn't so much that we had found the secret ingredients of a successful Cabinet department, of course, but that no one knew any better.

With Glenn's VA bill finally finished, we began the process of selling it to other committee members and staff. Our pitch was really quite simple. First, the bill had four fewer political appointees than the House measure, allowing the president to select a secretary, deputy secretary, up to four assistant secretaries, an inspector general, general counsel, and the chief medical and benefits directors.

Much more importantly for precedent, the bill also restricted the number of secondary political appointments in the new department—that is, appointments *not* subject to

Senate advice and consent. Under existing law governing the career civil service, the new secretary of veterans affairs would have been able to appoint another twenty-five to thirty noncareer, or political, members of the Senior Executive Service (SES), and an unlimited number of personal and confidential assistants. The SES was created in 1978 as an elite corps of six thousand or so top career servants, with up to 10 percent of the total selected on a noncareer basis by the president as political appointees.

It was Glenn's view that large numbers of such political appointees squeeze out most of the opportunities for career officials to participate in the governance of a department. Whatever we thought at the moment about the caliber of talent in the veterans benefits program, we had to stick with our basic belief in giving career civil servants the chance to rise to the top of the new department. Under Glenn's bill, therefore, the secretary would be restricted by three provisions: (1) a limit on the number of noncareer senior executives, (2) a limit on the number of personal and confidential, or Schedule C, assistants available to each political appointee, and (3) a prohibition against taking political affiliation or political qualifications into account for nonpolitical appointments.

As far as I was concerned, these were by far the most significant items in the entire bill, for they sent the message that political and career officers would have to work together, that there would be a limit to the politicization of the new department. Basically, the three provisions meant that the secretary would have a total of only twenty to twenty-two additional political appointments within the new department. By using the term "notwithstanding," we made clear that the secretary would be governed by this bill first, not the more flexible provisions of the civil service statute located at Title 5 of the U.S. Code.

Still more important for preventing politicization was the section of Glenn's bill that created up to fifteen deputy assistant secretaries who would work under the four assistant secretaries. From an agency management viewpoint, these deputies would occupy the critical layer where the three dozen or so political leaders finally met the 240,000 civil servants. By requiring that at least two-thirds of these fifteen appointments be career civil servants, our bill sent a strong message to the new department that there was room at the top for them. Were the bill successful, it would become a model for restricting political penetration of other federal agencies and departments.

Once the formal markup began not-so-promptly at 9:50, most of the committee members were willing to defer to Glenn. No matter that I spent most of the night before markup drawing organization charts describing the new department, most of the committee members simply didn't care. No matter that I had secured enough "proxy" votes from Democrats who would not be present to defeat any amendments that might come up. This was hardly the most exciting bill of all time, and with judicial review off limits, there was little cause for controversy. With the committee members seated around a conference table in the well where the witnesses normally sat, the markup of S. 533, The Department of Veterans Affairs Act, came and went without incident. So did S. 2037, The Presidential Transitions Effectiveness Act. Although the markup lasted roughly an hour, almost forty minutes was spent standing around waiting for the quorum to arrive. "Is that Nunn?" "No, he's not coming." "What about Pryor?" "Should be here in ten minutes." "Where's Levin?" "He's got another markup right now." "What about Stevens?" "He'll be late."

In fact, the only controversy of the day involved the "burial" of the old Department of Memorial Affairs. Under Glenn's bill, it would be absorbed into the new Veterans Benefits Administration. After a good deal of debate back and forth between Republican Heinz and Democrat Pryor, it was agreed that the committee would specifically note that the functions of Memorial Affairs would be administered by a deputy chief benefits director. Simple enough. With no further discussion, Glenn asked for a vote. Unanimous. Onto the next issue. Grand total time? Ten minutes.

As the organization chart for the new department suggests, Glenn's bill was not radically different from Brooks's. The old Department of Memorial Affairs was now a subunit of the new Veterans Benefits Administration, and there were four fewer assistant secretaries, but the overall structure was similiar. Like Brooks's bill, H.R. 3417, there was a secretary and deputy secretary with the normal responsibilities. The old Department of Memorial Affairs wound up under the new Benefits Administration in S. 533, but it could just as easily have been placed under an assistant secretary à la Brooks. There are only so many ways to draw the wiring diagrams.

This is not to say there were no differences. Rather, they were to be found not in the wiring diagram, but in the limitations on political appointees and the sundry provisions for search commissions and strengthening of the new department's inspector general staff.

All in all, the markup went extraordinarily well—no surprise amendments, no delaying maneuvers, no hard questions. Although there were six months left in the session, the legislative clock was accelerating.

All minutes are not created equal on Capitol Hill—a minute at the beginning of a Congress is much longer than a minute at the end, if only because staff find it so much more difficult to get time with the boss as the campaign season heats up. With the presidential primaries in full swing, with Massachusetts Governor Michael Dukakis and Vice-President George Bush virtually assured of nomination, the end of the session couldn't be far off.

More important, with a long queue of legislation already waiting for floor action, the pressure was on to file my two bills as fast as possible. The veterans gave us no choice on the VA bill. If we wanted the preelection planning provision to make any difference on the transitions bill, it had to be passed before the national party conventions, only three

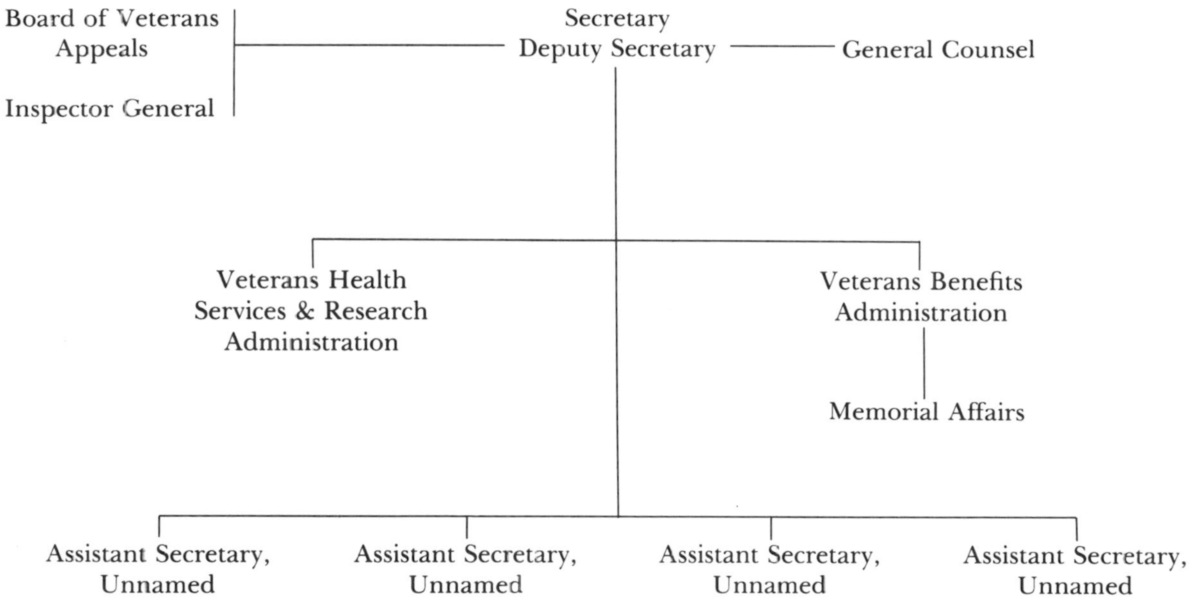

Figure 4. The Department of Veterans Affairs, S. 533 as reported

months away. It is not enough to simply pass a bill in committee. The bill must be packaged into a separate report, governed by strict Senate rules on format and style, and be presented to the Senate. Section 403 of the Congressional Budget and Impoundment Control Act of 1974, for example, requires an estimate of the potential cost of any legislation, paragraph 11 (b) (1) of Rule XXVI of the Standing Rules of the Senate requires a regulatory impact statement, while paragraph 12 requires a detailed statement of any changes in existing law made by the bill.

Above all else, however, a legislative report must provide some insights on just what the legislation actually means. Much as Governmental Affairs tried to make its intent clear in the texts of S. 533 and S. 2037, the legislative reports would help the president and the courts figure out what Congress meant if they needed help implementing or interpreting the bills.

The veterans elevation bill is an excellent example. While it is almost impossible to misunderstand the opening paragraph of S. 533—"The Veterans Administration is hereby redesignated as the Department of Veterans Affairs and shall be an executive department in the executive branch of the Government"—almost everything else in the bill is open to interpretation. That is the nature of legislation, of course. Much as we worked to refine the bill, there is always some wiggle room.

Indeed, the artful ambiguity began on the very first page of the bill. Just what did the Governmental Affairs Committee mean by the following sentence: "Notwithstanding section 212 of title 38, United States Code, the Secretary may not assign duties for or delegate authority for the supervision of the Assistant Secretaries, the General Counsel, or the Inspector General of the Department to any officer of the Department other than the Deputy Secretary"? Frankly, there was no record of the issue in the three hearings, nor was there any clarification at the markup—remember we only had a few minutes to explain the bill. Thus, the only way the new secretary or the courts could know what that paragraph meant was to read page twenty-one of the report:

> In addressing the need for a tighter organizational hierarchy and a clear chain of command, the Committee adopted three specific provisions in its elevation bill:
> 1. The legislation makes clear that either the Secretary or the Deputy Secretary of the Department will be responsible for supervising the Assistant Secretaries, the Inspector General, and the General Counsel. If the Secretary chooses to delegate those duties, the Secretary may only delegate to the Deputy Secretary.
> It is the Committee's intent that the Department have at least one official in the Office of the Secretary as the key official to whom the staff units report, and that the official be either the Secretary or the Deputy Secretary, *not a Chief of Staff or other staff officer who is not subject to presidential appointment and Senate confirmation.*[7] (emphasis added)

Only after reading the legislative report does the meaning of the sentence become clear: the Governmental Affairs Committee did not intend the new department to be run on a day-to-day basis by a chief of staff who was not subject to Senate confirmation, as had been done under then-Administrator Turnage. While we had no beef with chiefs of staff per se, we wanted to make sure the new chief operating officer at the VA was subject to advice-and-consent, and that meant either the secretary or deputy secretary would have to do the job.*

Just to make sure the point was not lost, the "section-by-section" analysis of the bill, also contained in the legislative report, reiterated the point: "It is the Committee's intent

---

* The reason for the growing use of chiefs of staff was obvious—the White House was forcing onto the departments deputy secretaries who were either not capable of doing the job or incompatible with the secretaries. As a result, secretaries were using their chiefs of staff to get the job done *around* their deputy secretaries.

that either the Secretary or Deputy Secretary have full responsibility for overseeing the internal operations of the Department. The principal officers of the Department are to report directly to either the Deputy Secretary or the Secretary."[8] Admittedly, a bit of overkill, but an unmistakable rule to live by for the new department.

Once past the section-by-section analysis and technical analysis, a legislative report can also convey important signals about a committee's priorities. For example, our VA report also raised a red flag regarding the number and quality of political appointments in the new department. Recall the caps on the number of political appointments? Here is how the legislative report explained the provisions:

> The issue in enacting such caps is not whether presidential and noncareer appointments are inherently positive or negative. . . . Rather, the issue is whether there is a compelling case for reducing a strong career presence at the top of VA in favor of more presidential and noncareer appointees. Given the VA's strong operational character and need for continuity of leadership, the Committee elected to impose limits on the number of potential political appointees as a barrier to any erosion of the Department's institutional capacity and long-term vitality.[9]

Again, the meaning becomes clear: the new secretary was not to flood the department with new political appointees.

Legislative reports also provide an opportunity to "wax poetic" about issues not addressed in the final bill. Even though Governmental Affairs had retreated from judicial review, the legislative report contained a long discussion of problems in the VA claims process. This discussion would be helpful if Simpson succeeded, as planned, to attach judicial review to the Cabinet bill as a floor amendment.

In addition, the committee report expressed the view that the Board of Veterans Appeals should abandon its bonus system. As noted earlier, we had discovered that the BVA had been exempted from the two government-wide bonus systems (merit pay and the performance management and recognition system) precisely because of the need to protect judicial independence and integrity, only to reestablish its own bonus system accountable only to the VA.

These kinds of exhortations may make the legislative staff feel better, but can be easily ignored on Pennsylvania Avenue. In this case, however, someone paid attention. Although Governmental Affairs was hardly the only critic, the Board of Veterans Appeals reluctantly abandoned its bonus system six weeks later. Chalk up one small victory to the committee, with plenty of credit to the Vietnam Veterans of American, who had filed suit against the VA in March attacking "assembly-line adjudication," and also to the Senate Veterans Affairs Committee, which had scheduled hearings on the issue for mid-June.

The committee report also took one last shot at the benefits process. In a somewhat unusual section titled "Additional Issues," the report summarized the now familiar problems at the VA: the cracks in the system, the fact-pattern study, the productivity pressure, and growing problems recruiting and retaining top-quality personnel.

The key question was whether the VA would ever provide the appropriate tools for its employees to do their jobs well. As the report argued, the answer was still in doubt: "the new Veterans Benefits Administration must have the personnel, computer capacity, training funds, and agency-wide leadership needed to ensure that all veterans receive the same quality of service regardless of where they live. It is the Committee's intent that the first Chief Benefits Director selected under the Department of Veterans Affairs Act address these problems, and that the first Chief Benefits Director be selected on the basis of demonstrated ability to provide the management leadership that these problems merit."

And what of judicial review? We could hardly deceive

ourselves that the legislative report would cause a revolution in the agency. After all, the VA had been insulted before with no appreciable results. Unfortunately, the only option available was to keep Glenn's options open, which we did with two simple sentences: "the Committee considered whether veterans should have the option of judicial review in the Federal Courts once all administrative options within the benefits process and the BVA are exhausted. The Committee withheld further consideration of this option pending action by the Senate Veterans Affairs Committee, which has jurisdiction in this matter."[10]

That last sentence was a clear signal to the veterans triangle that Glenn was willing to return to judicial review on the floor. That meant he was also willing to prevent S. 533 from reaching the floor until the Veterans Committee reported S. 11 for final passage. The Cabinet bill was to be a hostage in the fight for real reform.

Glenn clearly had the power to delay the process. The Cabinet bill itself would not be eligible for floor action until the Governmental Affairs report was filed with the secretary of the Senate, which required a signature from the chairman of the committee. Not only could we delay writing the report, Glenn could withhold his signature long enough to ensure that S. 11 and S. 533 could go to the floor together.

In addition, Simpson had already placed an advance hold on S. 533 whenever it reached the Senate calendar of business. A hold is nothing more than the exercise of an individual senator's freedom to prevent any measure, whether major or minor, from coming up for a vote. Since the Senate operates almost entirely by the unanimous consent of its members, legislation cannot generally be brought up for a vote unless all one hundred senators are in agreement, normally a routine matter. All a senator must do is call his or her party leader and say the magic words: "Hold!"

What Glenn and Simpson both wanted was to use the Cabinet bill as a hammer to drive judicial review through the House and Senate. Although the two bills had not been

linked explicitly, Cabinet status would not be allowed to
come up for a vote unless and until judicial review had
passed. Then the question would be whether Simpson could
win his motion to link the two bills.

The key to this new strategy at my level was simply to
get the Presidential Transitions Effectiveness Act passed before the Department of Veterans Affairs Act, and, in doing
so, give the Senate Vets Committee time to hold hearings
and a markup on judicial review. The last thing we wanted
was for S. 533 to make it to the floor before S. 11 was even
finished.* The fact was that I couldn't write two one-
hundred-page reports at the same time anyway. With the
Vets Committee ready to hold its first judicial review hearings on April 28, the transitions report became the perfect
excuse for a breather.

Unbelievably, we took no heat from the veterans groups
as we implemented the waiting strategy. It was as if Governmental Affairs no longer existed, as if we were but captured territory in some long march to the sea. The groups,
particularly the VFW, assumed that everything would run
like clockwork from now on, that there was no more cause
for concern.

Unfortunately, before moving on, I was to learn another
rule to live by. *Rule Six:* never, ever allow your senator's bill
to pass without first telling him or her.

We had filed the transitions report on April 20 and
started working immediately for passage by unanimous consent. As noted before, the Senate can do just about anything
it wants as long as no one disagrees. Conversely, the Senate
can do practically nothing unless all one hundred members
agree. As Oleszek notes, 98 percent of all Senate business

* Although Glenn and Simpson could have taken S. 11 as it was, it
made far more sense politically to wait for the Veterans Committee to
report its final bill. That way, they would avoid a skirmish over which
version of judicial review was better—the old S. 11 or the new. It was
better to wait.

is called up by unanimous consent, and virtually all non-controversial issues are enacted without debate.[11] A Senator rises, asks for unanimous consent to do X or Y, and, hearing no dissent, proceeds to act.

On most bills, including the Presidential Transitions Effectiveness Act, unanimous consent involves a two-step process. First, after the bill is cleared with both party leaders, normally a pro forma step, the unanimous consent is "hot-lined" by phone recording to every Senate office, thereby providing the chance for the single dissent. Generally, the phone rings, the senator or staffer listens to the recording, and normally hangs up, in so doing, signaling assent. Dissent is hardly more difficult. The senator merely calls his or her party leader's office and says no. Technically, such dissents are to be kept secret, though staff often ferret out the information.

Second, if no senator objects, the bill is written into a "script" to be read at the end of the legislative day by the majority and minority leaders. At that point, the process is entirely mechanical—the bill passes without debate along with dozens of other unanimous consent requests, creating a kind of "locomotive velocity," as former Majority Leader Byrd called it. Things move so fast it is hard to tell what is going on.

All went pretty much according to plan for the transitions act. Once filed, the transitions act was placed on the General Orders Calendar, one of only two scheduling calendars in the Senate. It popped up the following Monday, April 25, right there between The South Pacific Tuna Act of 1987 and a bill to authorize appropriations for the Federal Election Commission for fiscal year 1989.[12]

The effort to reach unanimous consent can produce an occasional compromise of its own, if only because unanimous consent increases the power of an individual senator. In this case, our primary Republican cosponsor, Ted Stevens (R-Alaska) wanted an amendment to the transitions bill giving Ronald Reagan a bigger moving allowance home.

Under the original transitions act, amended in 1976, Reagan was slotted to get $1 million to pack up and leave town at the end of his term. Apparently, that was not enough, for at White House request, Stevens proposed a $750,000 increase.

After working for weeks without success to get the White House to support the $200,000 preelection transition planning allowance, the request for a larger moving allowance was probably worth a fight. With passage so close, however, accepting the amendment was the better part of legislative valor. After all, it was a relatively small piece of change and might well be removed in conference with the House.

Thus, after checking with everyone I could think of, everyone, that is, *except* John Glenn, I accepted the amendment on his behalf. Stevens signed off on the agreement, S. 2037 was hot-lined, and placed in the script. At exactly 6:36 P.M., April 26, 1988, the Presidential Transitions Effectiveness Act was passed by the Senate. It was all over exactly 52 seconds later—believe me, I timed it. Months and months of work, hearings, phone calls, endless meetings, handshakes, disappointments, hassles, and it all took no more than one minute.

For those interested in the technical sequence, the committee's version of S. 2037, which had been marked up and passed April 14, would have to be amended by Stevens before Glenn's original version of S. 2037, introduced February 4, could be completely replaced by the final version of S. 2037, which is known in legislative jargon as an amendment in the nature of a substitute. Here's how the "debate" went. Remember that only three people were in the Senate chamber at the time: the majority and minority leaders and the presiding officer:

Mr. Byrd. Mr. President, I ask unanimous consent that the Senate proceed to the immediate consideration of Calendar Order No. 616, S. 2037.

The Presiding Officer. Without objection, it is so ordered.

The clerk will report.

The assistant legislative clerk read as follows:

[The complete text of the Presidential Transition Effectiveness Act was inserted in the record here.]

Amendment No. 1979

Mr. Dole. Mr. President, I send an amendment to the desk in behalf of Mr. Stevens and ask for its immediate consideration.

The Presiding Officer. The clerk will report.

The assistant clerk read as follows: ⸴

[The text of Stevens's amendment, which happened to be the 1,979th amendment in the one hundredth Senate, was inserted in the record here.]

The Presiding Officer. Is there further debate on the amendment? If not, the question is on agreeing to the amendment of the Senator from Alaska.

The Presiding Officer. The bill is open to further amendment. If there be no further amendment to the proposed, the question is on agreeing to the committee amendment in the nature of a substitute, as amended.

The committee amendment in the nature of a substitute, as amended, was agreed to.

[Glenn's original version of S. 2037 was erased by the Committee's marked up text. Statements from both Glenn and Stevens were inserted in the record here as if they had read their statements live.]

The Presiding Officer. The question is on the engrossment and third reading of the bill.

The bill was ordered to be engrossed for a third reading, was read the third time, and passed as follows:

[The final text of the Presidential Transitions Effectiveness Act, as amended by the committee's marked up and amended version, was inserted here. Once engrossed on blue paper, the bill is sent to the House for the next step, usually a conference to iron out any differences.]

Only two small problems. First, we had forgotten that the House had already passed its transitions bill. Therefore, we had to construct another unanimous consent agreement three days later to amend H.R. 3932 with the new text of S. 2037. The bill retains the number of the chamber that moves first.

Second, I had never checked with Glenn about the Stevens amendment. It was a classic case of staff imperialism, I suppose, and the fact that I was under marching orders to get the bill passed as soon as possible was no excuse. Because almost everything is done by phone and because so many staff have their senator's proxy, the bill could move without even the slightest whisper from Glenn to the majority leader.

Glenn apparently didn't know his bill had passed until I ran into him in a hallway and offered my congratulations. "Congratulations for what?" he asked. "Well, your transitions bill passed," I replied. "Didn't you think I might want to know?" he answered. Only then did I realize I had never called my own senator.

Rule Seven: whatever you do, work for a senator with a sense of humor and a willingness to forgive.

6

Showdown at Peanut Brittle Gap
(Floor Action)

THAT ELECTION IS always on the mind of the Senate was never more obvious than when the Senate chaplain rose to give the opening prayer on August 3, 1988:

> Sovereign Lord of history and the nations, we pray for the Senators running for reelection. Thou knowest the tensions inevitable between campaigning and business as usual in the Senate. Thou knowest the ambivalence inescapable in delicate decisions when voting against conscience for the sake of constituent approval is so compelling. Give wisdom to those who direct their campaigns—give the Senators special persuasiveness in speech—hold them to truth—and provide wherever needed adequate campaign funds. We pray in His name through whom Thou dost promise to supply all our needs according to Your riches in glory. Amen.

Although there are always prayers for reelection on the Senate floor, rarely are they spoken out loud,[1] and certainly not without a word or two on behalf of the thirty or so senators thinking about the presidency.

Having won reelection by an overwhelming margin in

1986, election prayers were not on John Glenn's agenda that summer. Nor were presidential hopes. After a disappointing run for the Democratic nomination in 1984, Glenn had renounced any interest in another try early in the 1988 campaign. "I humiliated my family, gained sixteen pounds and went over $2.5 million in debt," Glenn said of 1984. "Outside of that, it was a great experience."

Nevertheless, with Massachusetts Governor Michael Dukakis the nominee-apparent almost six weeks before the nominating convention, all thoughts turned to the vice-presidency. Suddenly, at least for some on Glenn's staff, vice-presidential prayers became the order of the day. Although Glenn never ran for the nomination, his name was bound to come up as a possible match for Dukakis—Duke the liberal, Glenn the moderate; Duke the relative unknown, Glenn the national hero.

Remarkable how the vice-presidency surges to the front page every fourth summer. Although the job has grown dramatically over the past three decades, including a substantial role in shaping administration policy and a West Wing office, a vice-president's success still depends almost entirely on the president's willingness to listen.

Even with the risks that come with a post steeped in relative obscurity, the vice-presidency has become *the* job for all reasons and all seasons—a great place to start up the political ladder for a run to the presidency. Not only does the job provide ample opportunities to build allies for future campaigns, it provides on-the-job political training and one of the nicest homes (at the Naval Observatory) in northwest Washington. That, plus four years of free media exposure, can transform relative unknowns into household names.

For someone who wants to shape national policy, what better job to take, short of the presidency itself, than the vice-presidency? As Walter Mondale clearly proved as second-in-command to Jimmy Carter, a vice-president can have a substantial impact on the president's foreign and domestic agenda and can become a player to be reckoned with inside the White House. The days when Hubert Humphrey, vice-president to Lyndon Johnson, could describe being in the office as "like standing naked in a blizzard with nothing but a match to keep you warm" are now over.

For someone who savors the spoils of victory, what better circumstance for pomp than being in the second-highest office in the land? Vice-presidents are like most other politicians—they like red carpets and limousines, first-class service, bands, and salutes. The vice-presidency now provides more perquisites per square inch, and its incumbents are treated with more dignity and greeted with more elan, than ever before. They have their own seal of office, their own staff, *Air Force Two*, and their own song, "Hail, Columbia."

Just about the only thing the vice-presidency *cannot* do is repair a damaged reputation—it is probably the worst office in America from which to convince the public regarding one's basic character or leadership qualities. The office can enhance, but it cannot repair. Ask Dan Quayle.

Enter John Glenn in 1988. Because he came from northern state considered essential for a Democratic victory (twenty-three electoral votes), and because he had the requisite foreign and defense experience to balance Dukakis, Glenn became the front-runner for the second spot on the ticket. Early in June, *Newsweek*'s "Conventional Wisdom [CW] Watch" rated the four Democratic front-runners (Glenn, the Rev. Jesse Jackson, Indiana representative Lee Hamilton, and senator Sam Nunn) as follows:

Glenn:	Up	All systems go. Jackson's campaign manager says he'd be "almost unbeatable."
Jackson:	Down	He'll be "considered," along with all other native-born Americans over 35.

| Hamilton: | Down | Indiana Rep. was run up flag-pole. Nobody saluted. Demoted to CW secretary of state. |
| Nunn: | Down | Spring CW: The obvious choice. Summer CW: Forget him.[2] |

By the end of the month, the "Watch" still had Glenn moving up, Nunn and Jackson still moving down, and no mention whatsoever about Texas senator Lloyd Bentsen. Indeed, if the rumors were remotely accurate, Glenn was IT. Political experts like Jack Germond, Roland Evans, even former Agnew speech writer-turned-columnist Pat Buchanan said Glenn. High-priced consultants said Glenn, too, although it all depended upon who was paying the price. Every Ohio politician from the governor on down said Glenn. Andrew Young, a Jesse Jackson supporter and mayor of Atlanta, said Glenn. Even George Bush said Glenn would be tough, an endorsement that probably did more damage than good—did his polls tell him something?

By the end of June, only Glenn and Hamilton were still in the running—Nunn and New Jersey senator Bill Bradley had pulled their trial balloons down early, perhaps preferring their own shot at the presidency in 1992 or 1996. More to the point, Glenn had weathered remakably well, surviving a month of press pounding relatively unscathed. His public tryout with Dukakis during a campaign swing in Ohio was especially effective, and despite a smattering of bad stories— New York's *Villge Voice* ran a piece on Glenn titled "It Came from Outer Space"—he had become the "obvious choice" on virtually every list. "Still defying laws of gravity," *Newsweek*'s "Watch" opined in July. "Will he stay in his capsule or spin into his usual Gaffe Zone?"[3]

There are perils in taking a vice-presidential boomlet seriously, of course. What the great Washington rumor mill gives, the presidential candidate often takes away. Only one person, Michael Dukakis, mattered in this campaign—not the consultants, not the columnists, not even George Bush.

The more Glenn seemed the obvious choice, the less he became the likely choice.

More importantly, Glenn's visibility as a potential running mate and the onward rush of the national conventions clearly altered our strategy for the VA bill. Simply put, the legislative window was closing. Democrats would be out for their convention in mid-July; Republicans in early August. With the fall campaigns already heating up, we would be lucky to have any time past September.

Moreover, our committee had almost no time with Glenn during June. Because the choice of a running mate is often the first significant decision a given candidate makes, virtually every corner of Glenn's life was inspected, audited, investigated, and probed. The risks are obvious. Pick a new face like Spiro Agnew (1968), Thomas Eagleton (1972), Geraldine Ferraro (1984), or Dan Quayle (1988), and spend the rest of the campaign month sorting through skeletons in the closet. Pick a known quantity like Richard Nixon (1952), Lyndon Johnson (1960), Walter Mondale (1976), or George Bush (1980), and spend the rest of the campaign trying to convince the public you know how to take a risk.

The Cabinet bill was filed May 12, 1988, placed on the Senate calender the very next day, Friday the 13th, as General Order No. 665, right before a bill authored by Lloyd Bentsen to create a plant-stress and water-conservation research laboratory in Lubbock, Texas.

The greatest challenge now was to get the bill up for a floor vote, no small task in the modern Senate. Party leaders no longer carry as much weight as they did in the past, while individual members carry much more. "Senate rules put few constraints upon senators' floor activism," writes political scientist Barbara Sinclair. "A senator can hold the floor indefinitely unless the Senate is willing to invoke cloture, which requires an extraordinary majority. A senator may offer an unlimited number of amendments, and in most cases those amendments need not even be germane."[4] Consider five different ways to impede debate on any given bill.

Hold the Bill. A senator is always free to simply pick up the phone, dial the majority or minority leader, and place a hold on any bill, thereby stopping it until someone figures out how to satisfy the objection. Since the Senate operates almost entirely through unanimous consent, one senator's dissent is enough to impede action on even the most important bills. "It used to mean that putting a hold on something meant simply that you would be given twenty-four hours notice that this thing would come up, so you could prepare for that," one staffer explains. "And, of course, when you put a hold on something, it puts the people, the sponsors, on notice that you had some problems and it would be in their interest to come and negotiate with you. But four or five or six years ago, it started to mean that if you put a hold on something, it would never come up. It became, in fact, a veto."[5]

Ask for a Favor. Even if a senator is persuaded to withdraw a hold, he or she may continue to frustrate action by exercising personal privilege. In the modern Senate, there is no reason not to. The Senate leadership is very accommodating, for example, toward individual senators who need an extra day to prepare for floor debate or another week to ready an amendment. If a senator cannot be in town on Tuesday, a vote can always be scheduled for Wednesday, and if not Wednesday, then perhaps Thursday next. "Everyone who wants to be accommodated is accommodated," one senior staffer explained to *Congressional Quarterly* reporter Alan Ehrenhalt. "If someone doesn't want a vote on Monday, there's no vote on Monday. The leadership just coordinates the individual requests."[6] Any senator who wants to slow down a bill need only schedule a meeting out of town at the right moment and phone in a request for postponement. It is that simple.

Talk a Bill to Death. Once a bill is actually called up for debate, a senator is always welcome to launch a good old-fashioned filibuster, holding the floor unless and until three-fifths of the Senate votes to end the debate. According to congressional scholar Charles O. Jones, the word "filibuster" is derived from the Dutch, French, and Spanish words meaning freebooter or buccaneer.[7] In Congress, it means talking a bill to death, a practice made common as more buccaneers have joined the Senate. Indeed, according to Barbara Sinclair, as floor time became increasingly precious from the 1950s to the present, "a filibuster's impact upon the Senate's functioning intensified; when floor time is scarce, a senator need not obstruct the flow of business for long to have a devastating impact upon the Senate's schedule. Consequently, the filibuster, actual or threatened, became a more powerful weapon."[8] Whereas there were only two filibusters from 1955 to 1960, there were an average of twelve *per Congress* in the past decade. Since a single filibuster can involve hundreds of hours of negotiation and debate, they are particularly frustrating toward the end of the session, when every minute of floor time is dear.

Bluster. Even after a filibuster is defeated, a senator is welcome to employ a "post-filibuster filibuster," using every device in the book to clog the Senate with debate. "If a senator is willing to make full use of his individual powers," Sinclair argues, "he can continue to prevent Senate action by calling up amendments offered before cloture was invoked, by demanding roll-call votes on those amendments and insisting on repeated quorum calls, and by calling for the reading of amendments, conference reports, and the *Journal*."[9] Bluntly put, a single senator can slow the legislative process to a halt simply by digging in. By offering one amendment after another, debate can linger on for weeks, eventually forcing the Senate to choose between the single bill at hand or the rest of the legislative agenda. Given the onward press of the calendar, death by amendment is a very real threat, indeed.

Amend. A senatore need not offer five hundred amendments—as Senate liberals Howard Metzenbaum (D-Ohio) and James Abourezk (D-S.Dak.) did in a post-filibuster filibuster of President Carter's energy bill in 1977—to slow down the process. One or two carefully crafted amendments can be quite sufficient. Just about the last thing the Senate leadership wants is to bring up a noncontroversial bill for a quick vote only to discover a couple of amemdments waiting in the bushes. On most legislation, therefore, the Senate leadership is extraordinarily risk-averse. Even the hint of impending battle on something like the Department of Veterans Affairs Act can be enough to move the bill down the legislative queue.

Whether used separately or in combination, whether actually employed or merely threatened, the tools of obstruction have made Senate floor action much more unpredictable. Moreover, when these tools are used in conjunction with real amendments like judicial review and legitimate controversy, moving a bill through the Senate can be a miracle at best.

Unfortunately for the majority leader's scheduling office, the 1970s and 1980s ushered in a new era in controversy on the floor, making even relatively noncontroversial legislation targets for amendment. As Sinclair's research clearly shows, not only are more bills now subject to amendment, more amendments are now offered on each contested bill—one in five bills during the 1980s was subject to ten or more roll calls in which each senator must stand up and announce his or her vote![10] Although the Senate is still quite capable of passing something like the Presidential Transitions Effectiveness Act with barely a murmur, more and more bills generate intense controversy.

Despite all the rhetoric about the need to make careful choices, despite all the worry about wasted time, senators themselves have created the incentives for legislative wheel-spinning. Blustering, filibustering, and holding are sure ways to make the evening news, to achieve a visibility beyond one's years. "Senators regularly hold 'must' legislation hostage and extract a ransom in policy concessions," Sinclair concludes. "One senator or a small group of senators may be able to block altogether consideration of less-than-top priority legislation. A large minority may be able to stop passage of even major legislation favored by a Senate majority. Thus minorities, even small ones, can wield inordinate influence over legislative decisions."[11]

The Department of Veterans Affairs Act is a case in point, although one might quibble with Sinclair's view that minorities employ *inordinate* influence. From my vantage point, inordinate is entirely in the eyes of the beholder. Largely because of a dogged Wyoming stubborness, Simpson had not backed down an inch from his promise to offer judicial review as an amendment to the Cabinet bill. He had placed a standing hold on S. 533 until S. 11 was ready. I have absolutely no doubt that Simpson would have filibustered had the Senate leadership tried to steamroll the Cabinet bill through. If he wielded inordinate influence, I thought it was all to the good.

Even without Simpson's hold, S. 533 was backed up behind hundreds of other bills awaiting Senate action, bills with a much greater claim to consideration, bills with their own holds and threatened filibusters. The Senate floor toward the end of a session is something like Chicago's O'Hare Airport during Christmas break, only more crowded.

Just consider the majority leader's agenda for the week of May 16, and ask where anyone could have found the six hours needed to debate S. 533 and judicial review. Recall, for example, that the Intermediate Nuclear Forces Treaty was Reagan's top priority in the spring of 1988, the first significant arms control treaty in a decade. Also note that the trade bill was one of the top issues in a campaign of mostly nonissues, a rare opportunity for the Democrats to take a stand against the administration:

Week of May 16

1. *Defense Authorization Bill*, S. 2355 (Cal. No. 646)

2. *Intermediate Nuclear Forces Treaty*

3. *Bill Banning Plastic Handguns*, S. 2180 (Cal. No. 668) (if possible)

4. *Genocide Convention Implementation*, S. 1851 (Cal. No. 655) (if possible)

5. *Corporate Takeover Legislation*, S. 1328 (Cal. No. 502) (if possible)

6. *Budget Conference Report* (if available)

7. *Conference Report on Japanese Wartime Reparations*, H.R. 442 (when available)

8. *Possible override of the President's Veto of the Trade Bill*, S. 2 (if available)

Why S. 533 was on hold should be quickly apparent. Just because it was Order Number 665 made no difference at all. Items were pulled from the list based on Senate willingness to act, relative importance, and political pressure.

Thus, throughout most of May and June, there was simply no room at the inn for the Department of Veterans Affairs Act and its associated amendments. It hardly mattered, of course, for we had already encountered a flurry of objections to floor consideration. Cabinet status wasn't going anywhere in a hurry.

More importantly, waiting clearly favored Glenn and Simpson. For the first time in memory, Sonny Montgomery was talking about some kind of judicial review bill in the House, and the big veterans groups were starting to coalesce around a possible compromise. The Senate Veterans Affairs Committee had held its judicial review hearing April 28, and was on course toward a markup of S. 11 in late June.

The only problem was that waiting drives staffers crazy. Indeed, much of what staffers do is wait. They wait to get into meetings, and wait to get out. They wait for their boss, wait for their bills, wait for their lunch, and sometimes even wait to start waiting. Most staffers quickly invent ways to kill time, whether by watching the Senate floor debates on their cable television or wandering through the hallways in constant search of conversation. Unfortunately, my habit was making a popcorn or ice cream run, not the easiest way to keep my naturally slender shape. Everyone has to sacrifice something in the legislative process, but woe to the architect who planned a snack bar within walking distance.

Just about the only constant during this long waiting period was the VA's continued opposition to judicial review. The agency was locked into an unyielding defense of its system, unable either to acknowledge the need for improvements or the cumulative evidence of its mistakes. The VA's primary motive was pure survival: judicial review would require a massive change in standard operating procedures, ones that the VA was not sure it could meet.

Indeed, there were times when the VA would have been better off taking the Fifth Amendment against self-incrimination than testifying. "VA would be thrust into a unaccustomed adversarial role of developing evidence to refute a claimant's contentions in order to assure that the record supports denial of an unmeritorious claim to the satisfaction of a reviewing judge," the General Counsel testified at a Senate Veterans Affairs Committee hearing on judicial review in late April. "The Agency would have to document every factor and consideration that led to denial of a claim, that is, 'build the record.' Every procedural step would have to be recorded, including minor ministerial actions."

Increasingly, even the most ardent supporter of the VA's so-called nonadversarial, informal system was asking "what's so bad about that?". The notion that the VA should have to meet some minimum standards or that the agency should have to tell veterans exactly why their claims had been denied no longer seemed so ridiculous, not with the overwhelming evidence that the system was breaking down. "In the judgment of the American Legion, the system may not be 'broke,' but there are very clearly a number of chronic problems affecting veterans and the agency's ability to fulfill its mission," the American Legion representative had testified before the U.S. Senate Veterans Affairs Committee on April 28. "In this regard, we must conclude that the pressing nature of the problems had sapped much of the vigor and vitality of the agency. They clearly have had a dramatic and very negative effect upon morale throughout the field stations and in the Department of Veterans Benefits as a whole."

Indeed, by June, the question was not so much *whether* judicial review, but *how*. In fulfilling its promise to Glenn to review its position on judicial review, the American Legion had adopted a resolution endorsing a limited reform. Although the Legion could still not bring itself to support full court access for veterans, the terms of a compromise were clearly emerging: veterans would get some kind of independent court review, internal procedures would be tightened, and the Board of Veterans Appeals would be reformed. If the Legion had not completely erased the *Post*'s "Featherweights" editorial, it certainly affirmed the momentum toward compromise.

Much of that momentum was fueled by a public opinion poll showing overwhelming support for judicial review among veterans themselves. Admittedly, the question asked by Cambridge Survey Research on behalf of the Vietnam Veterans of America was tilted toward a response in favor of review:

> With one exception, Americans have the right to take a government agency to court if they disagree with a decision made by that agency. This right, called the right of 'judicial review,' is currently denied to veterans in disputes with the Veterans Administration, known as the

VA. When veterans disagree with a decision of the VA, the VA itself reviews that decision and makes a final judgement which cannot be appealed in court. Some people feel that this denies veterans fair treatment. Others say that the current system has treated veterans fairly. Which of the following statements comes closer to your point of view:

> The current system used by the VA to handle veterans' claims is fair. There is no need to change the system by subjecting the VA to judicial review.

> Veterans should have the right to appeal administrative decisions to the courts. The VA should be subject to the same judicial oversight as every government agency.

Talk about an easy choice. What right-thinking veteran would deny a buddy what every other American already had? Given a choice between a system run by "little 2-by-4, squint-eyed experts, fumbling around under their desks and issuing pronunciamentos," as Huey Long called the VA bureaucrats back in 1933, and one that guaranteed a day in court, what decent God-fearing American vet wouldn't cast a vote for judicial review? What was surprising is that *only* 72 percent of veterans favored judicial review in the poll. The outcome might have been very different had the pollsters given veterans a choice between a friendly, neighborhood system that gave every applicant the benefit of the doubt versus a system run by greedy lawyers.

The question for political scientists and philosopher kings is whether public opinion should have played any role at all in what the Senate was about to do. Both sides were letting public opinion drive the policy process, public opinion that was likely to be either misinformed or easily manipulated. Recall the letter from the local American Legion commander in Ohio.

Early in the process, some of the veterans groups had manufactured letter campaigns based on scare tactics about lawyers' fees and endless delays. Now, late in the process, another veterans group was advertising 72 percent support for judicial review based on a polling question hardly anyone could answer fairly. The truth of the matter was that judicial review was not well understood by most veterans. It was a complicated issue at best. Perhaps this was one where the Senate and House should have made a decision based on the technical merits of the case.

More to the point, public opinion could not resolve the remaining differences on judicial review, particularly the growing concern over the *locus* of judicial review. Would veterans appeal directly to the federal courts around the country or be forced to take their cases to a specialty court established for veterans only?

The answer looked to be a specialty court. Federal judges were so concerned about preventing an increase in their already heavy case loads that some even lobbied Congress to go the specialty route.* Under Article I, Section 8 of the Constitution, Congress is free to "constitute Tribunals inferior to the Supreme Court." Such courts are completely independent of the federal judiciary created under Article III, and are technically not even in the judicial branch.[12] Judges in specialty courts may wear robes and their courts may have judicial seals, but they are not part of the federal court system. Nor do they have the life tenure of federal judges.

To establish a specialty court for veterans and call it judicial review was stretching the term a bit, particularly if the court was located only in Washington, D.C. Not only are most specialty courts seen as an appendage of their agency, they are often subject to oversight by the primary authorizing committees, in this case the House and Senate Veterans Affairs. Thus, veterans would still not have the

---

* There is a profound lack of comity between Congress and the judicial branch. Neither understands the other well. The lack of underlying appreciation for the political and work-load pressures in each branch often comes to the fore when one branch needs something from the other.

same rights as most Americans to take their case to court wherever they happened to live. Nor would they have the same rights of appeal upward to the U.S. courts of appeal and Supreme Court. More troubling, the veterans triangle might end up capturing the specialty court, too.

Despite the progress toward an agreement with the House on judicial review, it appeared that the only way to motivate Sonny Montgomery was to tack the issue onto the Cabinet bill. "Cabinet status is about the only thing Sonny truly cares about in the One-hundredth Congress," one House staffer argued at the time. "Hold it hostage for judicial review, and we finally have a chance over here."

That was exactly what Simpson intended. "In the House, my dear friend Sonny Montgomery, who is a remarkable chap, has indicated his willingness to hold hearings and a markup, but he will not allow the bill to go to the floor," Simpson explained to one of the veterans groups later in the summer. "Sonny is a very fair man, and it is good to have him in public office—honest and up-front. . . . [My] amendment is absolutely necessary in terms of securing House consideration of the issue, since Sonny has indicated quite clearly that the judicial review bill will not go to the floor from his committee."[13]

Simpson had ample cause for suspicion. The Senate had sent the bill over four times on its own and once as an amendment to a veterans compensation measure. Each time the bill disappeared without a trace. The House Veterans Affair Committee had become a veritable Bermuda Triangle for judicial review bills—I half expected the bills to show up one day stepping out of a spaceship.

Nevertheless, the House Veterans Committee was sending out signals of compromise. A headline in the June 5 *Washington Post* suggested that "Longtime Foe Montgomery to Consider Benefit Claims Compromise." The *Post* also reported that the veterans groups were no longer absolutely opposed, "part of the price that Sen. John Glenn (D-Ohio) extracted from the American Legion for his willingness to exclude a judicial review provision from legislation elevating the VA to Cabinet level." Finally, the *Post* reported that an unnamed Montgomery aide said "some kind of compromise on this is possible."[14] But Sonny Montgomery was nothing if not an artful politician. There are many ways to kill a bill, including lulling adversaries to sleep.

The question, as always, was how hard to push Montgomery, a question asked again as the key players met behind closed doors to discuss the judicial review amendment on June 22. Gathering in a hideaway office just off the Senate floor late in the day, Senators John Kerry (D-Mass.), Cranston, Simpson, and Tom Daschle (D-S. Dak.), and Rep. Lane Evans (D-Ill.) worked through the pros and cons of linkage.* Each of the senators had played a critical role in bringing judicial review through the Senate in past sessions, while Evans was a prime mover behind the measure in the House. Glenn was supposed to be there, too, but was tied up in another meeting. Weiss and I were there in his stead.

Alas, it was to be a very short meeting with no resolution of the jurisdictional problems in the Senate, for Cranston led off the meeting with a simple promise: if Montgomery killed a separate judicial review bill again, Cranston would link S. 11 to the yearly veterans cost-of-living adjustment (COLA) legislation coming up in August or September. With every House member up for reelection, such linkage would be impossible to defeat.

Simpson immediately countered that Montgomery would never go along, calling the recent signals from the House "bosh." Didn't everyone in the room know what Montgomery was already digging the grave for judicial review? How many times did the Senate have to cave in? Wasn't this the

---

* Daschle and Evans had worked together on judicial review before as members of the House Veterans Committee. Presumably, Evans was at the meeting to advise the group on possible reactions from the House.

best chance the Senate had had in years to force Montgomery to yield?

Simpson's passionate plea was not enough to sway Cranston, however, who was motivated by two simple concerns: he wanted to protect his committee's past investment in judicial review, and he had to maintain a civil working relationship with the chairman of his companion committee in the House. Both perfectly reasonable. It was very much a legitimate question of turf, one Glenn would have fought had another committee suddenly adopted his prize bill without permission. As one Veterans Committee staffer later put it, "We don't want to poke Montgomery in the eyes. We've got to deal with him on at least a half-dozen other bills this year. We just can't afford to make Sonny furious right now." The meeting had ended just about where it began—Kerry, Daschle, and Evans were doubtful, Simpson undeterred.

From Simpson's perspective, of course, making Sonny furious was hardly the question. Simpson had been pilloried by veterans groups in his home state, called an "asshole" by one local Legionnaire (a fact dutifully reported in the state's largest paper, the *Casper Star Tribune*[15]), and had been raked in the national veterans publications. Hardball is hardball, and Simpson was unmoved. Judicial review would be up as an amendment to S. 533 or S. 533 would never come up.

Although he did not expect to win, Simpson was impossible to ignore. The more I worked with Simpson's staff on the floor strategy, the more I admired him. I'd say that no one in the Senate wrote a better letter, delivered a better speech, or gave the veterans groups more grief. The following letter, directed to the national commander of AMVETS, was typical of Simpson's style:

Dear James:

That was a fascinating letter you cranked out there on June 2. I do appreciate having this opportunity to set you quite straight on the reason for and content of my "Dear Colleague" letter regarding judicial review and S. 533. You are obviously laboring under some great misapprehension, and I can only assume that you have not actually seen my letter.

Since that appears to be the case , let me reiterate just what I said in that letter. This village is a curious place to work. I've been the principal hard-charger for judicial review since I came to the U.S. Senate. My long-time support for judicial review, and my intention to offer a judicial review amendment to the cabinet-level bill, are not intended by me as an effort "to kill" the cabinet-level bill. That bill has widespread support, and it is sure to become law before the end of this Congress, with or without a judicial review amendment. There has been *no* indication whatever from the President or the Administration that the cabinet-level bill would be vetoed if there were a judicial review provision attached. That there "might be a veto" is one of those delicious Washington rumors which has circulated—babbled about in the halls by the opponents of judicial review.

What is clear is that this bill, S. 533, with its overwhelming support, offers the best chance for another widely-supported piece of legislation, judicial review. Judicial review legislation has passed four times and has always before been bottled up in the House Committee on Veterans' Affairs, in spite of overwhelming support among the members of the House. I've worked my butt off for it. . . . It is opposed by traditional veterans' organizations, who appear to have been threatened by the VA with various dire disincentives, including loss of VA office space that they now enjoy free of charge.

So don't try to twist my words or attempt to cover your own fanny by attributing to me a motivation that has nothing to do with my support for judicial review. You do me—and yourself—a great disservice.

In response to your question about my reference to "professional veterans," I refer to those who are paid handsomely (check the books) by veterans' organizations to lobby Congress day and night, and whose existence and exorbitant salaries are justified by fund-raising efforts poured out to the unsuspecting citizens, trying to represent to the American people that Congress is ever and always on the verge of lopping off all funding for veterans' programs, treating all veterans as second-class citizens, and cruelly killing off all benefit programs. What guff! Those are the "professional veterans" to whom I refer.

I trust you may now have a better understanding of my position. I regret that you felt you had to snidely characterize my letter and my motivation not only in writing that little dandy to me, but in forwarding your letter to all of my fine colleagues. I have a hunch that next time you will make an honest effort to correct the misapprehensions which you perpetrate—without my urging.

So, get the cloud of smoke out of your own eyes and the wax out of your ears.

With best regards from a fellow AMVET.

Most Sincerely,

Alan K. Simpson
United States Senator

Simpson was obviously in the mood for counterattack. In March, for example, he had asked all the veterans groups for information about how much they paid their top executives. "Would you please answer that?" he wrote the national commander of DAV in August. "That would be helpful. I think our colleagues need to know that information as they continue to receive a lot of heavy stuff from your organization about the fact that we do 'nothing' for the veterans. . . . Perhaps you could be doing more for the veterans if you did not have such a tremendous overhead and expense burden there. You might want to be looking into it. I intend to spend a great deal more time doing that. Do please stay in touch."

Much as I hoped Simpson would win, we all knew he didn't have the votes. Simpson simply could not protect his colleagues from the withering assault from the vets groups back home. As one senator after another said "no" to what seemed like a political suicide mission, it was clear the groups were working double-time to prevent any linkage between judicial review and the Cabinet bill. They might have changed their minds a bit on the general concept of court access, but were still dead set about carrying the idea forward in the Cabinet bill.

Those who favored linkage were now in an almost impossible bind. Under the most likely scheduling scenario, judicial review would be taken up as a separate bill immediately before Cabinet status. If it passed in its own right, every senator would have a reason to oppose linkage. "Thus, by the time Senator Simpson offers his amendment to S. 533," Cranston wrote his colleagues just before the two bills were scheduled for floor debate, "the Senate will have expressed its will with reference to judicial review, and I see no benefit to taking any further action on that issue."

Just to drive the point home, Cranston also raised the "killer amendment" argument: "Indeed, adding the judicial review amendment to S. 533 could very well jeopardize final action on the underlying bill this Congress in view of the nature of House opposition to judical review. Moreover, I believe it is quite likely that such linkage could very well substantially increase the difficulty of our reaching agreement with the House on any meaningful judicial review legislation."[16]

Much as Glenn tried to ease Cranston's jurisdictional concerns by promising to drop S. 11 from the Cabinet bill the minute the House passed its own judicial review bill, Cranston continued to defend his turf. Perhaps we would have felt the same had the Vets Committee taken up the Presidential Transitions Effectiveness Act or some other bill as part of their veterans COLA bill. After all, they had to deal with Montgomery day in and day out—long after we had cleared out, they would have to pay the price for poking him in the eyes.

We still had a chance to link the two bills on the floor, of course. Indeed, one of the marks of the modern Senate is the almost complete disregard for committee prerogatives on the floor. If committees are so powerful, how come so many noncommittee amendments pass? If committees are so influential, how come so many bills take on unrelated freight?

The answer, according to Barbara Sinclair, is simply that Senate decision-making is less committee-centered than it used to be. "As senators expanded the supply of resources and increasingly exploited the power that Senate rules vest in individual members," she writes of the 1970s and 1980s, "influence shifted from party and committee leaders to individual senators. Junior status no longer bars a senator from playing a major role, even a leadership role, with a committee. Party and committee leaders have much less control over the agenda of the Senate than formerly, while rank-and-file senators influence the agenda, positively and negatively, more than they did in the past."[17]

Whatever I thought of the shift in control as a political scientist, as a Senate staffer fighting for a lost cause, I had to hope Sinclair was right. Remember, though, that Simpson had already won a first victory. The fact was that judicial review and Cabinet status were already implicitly paired—S. 533 could not come to a vote before S. 11—and we would find out soon enough whether the two could be pulled together any tighter.

There is truly nothing quite as exciting as going to the Senate floor for a showdown. Even if one knows the outcome beforehand—and most of the time, one does—stepping onto the floor always gave me momentary pause. The feel of the thick pile carpet, the bright television lights, the stately desks each with a spittoon tucked neatly underneath, the hustle and motion, my own fading memories of high school civics, the history of the great debates, the very idea that Daniel Webster sat at a desk that is still on the floor, albeit occupied from 1987 to 1989 by Sen. Gordon Humphrey (R-N.H.), all conspire to create a sense of history every time one walks onto the floor. Chiseled into the marble on each wall is a great motto: "In God We Trust," "E Pluribus Unum," "Annuit Coeptis" (God favored our undertakings), and "Novus Ordum Seclorum" (A new order of the ages is born).

This debate was not likely to be Webster-like, but it was as close as I was to come to a great fight. The order of business said as much when it was finally published in the majority leader's calendar for the week of July 14. With judicial review right in front, Cabinet status was the hottest bill in the batch:

Week of July 14

1. *D.C. Appropriations*, H.R. 4776 (Cal. No. 770)

2. *Judicial Review of Veterans' Administration Decisions*, S. 11 (Cal. No. 790). After the Senate disposes of the D.C. Appropriations bill, under the provisions of a unanimous consent request entered on Thursday, July 7, the Senate will turn to the consideration of this bill. The legislation will be considered under an agreement reached on June 28.

3. *Cabinet Level for the Veterans Administration*, S. 533 (Cal. No. 655). It has been ordered by a unanimous consent agreement ordered on June 28, that the Senate proceed to the consideration of this legislation following the disposition of S. 11.

4. *HUD Appropriations*, H.R. 4800 (Cal. No. 762)

5. *Transportation Appropriations*, H.R. 4867 (Cal. No., 779)

6. *Interior Appropriations*, H.R. 4867 (Cal. No. 778).

7. *Defense Appropriations*, H.R. 4781 (Cal. No. 763)

The unanimous consent agreement on S. 533 had been negotiated in a series of phone calls and personal meetings between the various players and staffers. First the majority leader would call Cranston, who would talk to Murkowski or Thurmond or Kerry or Daschle. Then the minority leader would call Simpson, who would talk to Glenn or Heinz or Levin or someone else. Then one of the staff would float a specific agreement and see if anyone objected. Finally, if all the signals were good, the majority leader and minority leader would "hot-line" the agreement by recorded message to their respective senators, waiting for somebody to call in an objection.

We had been through the exercise six or seven times since early June, always with one senator or another calling in. Technically, we were never told who said "no"—holds on legislation are kept secret—but we could always find a lead by comparing notes with other staffers. It would be Simpson or Daschle or Kerry or even Cranston, all maneuvering to get the best deal for the debate.

Ultimately, the agreement itself was disarmingly simple, for the delays had not been about the agreement at all, but getting the judicial review bill to the floor in time. Under the agreement, there would be three basic amendments permitted—one on judicial review by Simpson, one on giving President Reagan the power to appoint the first Secretary of Veterans Affairs by Thurmond and Murkowski, and one cleaning up typos and grammatical mistakes in the bill. The majority and minority leaders had announced the draft agreement as usual by recorded phone message and no one objected. Since a time agreement binds the Senate, all players had to speak now or forever hold their peace. The final agreement read as follows:

>   —*Ordered*, That following the disposition of S. 11, the Senate proceed to the consideration of S. 533, a bill to establish the Veterans' Administration as an executive department, and that there be 1 hour debate on a Murkowski amendment relative to the appointment date for the first Secretary of Veterans' Affairs, that there be 3 hours debate on a Simpson amendment relative to judicial review, to be divided 2 hours under the control of

the Senator from Wyoming (Mr. Simpson), and 1 hour under the control of the Majority Leader or his designee, and that there be 30 minutes debate on a Cranston/Murkowski amendment relative to the organization of the Veterans' Benefit Administration.

Ordered further, That no other amendments be in order other than the committee reported substitute.*

Ordered further, That no motions to recommit the bill, with or without instructions, be in order.

Ordered further, That there be 2 hours debate on the bill, to be equally divided and controlled by the Senator from Ohio (Mr. Glenn) and the Senator from Delaware (Mr. Roth).

Ordered further, That there be 15 minutes of debate on any debatable motions, appeal, or points of order by the Chair for debate.

Ordered further, That the agreement be in the usual form. (June 28, 1988).

All we had to do now was wait for the majority leader to find roughly eight hours of floor time for the two bills.

As chairman of Governmental Affairs, Glenn would handle the time on his bill, recognizing speakers by giving them little pieces of the 120 minutes. As author of the key amendment, Simpson controlled his time, too. However, the fact that his opponents asked for only one hour to Simpson's two was a sign they knew they would win.

What is remarkable about floor procedure on a bill such as Cabinet status is the degree to which the Senate can resemble a finely tuned machine, even a computer, once it

* Recall that the committee bill was still in the nature of a substitute to Thurmond's original bill. The Senate would act on the committee bill as an amendment to S. 533, striking out every line of Thurmond's bill after the enacting clause. Once that substitution had occurred, this new version of S. 533 would be presented to the Senate in the nature of a substitute to the House bill, H.R. 3417, striking out every line of the House bill after the enacting clause, too, and sending the new version back to the other chamber. Subsequent to Senate passage of the amended H.R. 3417, the Senate asked for a conference and appointed its conferees.

decides to act. With a unanimous consent agreement locked down, the Senate can be remarkably efficient, the majority leader and the scheduling staff in full control.

Such was the case with both judicial review and Cabinet status when they came up for floor debate on July 11. Judicial review was handled with remarkable ease—an alternative to S. 11 supported by the Republicans and the American Legion was easily tabled, and final passage followed shortly thereafter by an overwhelming margin, 86 to 11. Unlike the earlier, much milder versions of judicial review endorsed by the big vets groups and likely to emerge from Montgomery's committee, the Senate bill would give veterans the right to challenge the facts of their case in any federal court. Veterans would still have to prove that the VA's decision was "so utterly lacking in a rational basis in the evidence that a manifest and grievous injustice would result if such finding were not set aside," that narrow standard crafted to mollify the federal judges, but at least they could go to court.

There was no great hurrah as the Senate clerk called the roll one more time on judicial review. ADAMS, ARMSTRONG, BAUCUS, BENTSEN, BIDEN. Unlike the House, where all voting is by electronic card, Senate roll calls are still called name by name. DECONCINI, DIXON, DODD, DOLE, DOMENICI. Not that there was much suspense on this one, however. The floor was about as quiet and unexciting as the local library. All the desks had been stocked with two sharpened pencils, a supply of legal pads, and a quill pen. Interestingly enough, there was no ink to be found. NICKLES, NUNN, PACKWOOD, PELL, PRESSLER, PROXMIRE, PRYOR. Senators wandered in and out, stopping occasionally to visit or to steal a piece of candy from an old roll-top desk in the corner, while staff lounged in the deep leather sofas waiting for debate to move on. STEVENS, SYMMS, THURMOND, TRIBLE, WALLOP, WARNER. Cranston had brought his own stash of peanut brittle to the floor, and quietly crunched off and on during the vote. Sitting next to Glenn and Weiss, only one chair away

from Cranston, it was all I could do not to steal a piece.
WEICKER, WILSON, and WIRTH.

The only way anyone could tell S. 533 was up was the
breeze from the entry of the senators heralding the new era
at the VA. Simpson was right about the vacuum that occurs
with a veterans vote, of course. The double doors leading
onto the floor from the second floor elevator bank flapped
open and shut with the herd of senators arriving to insert
speeches into the record, creating a bit of a breeze for Glenn,
Weiss, and me. One of the senators who wandered over to
ask Cranston about the upcoming vote accidentaly tipped
a tall glass of ice water onto my lap—an omen for the
evening.

The most puzzling opening statement came from none
other than Strom Thurmond, the original author, who rose
to thank the following groups for their hard work in winning
the elevation battle: "the American Legion, the Veterans of
Foreign Wars, the Disabled American Veterans, AMVETS,
the Paralyzed Veterans of America, the Military Order of
the Purple Heart, the Blinded Veterans Association, the
Jewish War Veterans, and the American Optometric Association." To this day, I'm not sure how the optometrists
got pulled in.

With the initial salvos over in less than an hour, Cranston
rose to offer the 2,546th amendment of the One-hundredth
Congress. The amendment had been drafted by the two
committee staffs to fix several mistakes in the Cabinet bill
and patch a political problem. Remember the VA's cemetery
system? Under S. 533, Governmental Affairs had folded the
old Department of Memorial Affairs into the new Veterans
Benefits Administration, thinking that there might even be
some budgetary savings from consolidating one very small
program into a very big one.

Unfortunately, as if to prove that no issue is too small to
fight, this simple change had prompted Senator Heinz to
demand an independent cemetery system. "The cemeteries
are essentially shrines," he argued, "with historical and per-

sonal significance, and should not be tied to the bureaucracy of veterans benefits." The fear, apparently, was that the Department of Veterans Benefits might lose bodies just as easily as it loses claims. To accommodate Heinz, and thereby avoid another floor amendment, the Governmental Affairs and Veterans Committee decided to add a proviso in the technical amendment creating a separate deputy benefits director to run the national cemetery system. As Glenn said in rising to support the amendment, "It is noncontroversial, as I see it. It would strengthen the bill, does not violate the Governmental Affairs commitment to a strong memorial affairs program. . . . I will be happy to accept it." Such is the art in avoiding conflict on the floor.* The amendment passed by voice vote without so much as a statement from Heinz. Next item.

The Thurmond-Murkowski amendment giving President Reagan the first secretary of veterans affairs appointment was more controversial, although we expected a straight party vote regardless of the debate. It wasn't that Glenn or his Democratic colleagues wanted to deny this great honor to Reagan per se. Rather, it just didn't make sense to have a secretary in place with only days remaining in Reagan's term. Moreover, the way the amendment was written, the new secretary would be at the top of a non-department—the real effective date for the department would still be January 21, 1989. Here's how the amendment read:

> Strike out section 20 and insert in lieu thereof the following:
> Sec. 20. Effective Date.
> (a) In General.—Except as provided in subsection (b), this Act and the amendments made by this Act shall take

* The amendment also gave us the opportunity to use my second favorite legislative term, "in lieu thereof," as in "pursuant to the requirement for a twenty-page typewritten paper, I submit in lieu thereof a brief handwritten note."

effect on such date during the 6-month period beginning
on January 21, 1989, as the President may direct in an
Executive order. If the President fails to issue an Executive order for the purpose of this section, this Act and
such amendments shall take effect on July 21, 1989.

(b) Secretary of Veterans Affairs.—Notwithstanding
subsection (a), the President may appoint, by and with
the advice and consent of the Senate, the Secretary of
Veterans Affairs on or after the date of the enactment of
this Act.

In other words, everything would go into effect sometime
after January 21, but before July 21, except, that is, for the
secretary, who could be appointed as soon as possible. Not
a headless horseman so much as a horseless headman. Although we had encouraged Murkowski's staff to draft the
amendment as narrowly as possible, whether narrow or not
it was simply bad public policy.[18]

Glenn was in fine form as he moved on what was clearly
a party-line issue. "Now what kind of nonsense is that?"
Glenn asked of the secretary of veterans affairs envisioned
under the Murkowski amendment. "He does not have a
department over which to preside. He cannot change policy
in this new department because there is no Veterans' Affairs
Department over which the Secretary is to preside. . . . So
I ask what on Earth is this new Secretary to do? Is this to
be an honor for the President going out?" After yielding
back the balance of his time on the amendment, Glenn
moved to table, or kill, the amendment. It all happened in
a matter of seconds:

Mr. Glenn: Mr. President, I yield back the remainder
of my time and move to table the amendment of the
Senator from Alaska.

The Presiding Officer. The tabling motion is not in
order until the remainder of the time of the proponents
has been yielded back.

Mr. Murkowski. I yield back my time.

Mr. Glenn. Mr. President, I move to table the amendment of the Senator from Alaska.

Mr. Murkowski. I ask for the yeas and nays.

The Presiding Officer. Is there a sufficient second?
There is a sufficient second.

The yeas and nays were ordered.

The Presiding Officer. The question is on agreeing to
the motion to table the amendment of the Senator from
Alaska. On this question the yeas and nays have been
ordered, and the clerk will call the roll.

Immediately at that, the clerk began reading the list of senators again, as bells sounded in every hallway, office, and
bathroom giving senators notice that they had 15 minutes
to cast their vote. The final tally was 52 Democrats yea, 43
Republicans nay, a straight party vote.

The Republicans were hardly seething about the defeat,
however. In fact, the atmosphere was friendly and relaxed;
Cranston continuing to munch, Glenn off to fetch a couple
of peppermints for himself and his hungry staff. (*Rule Eight*
to live by: Never reach for candy from the old roll-top desk.
Weiss had explained the rule to me sometime ago, assuming
rightly that I just might go for it.)

The real controversy was at hand as Simpson rose to
amend S. 533 with the freshly passed judicial review bill.
As he argued, "There is no other vehicle for this measure
than this particular train, and seeing it go separately out of
here, it will sit like a lump of clay."

Senators were hardly lining up for this vote, however. It
seemed like a reverse vacuum as they left the chamber.
Speaking with what was clearly heartfelt committment, for
example, Daschle had pulled back early in the debate:

If we had not been given our day in court here on
the floor just now with the passage of S. 11, I would have
supported that amendment. If there were no other vehicle remaining this year, I would have probably even

supported it in that case. But the fact is that should this amendment pass the Senate, it will not be kept in conference. The fact is that we have just been given a good, solid vote on S. 11. The fact is that our efforts today reflect a good-faith commitment from the House side that this issue will receive a vote in committee and on the floor. The fact is there will be other vehicles beyond Cabinet level to which we can offer an amendment should that be necessary.

Kerry was wavering, too, though he never rose to speak one way or the other. Cranston and Thurmond were obviously opposed—in fact, few members had ever seen Thurmond so animated, his face beet-red, demanding that the Senate let his bill go. "This is another matter," he shouted. "It is an extraneous matter. This amendment does not belong on this bill. We passed it as a separate bill. Let it go at that. You will jeopardize the whole thing."

Despite Thurmond's stem-winder, the debate hardly ruffled a feather. One of Simpson's opponents sat quietly at his desk reading a *U.S. News and World Report*, totally oblivious to the debate, his staff person occasionally instructing him to look up, look left, nod yes, and so forth, presumably so the Senate cameras wouldn't catch him ignoring his colleagues.

Not that the debate mattered. The Senate was apparently willing to give Sonny Montgomery the benefit of the doubt. Much as Simpson warned the Senate "either couple them or go through the same old stuff we have gone through for nine years and that is send it over there and watch it die in the great elephant graveyard," the two bills now seemed destined to remain on parallel tracks.

The only variable now was Glenn. We had prepared two statements for him, one in favor of the Simpson amendment, one against. The key paragraphs had a very different tone, reflecting our obvious effort to persuade Glenn to take the one we preferred:

Against	*For*
Mr. President, the Governmental Affairs Committee decided not to attach judicial review to the VA Cabinet bill. The Cabinet bill is a strong reform measure in and of itself and should be considered separately from judicial review. That does not mean, however, that I do not support judicial review. In fact, after listening to testimony before the Committee on issues involving the quality and timeliness of VA benefits decisions, I am more convinced than ever about the merits of this reform. Nevertheless, I must oppose the amendment to protect the integrity of the Committee's work.	Mr. President, I was roundly criticized in the *Washington Post* and a host of other papers for having made the decision not to include a judicial review provision in the elevation bill as it moved through the Governmental Affairs Committee. That decision was made after it was made clear to me that inclusion of judicial review would result in a sequential referral to the Veterans Affairs Committee with attendant delay in bringing the bill to the Senate floor. Now that the bill is on the floor, I rise to support adoption of the judicial review amendment offered by my good friend from Wyoming.

Ah, the search for recdemption. As Simpson made his case for linkage, Glenn shuffled the two statements back and forth. The safe thing would have been to declare victory and retire for the evening—after all, the key decision had been made months ago when Glenn said "no" to linkage in committee. The Veterans Committee had produced a good bill, and the Senate clearly had Montgomery's attention. Why take another beating? When he finally spoke near the very end of the debate, Glenn summarized his thinking in his first paragraphs:

I am very much aware that Senator Simpson's provison on this of judicial review is likely to go down in very ignominious defeat . . . I do not know whether he has a nose count on this or not. I have not made one, and I will not predict how many votes he will get on that. But I would guess the way things are looking, that it will not be too many.

But my question then is, How do I feel about that and having voted for the judicial review earlier today, do I think it is important enough that I would vote with him even in what I think will be a lost cause perhaps in what I beleive is an important thing for veterans.

Glenn then worked through his concern that veterans not be treated as second-class citizens, that they deserved the right to take their government to court just as much as other Americans did. Even as he worked through these initial paragraphs, I wasn't quite sure if Glenn would support Simpson.

He also summarized his conversations with the national veterans groups: "To date, I have not heard an argument which convinces me that veterans should continue to be denied the option to seek judicial review if they believe they have not been treated fairly with the VA's administration claims process."

He attacked the VA for its continued resistance to change: "I find it very hard to believe that forcing VA to develop a full documentary record is somehow undesirable. . . . Should not every veteran who is denied a benefit be told the specific reasons for that denial? Should not all the decisions be based on a careful reading of the record?"

He reviewed each piece of evidence from the Governmental Affairs Committee hearings, including the VA's own study of rating-board consistency: "Unfortunately in the four years since the study the personnel cuts have continued. . . . We simply do not know whether the problems have been fixed because the VA has never repeated the study and I can understand why."

He asked the Senate to consider the kind of society Americans would live in if they lost the right of judicial review:

That is a society few of us would want to live in. Yet our
Nation's veterans live in that kind of society today. Once
they exhaust their administrative options inside the VA,
they have no place to turn. They have no recourse if they
believe the VA's adjudication process has not treated
them fairly. They cannot submit their case for review by
an independent impartial judicial body. All other citizens
whose rights and freedoms these veterans fought and
died to defend have the right to judicial review and I
think it is long past time for veterans to have that right,
too.

At the very end of the statement, Glenn made his position
clear: "Even though I have every reason to believe that we
are probably going to go down and lose on judicial review,
I must, in good conscience, support Senator Simpson on
this." I was never prouder to be associated with him. He
had done what I thought was the absolute right thing, even
though he knew he would lose.

Alas, Glenn's statement had almost no impact. Senators
milled about, waiting for the debate to end, chatting about
this and that, complaining about the late hour, musing
about Dukakis and the vice-presidential nomination. In fact,
political scientists have long known that floor debate doesn't
matter much at all—"Few members are persuaded of the
merits of a policy by floor discussion, particularly on matters
of much importance or controversy," Steven Smith writes.
"Much of the talk on the House and Senate floors has merely
symbolic and theatrical purposes."[19] "Merely" wasn't exactly
the word I would have chosen, but Smith is right.

Even if Glenn's speech had made a difference here and
there—leading Christopher Dodd (D-Conn.) to vote with
Glenn and Simpson, explaining to no one in particular at
the time that "I happen to think they're right"—it was immediately answered by a string of opponents.

Thurmond: "If you go and put this amendment on here,
it may kill the whole bill. Why take the risk?"

Murkowski: "The amendment before us is steeped in

controversy. While the Senate has passed similar legislation four times, it died in the House each time."

Future majority leader George Mitchell: "The only way either of these two bills has any chance of being advanced is for them to advance separately. So the effort to combine them can only be an effort to defeat one or the other of them."

Cranston: "I believe the cause of judicial review and the cause of Cabinet-level status will plainly both be delayed, hampered, injured, and possibly we will not achieve our goals in either respect if we link the two issues."

Obviously, linkage was not to be. As Cranston took a last bite of peanut brittle, the Senate roll was called, and Simpson's amendment was tabled 83 to 11. Cabinet status would now move forward on its own, although still linked to judicial review in spirit, still a hostage if the House failed to act on its own judicial review bill.

It would be a mistake, however, to assume that Simpson and Glenn had lost completely. Even as the roll call was taken, Speaker of the House Jim Wright (D-Tex.) and Majority Whip Tony Coelho (D-Calif.) were putting pressure on Montgomery to let judicial review go. With two hundred-plus cosponsors in the House, judicial review was about to start moving, too, in no small measure because of the tremendous pressure from the Senate and the visibility generated by Simpson, Glenn, and Governmental Affairs. In that regard, Cabinet status had been redeemed. (*Rule Nine* to live by: take redemption when you can get it. It doesn't come around that often.)

As the evening drew to a close, Dukakis was making his decision, too. He hadn't been watching the Senate debate at all, of course. He had been sitting at his kitchen table with three or four top advisers working through his short-list of vice-presidential candidates. He knew that Ohio was critical to his chances for winning, but wanted to reshuffle the political cards a bit and desperately needed to do something dramatic. His advisers had told him that he could win Ohio with or without Glenn, that the real challenge was down South. Even if he didn't win Texas or Florida, maybe he could force Bush and the Republicans to spend some time and money defending their home turf.

Thus did Dukakis convince himself that his running mate wouldn't have to win a single state to be of great value. More significantly perhaps, Dukakis was already thinking of the historical parallels with 1960. Just as John Kennedy had selected a Texas senator, so, too would Michael Dukakis. Lloyd Bentsen was to be the choice.

Glenn did not seem particularly disappointed when he finally found out early the next morning. Like Jesse Jackson, he hadn't heard the news from Dukakis, but on his car radio. He came to the Senate floor for the final vote on Cabinet status, accepted condolences from a couple of his colleagues, and went back to the Dirksen Office Building to chair a Governmental Affairs Committee markup.

Incidentally, the Department of Veterans Affairs Act had passed, 84 to 11. Because the House had acted first, the final vote was not on S. 533, but on H.R. 3471 as amended by S. 533. It was hardly the most rewarding twenty-four hours for any of us, particularly John Glenn. We had lost on judicial review, Glenn had lost the vice-presidency, and we now faced a month of negotiation with the House over Cabinet status and presidential transitions.

7

Cabinet-Making 101
(Conference and Final,
Final Passage)

THINK OF A legislative conference as akin to making college basketball's "Final Four." After fighting for a year, surviving committee markup, and moving through the preliminary rounds on the House and Senate floor, all that stands in the way of a public law is a simple conference. Unfortunately, whether the goal is to get through the conference and into the Oval Office for a presidential signature or merely to slip past Michigan and Notre Dame for a turn at cutting down the championship net, both contests demand an absolute commitment to the game. That is where the similarity ends.

Unlike the Final Four, for example, conferences have very few rules and absolutely no referees. Games almost never start on time, and no one gets called for traveling. Created in 1789 during the very first Congress to help smooth the legislative process, conferences remain an entirely "extra-constitutional" device for resolving House-Senate differences.[1] Rather than pass a bill from one chamber to the other and back again until both could agree as envisioned by the founding fathers, a conference produces a single bill to be reported back to each chamber simultaneously in the form of a conference committee report.

Unlike the Final Four, conference rules often change in the middle of the game as committees reshape legislation outside the normal process. There aren't any television commercials or instant replays. Technically, conference committees are not permitted to go beyond the "scope" of the two bills to draft entirely new legislation. That would be a violation of germaneness standards in each body. In practice, however, conferences frequently resolve differences by doing just that. As Ronald Reagan once lamented, "You know, if an orange and an apple went into conference consultations, it might come out a pear."[2]

Unlike the Final Four, there are no trophies for good sportsmanship. This is an arena where the opponents barely speak to each other, let alone acknowledge the rules of the game. The fact is that the House and Senate have very little in common, least of all respect. It is said that it is farther from the House to the Senate than it is from Congress to the White House. If House members and Senators can work together long enough to hammer out a legislative agreement, it is a sure sign that they mean business.

Finally, unlike the Final Four, the secret to a successful conference is quiet influence, not slam dunks and three-pointers. Conferences are often private affairs, hidden from public view, with no play-by-play. Indeed, except for the most controversial legislation, staff play *the* prominent role in resolving differences, drafting compromises, and setting priorities. Oftentimes, a conference committee exists in name only—if the staff can get it done on their own with minimal "interference" from on high, so be it. The last thing a senator or representative wants is to sit in an endless meeting working through the technical details of a bill, especially toward the end of a session or during an election campaign. Members have far better things to do, for example, than decide whether the VA's old Department of Medicine and Surgery should be called the Veterans Health

Services Administration or the Veterans Health Services *and Research* Administration.

With judicial review off the agenda, the VA conference was likely to be a staff affair. With senators and House members en route to the national party conventions and a fall campaign in full swing, they would be available only on the most visible bills. And Cabinet status was not one of them.

By the time the VA Cabinet bill went to conference, the key House and Senate members had already agreed on the final version of the Presidential Transitions Effectiveness Act. The House might have passed the Senate-amended bill directly on to the president for signing but for one major problem: Government Operations chairman Jack Brooks simply would not yield on the Senate proposal to give $200,000 to each national party committee to do transition planning during the general election campaign. Granted, the parties would be getting $9 million in public funds for balloons, platform committees, fliers, and banners at the national committees. Granted, the candidates themselves would be getting $44 million. Nevertheless, in Brooks' view, the $200,000 of preelection planning was not defensible.

Glenn had known the preelection provision would be a problem for the House from the very beginning. As the chairman of the Government Operations Committee and the most senior member of the conference, Brooks's opinion would matter most, and he had called preelection planning a *National Enquirer* issue. Since one of the two parties would surely lose, at least half of the preelection transition planning funds would technically go to waste. "We have to run every two years over here," one of the key House staffers joked at one point. "We don't have the luxury of voting for these kinds of things every day like you do."

Thus, despite lobbying by a number of top Democratic advisers—former Carter domestic policy adviser Stuart Eizenstat wrote Brooks that "having been involved in the

Carter pre-election planning effort, I cannot overstate the frustrations of having to raise money to cover something so clearly in the public's interest"—Brooks would not recede. Like most conferences, each side had its "must list," and Brooks was betting that the Senate would fold on this one issue to protect the rest of the bill. That is exactly what we did on July 22, all without a single meeting of the "principals."

Much as Glenn wanted to create an incentive for doing a little advance planning, the preelection funding was not worth losing the entire bill, particularly the limits on private cash. We had made that calculation early on, too. Alas, the House would not fight the increase in Reagan moving expenses either, meaning I had no chance to correct my earlier mistake with Glenn.

With the agreement in hand, the House passed its version of the transitions bill by unanimous consent on July 26 and sent it back to the Senate, where it was passed by unanimous consent on August 2. The measure was signed by the Speaker of the House on August 3, the president pro tempore of the Senate on August 9, enrolled on parchment paper, and sent to the president of the United States on August 10. He signed it into law on August 17 without so much as a word—no elegant signing ceremony for this bill.

Technically, the House and Senate never had a conference on the transition bill, since neither chamber formally asked for a conference nor appointed conferences. Instead, the two committee staffs simply got together and worked through the differences. When finished, the House amended the Senate bill, then the Senate adopted the package and passed it on to the president. It was a process rather like the founders intended.

Although this was hardly earth-shattering legislation, I still remember how nice it was to see the president's signature across the bottom of Public Law 100-398, the Presidential Transitions Effectiveness Act. Whether he knew it or not, Bush's transition was just a little bit more effective because of that small bill. It was hardly like winning the NCAA championship—no trophy ceremony, no marching bands, no television interviews—but it felt good nonetheless. Very few staffers ever get to see an idea they worked on translated into public law, especially one that actually makes a small improvement in the way presidents do business. (Interestingly enough, Reagan did not use any of the moving home increase, having been able to get back to California for under $1 million.)

But just because we lost on the preelection planning provisions in this "quasi-conference" did not mean we had in any way been defeated. Most of the Senate bill emerged intact, and our willingness to recede on that one key provision with Brooks became a "chit" in the VA conference. Although every legislative conference is unique—there is no such thing as a standing conference committee, although it might not be a bad idea for the budget and appropriations process—conferences do not take place in a vacuum. Deals made in one conference affect deals made in another.

Although political scientists are prone to look at the won-lost score for each individual conference, it is far more appropriate to think of a running score over an entire Congress or more.[3] There is a natural tendency among members and their staffs to try to even things up from one conference to another. Thus, as we went to conference in late July on the Department of Veterans Affairs Act, a bill totally unrelated to the Presidential Transitions Effectiveness Act, we knew we had the political chits, or capital, to win most of the disagreements.

Debate over the VA conference had actually begun *before* the Senate passed S. 533 on July 12. The best way to influence a conference committee is to be a member, and the way to be a member is to get appointed in a unanimous consent request from the chairman and ranking member of the committee that authored the bill. That is why Cranston and Murkowski sent Glenn and Roth a letter on May 27 asking to be appointed as conferees. Although the letter came *before* passage—the Senate and House Governmental Affairs/Government Operations Committees routinely appointed members of other committees to their conferences—it was a signal that the Veterans Committee, most particularly its senior staff, intended to play a visible role in the Cabinet conference.

Despite the positioning, we could not have a conference unless and until the Senate passed a bill. However, the letter was a clear signal that our jurisdictional squabbling was going to continue to the bitter end.

Conferences do not just occur through spontaneous legislative combustion, of course. The dance begins when one chamber sends its bill to the other, a rather impressive step in which an emissary hand-carries a bill to the floor, and is heralded with great fanfare. In the Department of Veterans Affairs Act, the "Message from the Senate" was simple: absolutely nothing remained of the original text of H.R. 3471—the Senate had erased everything after the enacting clause, substituting S. 533, as amended by committee and the full Senate, for the entire House bill.

It was always possible, of course, that the House would merely accept the Senate version of H.R. 3471 and send it to the president for final signature. That sometimes happens—in fact, that is exactly what the Senate did on the transitions bill, accepting the House amendments to the Senate amendments to the original House bill. On the Cabinet bill, our natural view of things was that the House would just be better off passing our amendment and sending the bill onto the president. I even suggested the idea to my House counterparts early in our first conference meeting as part of the standard chatter that eases the negotiating process. "You know, we could always get this over fast if you all would just take our bill," I said. "Then how would you spend the rest of your summer?" was the predictable answer.

A conference does not begin with just a joke, however.

It takes a formal disagreement from one or the other body. Usually, the chamber that acts first on a bill is allowed to disagree, since its version is the one amended by the other body. Only when the "papers," or formal engrossed text, arrives by messenger can the House or Senate disagree. Given that the House Government Operations Committee staff had told us all along that our bill was over-specific, overlong, and overbuilt, we suspected the House would disagree.

And that is just what the House did on August 10, voicing its disagreement by unanimous consent and requesting a conference with the Senate to reconcile the two bills. At the same time the Speaker of the House appointed his conferees, eleven to be exact. No matter how many conferees each chamber appointed, however, there would only be two votes in the conference, one from the House and one from the Senate. One day later, the Senate responded by insisting on its amendments. In the same motion, the Senate agreed to a conference by appointing nine conferees, with Cranston and Murkowski listed among them.

There is no great secret about who gets appointed as conferees. Since committee members and staff have dozens of competing priorities, conferees usually end up being those who have expressed an interest in a bill earlier in the process or do not have a quick excuse to avoid being appointed. For the Cabinet conference, Glenn's list of nine included some of both. It took me the better part of a day to round up conferees number eight and nine, primarily because no one wanted to serve on the Cabinet bill. Cranston and Murkowski were on the list, in large measure because the Speaker's eleven House conferees included several Veterans Committee members, forcing us to balance their's with our's. Once these decisions were "messaged" to the House on September 7, the conference was on.

Long before all the technicalities were satisfied, however, the informal conference was in full swing. We had already met, majority to majority, with the House Government Operations staff to set the ground rules, particularly where the game would be played—alas, it was their turn to host, meaning we would ride the subway from the Dirksen Senate Office Building to the Capitol, walk up the escalators, go past the elevator stations, turn right at the meat freezer, into the underground tunnel, past the hidden offices, turn right past the coffee shop, under the House chamber, a quick left, elevator down two more subbasements, take the House subway to the Rayburn House Office Building, and trudge up to the Government Operations Committee room.

With a half-hour walk to and from the House for each meeting, the Governmental Affairs staff had plenty of time to muse about the long list of disagreements. Reading through the twenty-six page, legal-sized document showed that the disagreements began on the very first page of the two bills and continued at every turn. Even the language creating the department was sufficiently different to cause a potential fight. The informal side-by-sider showed the disagreement as follows:

Existing Law	H.R. 3471	S. 533
Title 38, Sec. 201, United States Code Establishes VA as independent agency	Sec. 2, *Redesignation*. Redesignates VA as Department of Veterans Affairs	Sec. 2 (a) *Redesignation*. Same language as Sec. 2 of H.R. 3471
Title 38, Sec. 210 (a), Establishes the Administrator of VA as the head of the agency	Sec. 2, *Establishment of Secretary*. Establishes the Secretary of Veterans Affairs, appointed by the President with Senate advice and consent as head of the De-	Sec. 2 (b) (1) *Establishment of Secretary*. Same language as Sec. 2 of H.R. 3471, but adds the subsection designation "(1)". Also adds the following new subsec-
Title 38, Sec. 212, Allows the Administrator to		

Existing Law	H.R. 3471	S. 533
assign duties to officers and employees of the VA	partment. The Department shall be administered under the supervision and direction of the Secretary.	tion "(2)" Notwithstanding Title 38, Section 212, United States Code, the Secretary may not assign duties for or delegate authority for supervision of the Assistant Secretaries, the General Counsel, or the Inspector General of the Department to any officer of the Department other than the Deputy Secretary
Contains no provision	Contains no provision	Sec. 2 (c) *"Office of the Secretary.—* The office of Secretary shall consist of a Secretary and a Deputy Secretary and may include an Executive Secretary[4]

The pattern was repeated page after page throughout the document. Either the House had no provision at all or a much more simple statement.

Many of the Senate provisions were mere bargaining chits to be traded for a half-dozen key provisions. The real trick in a conference is to figure out what the other side wants, what you are willing to give, and what you absolutely will not yield. "The overriding ethic of the conference committee is one of bargaining, give-and-take, compromise, swapping, horse-trading, conciliation, and malleability of all concerned," writes political scientist John Manley. "Firm positions are always taken, and always changed. Deadlocks rarely occur to the degree that the bill is killed. Someone gives a little, perhaps after an impressive holdout, in return for a little; compromise is the cardinal rule of conference committees. Small wonder that each side claims victory; because almost everyone does win—something, somehow, sometime."[5]

Thus, a successful conference involves knowing what you want and what you don't. Take our provisions establishing the secretary's office as an example. Much as we wanted to keep the secretary from using a nonconfirmed chief of staff to run the department, we were quite willing to "recede" to the House position in return for one or more of our top priorities. In fact, despite dozens of differences between the two bills, Glenn only put six provisions on his "must" list.

Item One: Glenn wanted a strengthening of the inspector general's office. All the Senate bill required was 150 additional staff positions for what was one of the weakest Offices of Inspector General in government. Nevertheless, the House Veterans Committee was ready to argue that the VA could not afford the positions, not with widespread nursing shortages at many hospitals. Much as we found it hard to believe that the VA couldn't reallocate 150 positions out of a total workforce of 240,000, Glenn was open to a counteroffer.

Item Two: Glenn also wanted a relaxation of the statutory restrictions on the secretary's reorganization authority—the one requiring congressional notification for reorganizations of units employing 2.5 or more people. It wasn't a sweeping reform by any means, but was clearly something worth doing as a gesture to the new secretary. The House had no provision and had already signaled that it would seek a compromise.

Item Three: Glenn wanted a tighter organization chart than the House. The Senate bill contained four assistant secretaries compared to the House eight, while both had left the specific duties of each assistant secretary up to the incoming team. We were perfectly willing to compromise at six, however, in the grand spirit of splitting the differences, as long as at least one of the six was placed in charge of information-resource management and another was named the chief financial officer of the VA, both concerns of the Governmental Affairs Committee.*

Item Four: Glenn also wanted to protect a Senate provision establishing a national Commission on Executive Organization and Management. This was a bit of an odd one for us. The commission was designed to examine the basic structure of the federal government, and had been attached to the bill at the very end of the process both as a favor to the former committee chairman, William Roth. Just as we had used a study to slow down the Cabinet bill in December, a national commission might slow down the flood of Cabinet bills that would likely emerge as other interest groups decided it was time to elevate their agencies, too.

Admittedly, the commission had little to do with the main thrust of the Cabinet bill, and was, therefore, nongermane in legislative terms. Nevertheless, Glenn supported the idea, and intended to cash the chit he earned in yielding on pre-election planning during the Presidential Transitions Effectiveness Act conference. Nongermaneness is always in the eye of the beholder.

Item Five: Glenn would not budge on any effective date

* Glenn had introduced a bill earlier in the One-hundredth Congress to create a chief financial officer for all of government. We had picked up our provision requiring a chief financial officer, or CFO, directly from that bill. In many ways, the Cabinet bill became a vehicle for setting a number of precedents: caps on political appointees, which are now showing up in other legislation; creation of a chief financial officer, which reflected a long-standing Glenn concern; and search commissions for top jobs, which will become more prevalent in coming years.

for implementation of Cabinet status that came *before* January 21, 1989, the day *after* Reagan left office, especially not with a straight party-line vote to kill the Thurmond-Murkowski amendment. This was an unconditional position—Glenn had already told us that he was willing to let the cabinet bill die over this single position and put the blame at the president's desk.

Item Six: Glenn wanted significant caps on the number of political appointees in the new department. This was another position where he did not intend to budge. The caps on the total number of noncareer executives and Schedule C personal and confidential assistants had to stay. Nor did Glenn intend to recede on provisions restricting the number of political appointments to the new deputy assistant secretary slots. Of all the items in the bill, this was the most important to me—not only would it set a precedent for reducing the number of political appointees in other agencies, but it would send a strong signal to the White House regarding the need for political and career executives to work more closely together.

In order to prevail on this must list, however, we needed a parellel "trade list." We did not expect the House to recede on everything, nor did we want them to. This was only one of many conferences between our two committees during the One-hundredth Congress. Skunking the House on the VA bill would affect future conferences on other bills, including some in which the Senate would have the shorter bill or weaker position. Put another way, running up the score only counts in the college football rankings.

Thus, even though we had a much stronger hearing record than the House, and even though something in a bill beats a nothing in a bill almost every time, we developed a short list of giveaways to sweeten the process. For example, we were quite willing to recede on the organization of the secretary's office, which the House characterized as micro-management, as well as our requirement for an annual report to Congress on the cost of raising the VA to Cabinet status, which the House viewed as needless hassling. We were also willing to accept pretty much any proposal regarding the old Department of Memorial Affairs—it hardly mattered to us whether the Department of Memorial Affairs was absorbed into the new Veterans Benefits Administration or became the "National Cemeteries System."

All in all, these provisions were "small beer" compared to the political-appointee caps, the increase in inspector general staffing, or the later effective date. We'd give a little, they'd give a little, and we'd all go home happy and secure in the belief that we had both won what we wanted.

The only obstacle in the conference would be the House Veterans Committee. How much would they play and what did they want? We knew the Senate VA Committee would support the Senate bill on most points—that was part of the implicit deal in the appointment of Cranston and Murkowski to the conference. Given what we knew of the House VA Committee on judicial review, we expected a fight on every issue.

What we were to soon discover was that the House Veterans Committee didn't care about the wiring diagrams either. Instead of fighting over the loosening of the reorganization authority or the political caps, the House Veterans Committee seemed most concerned about the size of the search commission for the chief medical and benefits directors. Apparently, Montgomery and his staff believed that fourteen commission members was simply too large a number for effective small-group communication. (The irony was that elevation of the VA would bring the size of the president's Cabinet to precisely fourteen.) That the House Veterans Committee, which had been the original driver behind the Cabinet bill, would make a federal case out of the number of search-commission members was pure paradox. Nevertheless, the House Veterans Committee staff expressed genuine outrage at the size of the search commissions, insisting on a reduction in the number of members allowed.

What was even more puzzling was that Montgomery and his staff wanted the earliest possible effective date. It was a way to give credit where they felt credit was due: to the president who paved the way for a Department of Veterans Affairs. Much as we reminded Montgomery's staff that the Senate had killed the idea on a party-line vote—all Democrats aligned against all Republicans—we obviously had our work cut out for us.

The VA conference itself began in earnest on August 11, right in the middle of my one-week summer vacation. Needless to say, I was less than enthusiastic about giving up even a day of vacation to spend five hours sitting around a table with fifteen other staffers—some willing, some bored—walking through a side-by-side on the VA bill.

Moreover, we had decided to skip lunch and meet just before noon, not because of some grand tradition specifying start times for legislative conferences, but because we thought hunger would drive us inexorably toward compromise before the snack bars closed at 5:00.

Given the rules needed to authorize a conference in the first place, it is surprising that there are almost no rules governing the process once it gets rolling. Whether at the staff or member level, meetings must always be public—unless they happen to be private. Agreements must always be circulated for comment—unless they happen to be secret. Votes are never taken, statements are never recorded, and quorums are never important—unless, of course, the participants decide otherwise.

Indeed, just about the only rule that appears to be fixed from conference to conference is to settle the easy issues early and hold the sharp disagreements for the principals. That is precisely what we did, saving the inspector general's office, the National Commission on Executive Organization, the effective date, and the number of assistant secretaries for later. Like most conferences, each side gave a little as we worked through the long list of disagreements one by one. Consider, for example, the effort involved in striking a deal on the medical director's search commission, an agreement summarized as follows in our staff notes on the meeting:

House Bill: Contains No Provision
Senate Bill: Creates Search Commission

Senate VA voices support for provision, notes need for professionalism in the new Department.

Senate Governmental Affairs argues that the commission creates a presumption that the search process will play a vital role in process of selecting an individual on merit, as it does in the selection of the Comptroller General of the United States. Such a process increases likelihood of selecting someone of competence. Constitutionally, however, President cannot be forced to pick from the list the commission submits.

House VA states no problem with general concept, but concerned about the size of the commission. Fourteen members is too many for effective communication; too much potential for endless meetings; confusing. Does not like provision calling for the commission to submit additional names if the President so requests.

General mutterings about the 14 problem—isn't that how many will be on President's Cabinet after VA elevation?

Senate VA agrees to drop provision calling for additional names if the President requests.

House Government Operations objects to dropping language calling for additional names. Said that, as in the case of the Comptroller General, such a provision could strengthen the President's hand in getting a nominee through the Senate confirmation process, presuming the President selects an individual recommended by the search commission.

Staff agrees to leaving additional name provision. Staff agrees to let House and Senate Veterans Committee develop proposal for fewer members of search commission.

Senate Governmental Affairs notes importance of having commission members with management experience.

There were dozens of other agreements during the first meeting. The House agreed to call the Department of Medicine and Surgery the "Veterans Health Services and Research Administration," instead of the "Veterans Health Services Administration," thereby damning all of us to learn a hopelessly long name or a snake-like acronym, VHSRA (pronounced "visś rah"). The House also agreed that the chief medical director would be selected without regard to political affiliation or political qualification.

"All we are doing is giving the Senate a reason to vote no," one Senate staffer said. "Our overwhelming tendency is to approve just about anyone the president nominates. All we're looking for is ammunition." "Words are just words," a House Government Operations staffer responded. "You could confirm an ax-muderer under this provision. This won't make much difference one way or the other, but if it is that important to the Senate, we'll pass." "Haven't we learned anything from confirming all those Reagan bozos?" a Senate Democratic staffer asked. "Yeah, you learned how to confirm bozos," was the House retort. Nevertheless, the House receded.

The House also dropped its provision requiring a veterans benefits office in every state, the District of Columbia, Puerto Rico, and the Phillippines, while the Senate dropped an obscure requirement regarding Office of Management and Budget review of VA congressional testimony. Surprisingly, the House barely blinked in receding on the political caps. "I don't apologize for being political," a House Democratic staffer said at the time. "We are pandering here to a perception which is demeaning to all of us, that we ought never to appoint people who will be responsive to the political will of an administration. But if this will make the Senate happy, the House can recede."

Reaching even the simplest agreement is rarely easy, however. Witness the problems in hammering out a solution to the number of assistant secretaries:

> House Bill: Eight Assistant Secretaries
> Senate Bill: Four Assistant Secretaries

Senate Governmental Affairs opens the bidding by offering compromise at five Assistant Secretaries as long as the fifth Assistant Secretary was designated to perform the functions of a Chief Information Resource Officer.

Senate VA opposes designating fifth Assistant Secretary functions.

Senate Governmental Affairs will not accept another Assistant Secretary without designating.

House VA asks that tasks of fifth not be specified, joins with Senate VA.

Senate Governmental Affairs argues that Committee favors consolidation/streamlining of top management jobs, and will not support more Assistant Secretaries without clear need.

House Government Operations asks House VA to give in on the specification issue; House VA says "no."

Senate Governmental Affairs says again that the need for consolidation was clearly demonstrated in hearings, in the National Academy of Public Administration recommendations, and in general sense of testimony. Also notes turnover in top jobs at VA.

General arguing back-and-forth for better part of 30 minutes. Senate Governmental Affairs apparently willing to sweeten the deal by increasing number of Assistant Secretaries to six, but only if two are designated: one for Information Resource Management and one for Financial Management.

House Government Operations says two options are on the table: (1) five Assistant Secretaries with one designated as Information Resources, or (2) six with one designated as Information Resources and one as Chief Financial Officer.

Senate VA says that six Assistant Secretaries is too many; suggests that language in bill should read "not to exceed five."

Continuing dispute about designating the functions of either the fifth or sixth Assistant Secretary.

Senate Governmental Affairs offers final deal: five Assistant Secretaries with no designation of functions.

> *Staff agrees to five assistant secretaries. Compormise lan-*
> *guage reconciling the two bills to be worked out by House and*
> *Senate Government Operations Committees.*

By now, it should be clear that much of what occurs in conference is sometimes argument for argument's sake. Basically, there are three decision rules for resolving differences. First, when the two bills have different provisions on the same issue—for example, the number of assistant secretaries—the two sides will split the difference.

Second, when one bill has a provision that the other bill doesn't—for example, the chief medical director search commission—the provision will almost always prevail. Something beats nothing every time, unless, of course, the provision is traded for something else. It is like baseball great Yogi Berra once said: "Good pitching beats good hitting, or vice versa."

Third, and most important, whatever the specifics of any given conference, each side will share the spoils whenever possible. If a word change here and there will make a provision more palatable, so be it. In conference scorekeeping, it is quantity, not quality, that matters. As long as the other side wins roughly as many times, even if the wins are on essentially trivial issues, there is a general sense of mutual adjustment. It is the *perception* of evenness that matters most.

By following these three simple rules, we resolved 80 percent of the disagreements in the first staff meeting. Of Glenn's six must items, we had already prevailed on three. The political caps were in; we had a deal on the reorganization authority; and we thought we had an agreement on five assistant secretaries.

In the meantime, the two veterans Committees were working on the number of search-commission members, an essentially harmless task that eventually led to a proposal for ten instead of fourteen. The conference also agreed to pull the old Department of Memorial Affairs back up from under the new Veterans Benefits Administration and make it a freestanding line, or operating, unit at a lower level than the new Veterans Health Services and Research Administration and Veterans Benefits Administration. As one of the House staffers remarked at the time, "you're telling us that the benefits process is a mess, that you need more staff in the VA inspector general's office to stay on top of the problems, yet you're willing to put the national cemetery system into that swamp? If they're losing files all the time, don't you wonder what they're likely to do with bodies?" We receded.

Unfortunately, within hours after the first meeting, we were informed that the assistant secretaries agreement was not acceptable. The House wanted six and no chief information resources officer, arguing that because neither bill ever mentioned the subject of information resources, such a requirement would be far outside the scope of the conference and therefore a violation of germaneness rules. We responded that we would take only six assistant secretaries with the chief information and chief financial officers. Conference rules are made to be broken, including germaneness, and the House quickly agreed.

As to the disagreement on the effective date of the new department, it was obvious that the Senate would prevail. Reagan would not get the first appointments. In just about every case, a preference backed by a roll-call vote clearly outweighs a preference backed by a general inclination. Thus, even before the next conference meeting in early September, the two Government Operations/Governmental Affairs staffs met to agree on a specific date *after January 21, 1989*, to present as a unified position to the House VA Committee—getting together in secret is not against the rules, of course, especially if it is for the express purpose of ganging up on someone else.

The best way to find an effective date was simply to consult the calender. We decided Memorial Day was too late, May 1 too Soviet, April 15 too taxing, and April 1 too foolish.

After a suitable bit of squabbling, we finally arrived on March 15, the ides of March. If the House VA Committee didn't like it, Glenn was more than willing to hold the bill for reintroduction in the 101st Congress.

Most of these issues had been resolved with a nod or a quick "okay" from one or the other side. In fact, conferences create a certain momentum once the big decisions are either made or set aside for later. Generally, everyone in a conference wants to get onto other business and everyone soon learns that "speechifying" is neither welcome or helpful. The less said about most issues the better.

The remaining issues on the agenda simply could not be resolved at the staff level, even after a second five-hour marathon in early September. Jack Brooks was still unalterably opposed to a national commission, and we had given all the ground we could on the inspector general provision, whittling down our original proposal from 150 to just forty positions. Glenn and Brooks would have to meet.

With a hundred other meetings on the calendar, however, it would be impossible to get all seventeen conferences together, nor would doing so make much sense. If Glenn and Brooks could agree on the inspector general and national commission provisions, the rest of the conferences would gleefully assent.

Technically, a conference between the two key committee chairmen is not a violation of conference rules either. Meeting on September 23 with two other Governmental Affairs members, Roth and Levin, the two chairmen bantered back and forth on committee business—the reauthorization of the Office of Federal Procurement Policy, the military base closure bill, government contracting, and a separate inspector general bill.

Occasionally, and only occasionally, did they talk about the VA. But when they did, it was classic conference politics—give a little, take a little. On the inspector general, Glenn said the Senate had to have at least forty new positions at the VA—"We've given enough on this, Jack," Glenn told Brooks. "You and I both feel the same about the inspectors general." "Well, then I guess old Sonny is going to have to swallow forty positions," Brooks replied. Moments later, discussing the national commission, Brooks said he had to have a trigger allowing the next president to cancel the commission if he didn't want it. "You know that'll kill it," Glenn and Levin both said. But they had no choice. They had to give, too.

Thus, in a span of less then two minutes, the VA conference was over. There would never be a full-dress conference meeting. Staff had their marching orders to find forty slots and a trigger mechanism for the commission. Ultimately, the trigger was surprisingly simple:

(a) Establishment.—
(1) Within 30 days after the effective date of this Act, the President shall make a determination as to whether the national interest would be served by the establishment of a commission to review the structural organization of the government. If the President makes a determination that such establishment is in the national interest, the President shall transmit to the Congress written notification of his intent to establish a National Commission on Executive Organization.
(2) If the President fails to transmit the notification under paragraph (1), this section shall cease to be effective 30 days after the effective date of this Act.

In short, all the president had to do to kill the national commission was *not* act. And that is just what President Bush did when it came time to decide.

With our two final agreements in place, we tallied up the score and wrote the conference report explaining the final agreements. Technically, a conference report is not just the text of the final bill. It is the "joint explanatory statement of the Committee of the Conference" which provides the detail on what happend in a section-by-section basis. Here is how the joint statement summarized the assistant secretary agreement:

Section 4. Assistant Secretaries
House Bill
   The House bill provides for 8 Assistant Secretaries, one of whom is to perform functions regarding the National Cemetery System and State cemetery grant program, and delineates other functions to be assigned by the Secretary to the Assistant Secretaries.

Senate Amendment
   The Senate amendment establishes not to exceed 4 Assistant Secretaries. The Assistant Secretary whose functions include budgetary and financial functions to be designated the Chief Financial Officer of the Department. The Senate amendment specifies other functions of the Chief Financial Officer. In addition, the Senate amendment deletes from the functions specified for performance by the Assistant Secretaries in the House bill the functions regarding congressional affairs.

Conference Agreement
   The conferees agree to establish not more than six Assistant Secretaries and to follow the Senate amendment with regard to the functions to be performed by the Assistant Secretaries. The conferees agree to follow the Senate amendment with regard to the Assistant Secretary whose functions include budgetary and financial functions as the Chief Financial Officer of the Department. The conferees agree that the duties and responsibilities assigned to this position are not intended to require or to encourage the compilation of agency financial statements. In addition, the conferees agree that one of the Assistant Secretaries, whose functions include information management, shall be designated as Chief Information Resources Officer of the Department. This individual will perform functions specified in the conference report.

   A conference report also provides opportunity to express legislative intent, whether through outright prohibitions on action or thinly veiled threats of future congressional oversight. The House insisted, for example, that the chief financial officer not be required to prepare financial statements, a red-hot issue for Brooks. Although the restriction was not carried in the formal bill, it was duly noted in the joint explanatory statement. In return, the Senate asked that the joint statement express "the intent of the conferees that the Secretary not create a chief of staff with line supervisory responsibilities over persons appointed by the President with the advice and consent of the Senate." Regardless of their actual impact in preventing financial statements or chiefs of staff, both statements softened the blow of receding, allowing each side to claim a little victory in the face of what was actually defeat.

In fact, the respective staffs often went out of their way to be good sports, smoothing out differences to make the conference a draw. That does not mean individual conferences do not have winners and losers, however. Of the six items on our "must" list, we had won three outright (effective date, political caps, reorganization authority), compromised to no one's advantage on two (assistant secretaries and national commission), and compromised to the House advantage on one (inspector general). Of the thirty or so disagreements, the final score was Senate 14, House 9, and split decision 5. By my admittedly biased view of what was a major issue versus minor, the outcome was even stronger in the Senate's favor:

	Major	Minor	Total
Senate Wins	11	3	14
House Wins	3	6	9
Split Decision	3	2	5

Thus do both sides go home happy, secure in the belief that they both win.

All that remained now was to polish the final conference report, get the signatures in the right place, run the report past the two chambers for their approval, and send it on to the president for the expected signing ceremony.

In the meantime, Simpson was being proven wrong about judicial review. Montgomery had indeed slowed the discussion to a glacial pace in dialogue about the respective value of Article III "federal" courts versus Article I "inferior" courts, as well as a hundred other details in what were very complicated bills on both sides.

However, Montgomery could no longer stop the bill. With time running out for the One-hundredth Congress, the House was moving forward with or without him. Miracle of miracles. Although Senate staffers like me are rarely privy to the internal politics of the "other body," we do pick up rumors along the way. According to the drum beat, the Speaker of the House and the majority leader were under great pressure from many of the younger members of the Veterans Committee to force Montgomery either to report out a bill or be prepared to be overridden on the floor. If judicial review did not emerge in some form by mid-September, preventing it from being attached as a "rider" to some extraneous measure would be almost impossible.

At last Montgomery was feeling the sting from veterans lobbying, for even the big groups were urging compromise. "The bill was being used to destroy confidence in VA," one lobbyist told me two years later. "We had to get it off the front pages." In August, for example, the House Government Operations Committee published a devastating report on the benefits process. Written by Rep. Ted Weiss (R-N.Y.) and his staff, and based on testimony before the Subcommittee on Human Resources and Intergovernmental Relations, the report destroyed any confidence that might have remained in the VA's benefits process. The first three findings confirmed everything we had been saying, while the fourth merely heightened concerns about having a strong and vigilant inspector general inside the agency:

A. The VA has understated the actual numbers of errors found in the claims processing programs and has provided misleading data to Congress regarding the number of errors.

B. Favoritism, undue emphasis on production quotas, and the failure to consider all medical evidence in some cases, have hampered the Board of Veterans Appeals from always operating in the best interests of veterans seeking reconsideration of claim denials.

C. The VA has discouraged agency employees who have attempted to expose unjust treatment of veterans seeking benefits.

D. The former director of the VA Compensation and Pension Service misrepresented material facts during his testimony before the subcommittee, improperly solicited gifts from veterans' service organizations, falsified education credentials provided to VA, and maintained an improper fund of donations from veterans service organizations while Director of the Milwaukee regional office.[6]

Montgomery immediately attacked the report as a blatant attempt to encourage judicial review, a not surprising conclusion given that the report's first recommendation for fixing the system was, indeed, that "Congress should pass legislation allowing veterans the right to judicial review." Here is how the report made its case:

a boundless bureaucracy, compounded by a minority of incompetent or unethical VA employees, does not always serve the needs of our veterans, as the committee's report has found. Sometimes VA officials, overly concerned with their personal status, cover up the agency weaknesses rather than exposing them. Too often, agency personnel become caught up in maintaining arbitrary, unrealistic production quotas instead of assuring that their work is of the highest quality. Fortunately, the committee believes these problems occur in a minority of cases. But what becomes of the veterans who suffer as the result of the misdeeds or honest mistakes of VA employees? Federal law prevents veterans from appealing VA decisions outside the VA in public court. Even if veterans were accorded this privilege available to all other citizens, they are further hindered by an antiquated law that limits fees paid to attorneys representing veterans to $10.[7]

All we could say was "Amen."

Even with momentum building in the House, Montgomery was reluctant to move. Only with a final threat from the leadership was he willing to report even a tepid version of judicial review. A much more aggressive measure authored by Ohio Democrat Lane Evans (of the earlier Senate discussions over linkage) had failed on a 22–9 vote in the House Veterans Committee. Nevertheless, when the House Veterans Committee passed Montgomery's judicial review bill 29–4 on September 15, the passage provoked a celebration. It was the first time a judicial review bill had ever passed.

Although it was always unlikely that Montgomery would ever support a strong judicial review bill, just about any H.R. would do. All that the supporters needed was a device to force a conference where the House could let the Senate prevail. For eight years, of course, Montgomery had allowed only three votes (total) on judicial review, two of which killed versions of the bill.

The nail-biting was not over, however. Because the House Judiciary Committee had received a joint, or simultaneous, referral on the Montgomery bill when it was introduced, the Judiciary Committee was entitled to make its opinion known, too. Had the committee decided to hold hearings or a markup of its own—both permitted under such a simultaneous referral—the bill would have stalled again. But under some lobbying from the House leadership, the Judiciary Committee decided not to act at all, thereby letting the bill move onto the floor for a final vote on October 3. The bill passed 400 to 0.

The tough question now was if the House and Senate could reach an agreement in time. On the one side was a bill that gave veterans a crack at the federal courts, albeit with the "so utterly lacking in a rational basis" standard for review. On the other side was a bill that consisted of little more than elevation of the old Board of Veterans Appeals to independent status as an Article I court, what one lobbyist called "the BVA in robes." Suffice it to say that the House Veterans Committee had produced the most limited bill possible, one hardly worthy of the name "judicial review."

Facing two such diametrically opposed bills with less than four weeks left in session, agreement seemed impossible. Our Cabinet conference had moved so fast that S. 533 now seemed destined to pass long before judicial review. Whereas we had filed the conference report and joint explanatory statement on October 3, the judicial review conference didn't even start until October 4. Without a miracle, the Cabinet bill would be on Reagan's desk by mid-October, while judicial review would likely languish and die.

The miracle came from none other than Alan Cranston. With the VA conference report in line on the floor, Cranston exercised his right to place a hold on action. The Cabinet bill could play a role in dragging the new Department of Veterans Affairs into the twenty-first century. That Cranston was the one to recognize the ultimate value of Cabinet status in motivating Montgomery was all the more satisfying given his role as the chief naysayer when linkage was defeated in July.

In his brief letter to the majority leader placing the hold, he finally cemented the linkage Simpson and Glenn had wanted all along. The linkage was still implicit, however, with the Cabinet bill to be scheduled for final, final passage only *after* judicial review. But whether Cranston called it linkage or not, a ruse by any other name stalled the same. His letter was great! Suddenly, Montgomery found renewed vigor for compromise on judicial review.

The Senate, however, had the edge on the most important issues. Although veterans would have to accept an Article I court instead of direct appeal into the federal judiciary (House wins), they would be able to take the facts of their cases to court (Senate wins), where those facts would be judged by a new seven-member specialty court called the Court of Veterans Appeals (House wins). The old eight-step benefits process would remain pretty much intact (House wins), but veterans would be free to appeal upward and outward once their internal appeals were exhausted (Senate wins). And veterans would finally be able to hire an attorney for a "reasonable" fee (Senate wins).

Most important, the two sides had agreed upon a much more aggressive standard of review. Luckily, the House won this one. Instead of "so utterly lacking in a rational basis," the new court would be allowed to overturn a decision that was "clearly erroneous." "I have repeatedly stood by the standard articulated in S. 11 as being narrow enough," Cranston explained on the Senate floor, "to avoid a flood of cases into the Federal Article III courts but broad enough to allow essential review in cases which include very flawed fact findings. However, in deference to the new forum in which veterans benefits cases will be reviewed, the standard for factual review in the U.S. Court of Veterans Appeals would be the clearly erroneous standard which is far broader . . . and should permit that court to engage in a full and fair review of BVA decisions on factual issues."

Whatever the reason for his change of heart—most likely involving a major trade—this standard of review would give the court a more aggressive tool for overturning VA decisions. The original standard was impossible to understand, and, moreover, it would have limited review to only the most extreme cases. (Ultimately, no one had ever understood what "so utterly lacking in a rational basis" meant, except as applied to the standard itself.)

The compromise had its weaknesses, of course, as all bills do. Veterans would remain locked in a separate system, one governed almost exclusively by the veterans triangle. Even the new Court of Veterans Appeals would not exactly be independent.[8]

The court's budget, for example, would be reviewed by the same Appropriations Subcommittee that reviews veterans benefit programs, with all that means for potential micromanagement. The court's appointees would be confirmed *not* by the Senate Judiciary Committee, but by the Senate Veterans Committee, with all that implies for potential pressure from the veterans lobby. Moreover, establishing the court as an independent body, would be difficult, if not impossible, for example, if its appointees all came from the veterans community and were merely passed on by the Senate Veterans Committee—that is, if the veterans groups demand their own seats on the court. By creating an Article I court, the veterans community protected the federal judiciary from an increased workload. Whether they also protected the veterans who would eventually appeal was still in doubt.

With the two conference reports in hand, all that remained were two quick voice votes in the Senate on October 18. The House had already passed the Cabinet compromise on October 8 and would pass the judicial review bill the next day, October 19. After little more than a ripple of debate, the Cabinet bill was finished. Once enrolled on parchment paper, the bill was sent to the White House, again by messenger. Less than a week later, Ronald Reagan signed the bill into law in an elaborate ceremony on the grounds of Fort McNair in southeast Washington. The formal process was recorded in the Governmental Affairs Committee Calendar as follows:

October 13, 1987.—Referred to the House Committee on Government Operations

November 16, 1987.—Reported to the House by the Committee on Government Operations (H.Rept. 100–435)

November 17, 1987.—Called up by the House under suspension of rules and considered by the House as unfinished business

November 19, 1987.—Messaged to the Senate and referred to the Committee on Governmental Affairs.

July 12, 1988.—Committee on Governmental Affairs discharged by unanimous consent.

July 12, 1988.—Passed in Senate in lieu of S. 533 with an amendment and an amendment to the title by rollcall vote: 84 yeas, 11 nays.

July 26, 1988.—Senate action messaged to the House.

August 10, 1988.—House disagreed to Senate amendments by unanimous consent and requested a conference. Speaker appointed as conferees: Messrs. Brooks, Conyers, Weiss, Frank, Montgomery, Edwards (CA), Horton, Walker, Lightfoot, and Solomon.

August 11, 1988.—Senate insisted on its amendments by voice vote.

August 11, 1988.—Senate agreed to conference and appointed as conferees: Messrs. Glenn, Sasser, Levin, Mitchell, Roth, Stevens, and Heinz. From the Committee on Veterans' Affairs: Messrs. Cranston and Murkowski.

September 7, 1988.—Senate action messaged to the House.

October 3, 1988.—Conferees agreed to file conference report and conference report filed in House (H.Rept. 100–1036).

October 3, 1988.—Conference papers messaged to Senate and held at Senate desk.

October 6, 1988.—House agreed to conference report by voice vote.

October 18, 1988.—Senate agreed to conference report by voice vote.

October 18, 1988.—Signed by the Speaker of the House.

October 20, 1988.—Signed by the President pro tempore.

October 21, 1988.—Messaged to the President.

October 25, 1988.—Signed into law (Public Law 100–527).

The Department of Veterans Affairs Act was the 527th Act passed in the One-hundredth Congress. Almost a year to the day that H.R. 3471 had been introduced in the House, veterans had their department. But what the formal register did not record was the rather unceremonious passage of Public Law 100–687, the Veterans Judicial Review Act of 1988, signed into law November 18, with no grand parade, military bands, honor guards, or film crews present. Thus, veterans also had judicial review. For me, Cabinet status had been redeemed.

Epilogue
Business as Usual?

ALMOST A YEAR to the day after Ronald Reagan signed Public Law 100–527, the Department of Veterans Affairs Act, in that gala ceremony, I wandered by the VA headquarters on Vermont Avenue, N.W. The new department had come into being March 15, 1990, just as required by statute.

On the outside, the building was still dedicated to those who bore the burden, and the White House was still across the park. The only noticeable changes were the new limousines parked outside and a beautiful new seal on the front door. Instead of an eagle perched at rest, as on the old seal, this one had an eagle in full attack, claws grasping, two American flags, with gold braids and stars in abundance.

On the inside, the department had a new secretary, deputy secretary, and a revamped organizational structure. The secretary was one of George Bush's old friends from Congress, former Republican Rep. Edward Derwinski, and the deputy was none other than Anthony Principi, former staff director of the Senate Veterans Affairs Committee under Simpson and one of the most reasonable congressional staffers I had worked with during the Cabinet debate.

The appointments lent credence to the National Academy of Public Administration's view that Cabinet elevation might improve the quality of presidential appointees. The NAPA report was absolutely right. First, the VA appointees were generally top-notch, ready to provide the leadership the new department sorely needed.

Second, and perhaps even more importantly, gone were most of the players from just six months before—the former administrator, who had once argued that the change in status would not make one iota of a difference, was out of office, while the general counsel, who had led the charge against judicial review, was awaiting confirmation as one of the seven judges on the new Court of Veterans Appeals, not necessarily an auspicious sign for the independence of the new court.

Gone, too, were the chief medical and benefits directors, both asked to leave. The new team was making all the right moves, disturbing the culture just enough to create the tiniest possibility for change, a fact not lost on the *Washington Post* in another editorial on Cabinet status titled "Good News From Veterans' Affairs." Again, the first and last paragraphs give the general gist.

> Veterans Affairs Secretary Edward Derwinski and his deputy Anthony Principi have begun an extraordinary effort that both needs and deserves support. The heretics are studying the veterans benefit structure with an eye toward rationalizing it. . . .
>
> Some of the veterans groups are already complaining that the secretary and his deputy are, as one put it, "conspiring to eliminate veterans' entitlements." Depending on the recommendations made, there could be resistance within the Office of Management and Budget as well; not all of the steps in contemplation would cut costs. Nor is it clear that the jealous veterans committees in Congress will finally let former representative Derwinski do what needs to be done. But the idea that a leader of the agency is even considering such constructive steps is progress of

a kind the veterans groups did not envision when they urged elevation of the old Veterans Administration to increase its visibility and clout.[1]

This is not to say that Derwinski and Principi were absolutely perfect, however. Derwinski started his term talking about establishing a commission to reduce the number and mission of VA hospitals, both as a way of achieving cost savings and redistributing health resources to the South and West, where the veterans population was growing fastest. Modeled on a similar commission that resulted in the closure of several hundred military installations, Derwinski's idea went over like a lead balloon with the veterans groups. They hadn't fought for Cabinet status only to have the first secretary start dismantling the system.

Derwinski also proceeded to follow the letter of the law in appointing the search commission to select the new chief medical director. In appointing two representatives of veterans served by the VA—that is, "veterans groups," as required by the convoluted language drafted to satisfy the Senate Veterans Committee—he picked the two largest groups, the American Legion and VFW, and not the third largest, the Disabled American Veterans (DAV).

Naturally, the DAV resented the decision, announcing the end of the honeymoon with the new secretary in a letter to the president of the United States and all 535 members of Congress: "Needless to say, the DAV is deeply troubled by your decision to exclude us from the [Chief Medical Director] search process. It has cast a pall upon our support for and activities on behalf of a wide range of VA programs and services that would not otherwise be possible. Worst of all, it has called into question the sincerity of your Department's commitment to this nation's veterans."[2] The two Veterans Committees reacted to this great crisis by immediately introducing legislation to expand the two search commissions by two members each. Welcome to the VA, Mr. Secretary.

In spite of an occasional stumble, the new secretary and deputy secretary were clearly moving to take hold of the department, quickly earning a reputation for pragmatism, while taking full advantage of their authority to define the functions of the six assistant secretaries. Most of the decisions made eminent sense—assistant secretaries for finance and planning (chief financial officer); information resources (chief information resources officer); human resources and administration; acquisition and facilities; and congressional and public affairs. The new team also took full advantage of their honeymoon to streamline the agency, eliminating an entire layer of unnecessary management within the health-care system. The official departmental organization is summarized in Figure 5.

Just about the only curiosity was the creation of a sixth assistant secretary for "Veterans Liaison and Program Coordination," combining the responsibility for keeping the veterans groups happy with the responsibility for evaluating and coordinating programs, hardly what one could call a compatible mandate. We had sought to discourage such a structure with our committee report on the need for a strong program evaluation capacity inside the VA, the only blemish in what was otherwise a firm consolidation of the headquarters octopus. Placing the unit responsible for objective oversight in the same suite with the unit responsible for schmoozing the veterans groups would create nothing but pressure to cool the oversight.

Things were progressing even more smoothly at the newly created Court of Veterans Appeals, but perhaps not quite as Congress had intended. If the whole point was an independent court, questions were being raised by the initial appointments. Although the new appointees were all of good character, one was a former congressman (but not a former member of the House of Veterans Committee) who had been defeated running for the Senate in 1986, another was the former general counsel of the VA who had fought for years against the very concept of judicial review, and a

Figure 5. The Department of Veterans Affairs, as Implemented in 1989

Court of Veterans Appeals*

Board of Veterans Appeals

Inspector General

Secretary
Deputy Secretary

General Counsel

Veterans Health Services & Research Administration

Veterans Benefits Administration

National Cemetery System

Assistant Secretary, Finance & Planning

Assistant Secretary, Information Resources

Assistant Secretary, Acquisition & Facilities

Assistant Secretary, Human Resources & Administration

Assistant Secretary, Congressional & Public Affairs

Assistant Secretary, Veterans Liaison & Program Coordination

* The Court of Veterans Appeals is independent from the Secretary of Veterans Affairs.

third was a former staff director of the Senate Veterans Affairs Committee, a longtime advocate of judicial review. If the veterans triangle had not captured the court entirely, it did have some very old friends on board.

More important, reading through the final legislation after the dust had settled, it became increasingly obvious that the reform was hardly as sweeping as those in Congress thought.

First, much as everyone thought the ten-dollar limitation on attorneys' fees had been lifted, Congress had actually imposed a complete fee *prohibition* on most of the administrative process. According to Section 104 of the Judicial Review Act, "a fee may not be charged, allowed, or paid for services of agents and attorneys with respect to services provided before the date on which the Board of Veterans' Appeals first makes a final decision in the case."[3]

So, good intentions notwithstanding, Congress actually took a step backward. Attorneys would all but disappear from the early stages of the benefits process, coming in only after veterans had already lost their case at the Board of Veterans Appeals. It just made no sense. Granted, average veterans would still do well—they would retain a veterans service representative who would handle their case with ease. But, veterans with difficult of time-consuming cases would still get short shrift. Heaven forbid that they be allowed to retain counsel early in the process, build their cases as effectively as possible, and win at the preliminary stages.[4]

Second, the Judicial Review Act left the old veterans benefits process pretty much intact. Veterans would still go through the regional benefit offices on up to the Board of Veterans Appeals, with possible detours and remands back and forth along the way, and only after exhausting all internal options, up to the Supreme Court. In morning's light, this was but another variation on the old theme of separatism. Even if a case went up to the Court of Veterans Appeals, it could be reviewed only on the evidence in the file *and only then on* the degree to which the facts had been erroneously interpreted. There could be no "de novo," or review from scratch, by the court. Further, once the Court of Veterans Appeals made its final decision, there could be no further appeal into the federal, Article III, courts on the facts of a case.

This is not to argue that the Judicial Review Act was mere window dressing. It did provide a counterweight of sorts to the productivity pressure within the VA, encouraging at least some greater investment by Congress in new resources, employees, and computers for an old benefits process, thereby adjusting the power structure ever so slightly between the VA benefits and medical programs. Future benefits directors would have greater leverage in the fight for resources to do their jobs, protected in part by judicial robes. Although there were still questions about the independence of the court, its first decisions showed an admirable willingness to take on the VA.

Ironically, the court's very first decision involved Gordon Erspamer, the attorney whose decade-long fight against the VA had inspired final passage of the Judicial Review Act. Erspamer had filed on behalf of his mother as soon as the new court had a mail drop. In its ruling, the court clearly sided with Erspamer, first slapping the VA for taking ten long years to resolve Erspamer's case, then warning that it would grant retroactive benefits if the VA did not act within six months. The court was flexing its muscle, arguing that it did, indeed, have the power to reopen cases filed before the Judicial Review Act had passed.

The new department must have been listening. Two months later, the VA granted Mrs. Erspamer benefits.

Appendix
How the Senate Decides

I LEARNED MANY lessons in the fight over Cabinet status, not the least of which was the amount of time and commitment it takes to move an idea like judicial review through to passage versus the rush to judgment on bills like Cabinet status. For those who study Congress, however, this case study is probably most interesting for showing differences among Senate decision-making styles.

At times, for example, Glenn acted like a small-town neighbor, trading a favor here and a favor there to get his transition bill through. At other times, he behaved more like a university professor, struggling to teach his colleagues the value of judicial review. Still other times, he operated as a political garbage man, opening S. 533 to a stream of issues unrelated to the specific purpose of the bill, which was, after all, to elevate the VA to Cabinet status, not redress past benefit grievances.*

---

* Those who might be offended by the use of the word "garbage" to describe how senators make choices should note that the term comes from the original research on the subject, and does not reflect my view that bills coming from such a process are, in fact, garbage.

From my perch in Governmental Affairs, I saw at least six different decision-making styles among the key players on Cabinet status. The six styles and their key characteristics are summarized in Appendix Table 1.

Style number one is the senator as a *rational actor*. The senator thoughtfully weighs all the options, carefully calculates all the odds, assesses every possible preference, and uses complete information to make the perfect choice. The only time I saw anything resembling a perfect weighing of information was at the very final stages of the legislative process, when the Senate used unanimous consent agreements to schedule final passage. The fact is that unanimous consents are a perfect indicator of Senate preferences. Either everyone agrees or the UC fails.

Style number two is the senator as a *university teacher*. The senator accepts the fact that rational decisions are almost impossible and pursues instead the imperfect search for truth. The primary interest is not perfect decisions, but better ideas, and the understanding that comes with reflection and study. Although many senators saw themselves as great teachers, few could compare with Daniel Patrick Moynihan (D-N.Y.) whose study of welfare led to passage of the Family Support Act in 1988. It was the nation's most comprehensive welfare reform in two decades.

Style number three is the senator as a *business tycoon*. The senator engages in the art of the deal, buying and selling legislative ideas in pure pursuit of a winnable package.[1] Call it logrolling, coalition-building, or corporatism, decisions get made when enough senators join forces to propel an issue forward. The main currency of this political economy is the number of floor votes a senator can deliver.

Style number four is the senator as a *medieval warrior*. Of all the Senate decision-making styles, this is the easiest to recognize. Just look around for the blood and gore. Here, the goal is nothing short of total victory—no compromise, no prisoners. It hardly matters whether a senator has the

Table 1: Senate Decision-Making Styles

	Rational Actor	Professor	Tycoon	Warrior	Small-Town Neighbor	Garbage Collector
Central Activity	Analysis	Studying	Buying/Selling	Arming	Browsing	Coming/Going
Decision-making Mechanism	Equation	Understanding	Investment	Battle	Barter	Exhaustion/Deadline
Primary Skill	Calculation	Teaching	Art of the Deal	Fighting	Befriending	Confusing
Primary Resource	Perfect Information	Ideas	Products	Strength	Favors	Time/Energy
Strengths	Purity of Choice	"Good" Policy	Preservation of the Market	Total Victory	Goodwill	Gridlock
Weaknesses	Cost	Impatience/Boredom	Competition for Investors	Lasting Enemies	Selection	Chaos

best idea or not. The issue is raw political power. And to the victor belongs the spoils.

Style number five is the senator as a *small-town neighbor*. Here, the Senate behaves as a kind of "Mayberry" of the legislative world, a place where decisions get made through friendly give-and-take, where senators help each other because that is the neighborly thing to do. On small bills and routine business, senators often turn into pals, visiting their corner store (a committee or subcommittee), browsing about for their groceries (a favor on a bill, a pet project for a constituent, a judgeship for an old friend), and charging their goods on a tab to be paid in kind later. The simple rule of life is do unto other senators as you would have other senators do unto you.

Finally, style number six is the senator as a *garbage collector*. This is the hardest of the styles to recognize, if only because it requires a complete and total suspension of a belief in the senator as a rational actor.[2] Instead of searching for perfect decisions, garbage collectors spend their time looking for opportunities to use a given bill as a vehicle for addressing unrelated issues, or "garbage". Sometimes, they merely want to use a bill like Cabinet status to carry other issues that would never pass on their own. Other times, as I learned, making a bill into a garbage can is a way of slowing the process to a standstill. Gridlock is not always bad, particularly if a senator wants the time to draft an alternative.

All six Senate decision-making styles were present in the One-hundredth Congress. Not only did decision-making styles vary across the issues I worked on (Cabinet status involved more fighting than the transition bill), the styles changed along each step of the legislative process on each separate bill.

As Appendix figures 1 and 2 suggest, even the order of the steps was different for the two bills—the Cabinet bill was on the president's agenda very early in the legislative calendar, while the transitions bill caught the president's attention only after it had passed the Senate.

Although the two charts involve a number of judgment calls, they illustrate the importance of *how* the Senate decides to *what* the Senate decides. That Glenn and his staff became garbage collectors during the fact-finding stage of Cabinet status, for example, bought enough time and controversy to eventually link the Cabinet bill to judicial review, thereby altering what would have been likely defeat for judicial review on its own.

Here is how the story of the Department of Veterans Affairs Act is retold using Appendix Figure 1.

(1) The bill reaches the Senate agenda through natural buying and selling among business tycoons. Senators sign onto the bill to satisfy constituents as represented by the veterans lobby. No one expects the bill to go anywhere—sponsorship is a low-cost investment.

(2) The president becomes interested through a somewhat different process. Although it is still not clear why President Reagan said "yes," particularly given his earlier pledge to dismantle the departments of Energy and Education, the decision appears to resemble a small town, laden with nostalgia toward America's veterans and their perceived need for greater care.

(3) The Senate Governmental Affairs Committee accepts the issue because of the sheer political pressure and momentum characteristic of warriors as senators like General Strom Thurmond go to battle. The committee has no choice, lest its members be slaughtered. The bill is pushed by wave after wave of lobbyists demanding space on the committee agenda, putting members and staff under seige.

(4) Fact-finding moves forward as Glenn's garbage crew embarks on a detailed assessment of any and all issues that might be candidates for the Cabinet bill. This process lasts six months, delaying progress as judicial review moves forward in the Senate Veterans Affairs Committee.[3]

Figure 1. The Vets Get a Department ("X" Marks the dominant style)

	Rational Actor	Professor	Tycoon	Warrior	Small-town Neighbor	Garbage Collector
1. Senate agenda			X			
2. President's agenda					X	
3. Committee agenda				X		
4. Fact-finding						X
5. Drafting		X	X			
6. Markup		X		X		
7. Committee passage		X				
8. Floor amending				X		X
9. Senate passage			X			
10. Conference		X	X	X		
11. Final passage	X			X		

Figure 2. The President Gets a Transition ("X" Marks the Dominant Style)

	Rational Actor	Professor	Tycoon	Warrior	Small-town Neighbor	Garbage Collector
1. Committee agenda					X	
2. Fact-finding		X				
3. Drafting		X				
4. Markup		X		X		
5. Committee passage		X				
6. Senate agenda			X			
7. President's agenda			X			
8. Floor amending				X	X	
9. Senate passage	X		X			
10. Conference				X		
11. Final passage	X					

(5) Drafting occurs as Professor Glenn and others on the committee consider a number of recommendations for improving the operation of the new department. Hearing testimony supports the key components of the bill.

(6) Markup also occurs in a university setting, as the committee accepts the recommendations in a formal bill. However, objections regarding judicial review force the committee to back away from any linkage of the issues at markup and threaten a more extensive floor fight later.

(7) Committee passage is essentially a small-town picnic, a celebration of the committee's work among a neighborly crowd.

(8) Floor amending involves both warriors and garbage collectors. The effort to give President Reagan the honor of appointing the first secretary of veterans affairs fails on a straight party line-vote, while the final attempt to link the two issues of judicial review and Cabinet status also fails by an overwhelming margin.

(9) Senate passage allows all parties to coalesce around the final bill, permitting eighty-four senators to say "aye" regardless of how they voted on the two floor amendments. The corporation succeeds in letting the Senate have its cake and eat it too.

(10) Conference is a combination of deal-making, fighting and small-town favors as the two chambers work through one disagreement after another.

(11) The bill passes only after judicial review finally clears, thereby reflecting the continuing war over linkage. Final passage, however, involves a unanimous consent process, which makes the Senate look like a collection of rational actors. Once the judicial review bill passes, the Cabinet bill follows immediately as the majority and minority leader read their prepared scripts.

Here is how the story of the Presidential Transitions Effectiveness Act is retold using Chart Two:

(1) The Governmental Affairs Committee moves ahead purely because Professor Glenn is interested and because

the committee has traditionally allowed such leeway as part of its internal customs. Glenn asks other members to participate in developing a bill.

(2) Fact-finding involves seminars with the small number of experts knowledgeable about how presidential transitions might be improved.

(3) Drafting reflects recommendations emerging from extensive hearings on presidential transitions, including representatives from the national parties and past campaigns, again taking on elements of a college seminar.

(4) Markup involves a mix of medieval warfare as an effort to strip the Senate bill of preelection planning is quashed without a formal vote, then becomes a quiz on Glenn's lectures on strengthening the transitions process.

(5) Committee passage is congratulatory, smooth and near-rational.

(6) The bill reaches the Senate agenda as both a small-town favor and an acknowledgment of Governmental Affairs, Inc.

(7) The bill finally reaches the president's agenda when the potential for an increase in moving support catches the staff's attention.

(8) As a result, Senate passage becomes dependent upon getting the Republicans to buy the White House deal. The outgoing president must have an increase in his moving allowance. Rather than fight, Glenn (more specifically, his staff) agrees to a floor amendment.

(9) Senate passage occurs by unanimous consent long after most senators have gone for the evening as the majority and minority leaders rise again with prepared scripts. As one reviews the transcripts the following day, the Senate looks remarkably deliberative, even rational.

(10) The quasi–conference is a small-town affair as the two chambers work out any disagreements through friendly barter. The Senate yields on preelection planning in return for a future favor on the Cabinet bill.

(11) Final passage is "programmed" and predictable

once the House has acted, again making senators look like rational actors.

As figures 1 and 2 suggest, senators are not always successful in getting their colleagues to accept a given decision-making style. Much as Simpson and Glenn tried, for example, to teach the Senate about the importance of linkage between Cabinet status and judicial review, his opponents were successful in turning the vote into an armed struggle. In fact, the styles can be said to ascend and descent depending upon a number of factors, summarized in Table Two.

First, each style requires differing amounts of *time*. Garbage collectors can operate only with huge amounts of time, since it takes so long to clear out the unrelated issues once they enter the "garbage can" called a decision.

Second, each style requires differing amounts of physical and intellectual *energy*. My general view is that rational actors, professors, tycoons, warriors, and garbage collectors all need more stamina than small-town neighbors.

Third, each style requires differing levels of *information*. Clearly, rational actors need an almost impossible amount of information, while small-town neighbors need only to know where their friends live.

Fourth, each style demands differing amounts of *expertise*. Winning a battle or selling a legislative product takes more expertise than meandering over to the corner store for a favor or picking up the trash.

Finally, each style demands a differing level of *political capital*. Political capital involves little more than a senator's ability to deliver votes on the floor. Although a senator's support back home would certainly affect political capital—votes in the most recent election, public approval, and such—such *external* measures of political standing are far less important than the *internal* support a member can deliver on any given issue. Clearly, medieval warriors and

Table 2. Resources and Senate Decision-making Styles

Resources	Rational Actor	Professor	Tycoon	Medieval Warrior	Small-town Neighbor	Garbage Collector
Time	High	High	Mod.	Low	Low	High
Energy	High	Mod.	Mod.	High	Low	High
Information	High	Mod.	Low	Mod.	Low	Low
Expertise	High	Mod.	High	High	Low	Low
Political Capital	Low	Low	High	High	Low	Low

business tycoons need some minimal amount of capital to operate. Collecting garbage and teaching involve much less.

From my perspective as a former staffer, the critical question is whether any one of the six models is somehow better than the others for making "good" policy—that is, policy that is somehow more in the public interest. Perhaps Congress should ban garbage collectors—after all, the resulting policy is hardly rational.

Although garbage collectors and medieval warriors may seem less appealing than small-town neighbors and university professors, there is no one congressional model that works best for producing good policy. Congress is a human institution that adapts its decision-making process to changing issues and changing needs. That may mean Congress will occasionally look like a medieval battlefield, littered with the corpses of fallen adversaries. After all, politics is politics.

These words of reverence for politics nothwithstanding, and admitting my own professional bias, my general view is that teaching generally produces better legislation than fighting, especially in veterans policy. Unfortunately, building a great center of learning can be particularly difficult when there is no accepted curriculum, no independent source of information, no research base outside of the lobbying community itself, and not one major book or research article in fifteen years! Such was clearly the case in veterans policy.

In contrast to the two decades of research which finally produced a consensus on welfare reform in the mid-1980s, veterans policy is hardly an area of academic interest, in spite of the size of the bureaucracy and scope of the programs. This is no small reason why veterans policy has remained aloof from hard inspection over these many years.

Again admitting my bias, Glenn's presidential transitions bill was forged through careful study and hearings, based on a body of work developed over a decade or more. Although there was some good old-fashioned horse trading along the way, Congress ended closer to the ideal policy on the transitions bill than on Cabinet status for the VA, largely because of the work by many who had gone before. Ultimately, a similiar effort is needed by those inside and outside the veterans triangle, and, hopefully, among those who read this book.

Notes

Notes to Chapter 1

1. For an excellent history of Hoover's relationship with veterans, see Donald J. Lisio, *The President and Protest: Hoover, Conspiracy, and the Bonus Riot* (Columbia, Mo.: University of Missouri Press, 1974). The figures in this initial section are drawn from chapters 1 and 2.

2. Lisio, *The President and Protest*, p. 8.

3. These statistics are drawn from *Annual Report of the Veterans Administration* (Washington, D.C.: Veterans Administration, 1987).

4. Hugh Heclo was the first to coin the term "issue network," arguing that iron triangles were of declining usefulness in describing how Washington works. According to Heclo, "Iron triangles and subgovernments suggest a stable set of participants coalesced to control fairly narrow public programs which are in the direct economic interest of each party to the alliance. Issue networks are almost the reverse image in each alliance. Issue networks are almost the reverse image in each respect. Participants move in and out of the networks constantly. Rather than groups united in dominance over a program, no one, as far as one can tell, is in control of the policies and issues." See Hugh Heclo, "Issue Networks in the Executive Branch," in A. King, ed., *The New American Political System* (Washington, D.C.: American Enterprise Institute, 1978), p. 102.

5. The quote is from Michael Leaveck, an official with the Vietnam

Veterans of American, in Kirk Victor, "A Different Drummer," *National Journal* 20, no. 11, March 12, 1988, p. 670.

6. Gilbert Steiner's work on veterans policy still stands as the best short piece on the subject. See *The State of Welfare* (Washington, D.C.: Brookings Institution, 1971). He is one of the very few welfare scholars who mentioned veterans policy as part of the overall American safety net. Most other scholars concentrate on social security, Aid to Families with Dependent Children, food stamps, and various state and local general assistance programs, completely ignoring the enormous impact of the VA's benefit programs on poverty among all veterans.

7. Indeed, the VA has been very slow to equip its hospitals for the growing number of women veterans.

8. See, for example, Veterans Administrations Office of Inspector General, "Report of Followup Audit: Civilian Health and Medical Program of the Veterans Administration," Report No. 7R8-AO8-115, September 23, 1987, which found that roughly 30 percent of the participants in the CHAMPVA program from 1983–86 were ineligible. In 1987, the inspector general estimated that the VA would spend $14.2 million on care for dependents and survivors who were ineligible.

9. See Jeremiah Hurley, Daniel Linz, Emmett Swint, and Meredith Spear, "Assessing the Effects of the Medicare Prospective Payment System on the Demand for VA Inpatient Services: An Examination of Transfers and Discharges of Problem Patients," unpublished report for the Veterans Administration Department of Medicine and Surgery, undated. The study compared the number of problem admissions at VA hospitals in the year preceding implementation of the new Medicare cost-containment system and the year after, finding increases in transfers of patients of from 27 to 41 percent.

10. U.S. General Accounting Office, *VA Benefits: Law Allows Compensation for Disabilities Unrelated to Military Service*, Report No. GAO/HRD-89-60, July 1989, p. 16.

11. GAO, *VA Benefits*, GAO/HRD-89-60, p. 28.

12. GAO, *VA Benefits*, GAO/HRD-89-60, pp. 25-27.

13. Harvey Sapolsky, "America's Socialized Medicine: The Allocation of Resources within the Veterans' Health Care System," *Public Policy* 25, no. 3 (Summer 1977): 361.

14. These data are drawn from an internal VA report, "Veteran Eligibility and the Furnishing of Health Care," and cover the first three quarters of 1988. My sources in the VA say the percentages are representative of recent years.

15. An internal source provided this estimate as a rough figure. My source cautioned that the VA would never acknowledge such a

high number if only because of the politics involved in admitting that so many admissions were related to alcohol abuse.

16. Veterans Administration, *Survey of Aging Veterans* (Washington, D.C.: U.S. Government Printing Office, 1984), pp. 117–32.

17. James Christian and A. Joan Adams, "Benefits of a National Health Care System for Veterans: The Maryland Perspective," internal unpublished paper, March 1985, pp. 5–6.

18. GAO, *Better Patient Management Practices Could Reduce Length of Stay in VA Hospitals*, Report No. GAO/HRD-89-52.

19. Committee on Government Operations, U.S. House of Representatives, Report No. 100-74 (Washington, D.C.: U.S. Government Printing Office, April 30, 1987).

20. Committee on Government Operations, Report No. 100-74, p. 11.

21. GAO, *VA Health Care: VA's Patient Injury Control Program Not Effective*, GAO/HRD-87-49, May 1987, p. 24.

22. See Veterans Administration, Department of Medicine and Surgery, "White Paper: Malpractice," January 22, 1988, for the data; see also Veterans Administration, Office of Inspector General, "Final Report: Followup Audit of Medical Malpractice Claims," Report No. 7AB-A17-058, March 31, 1987.

23. Quoted in Julie Kosterlitz, "Graying Armies," *National Journal*, 20, no. 11, March 12, 1988, p. 668.

24. These and other figures about the numbers and age of veterans are drawn from the *Annual Report of the Veterans Administration* (Washington, D.C.: U.S. Government Printing Office, 1987).

25. These numbers are drawn from the 1987 *Annual Report of the Veterans Administration*; additional data on the aging of the veterans population can be found in Congressional Budget Office, *Veterans Administration Health Care: Planning for Future Years* (Washington, D.C.: Congressional Budget Office, April 1984); Veterans Administration, *Health Care of the Aging Veteran*, Report of the Geriatrics and Gerontology Advisory Committee (Washington, D.C.: U.S. Government Printing Office, 1983); and Terrie Wetle and John W. Rowe, *Older Veterans: Linking VA and Community Resources* (Cambridge, Mass. Harvard University Press, 1984). I owe a debt of gratitude to the many VA staffers who helped me understand some of these issues. In particular, Marjorie Quandt and her staff in Strategic Planning of the Department of Medicine and Surgery were always willing to answer even my most trivial question. My mistakes are, of course, mine alone, and do not betray a lack of knowledge on their part, but a lack of learning on mine.

26. Kosterlitz, "Graying Armies," p.668.

27. Kosterlitz, "Graying Armies," p. 668.

28. Norman Hearst, Thomas Newman, and Stephen Hulley, "Delayed Effects on the Military Draft on Mortality," *New England Journal of Medicine* 314, no. 10 March 6, 1986, p. 620.

29. The best description of the Vietnam War from the veterans viewpoint comes from Myra MacPherson, *Long Time Passing: Vietnam and the Haunted Generation* (New York: Signet, 1985); see also Laura Palmer, *Shrapnel in the Heart: Letters and Remembrances from the Vietnam Veterans Memorial* (New York: Vintage, 1987).

30. Quoted in Victor, "A Different Drummer," p. 671.

Notes to Chapter 2

1. Most of these work-load statistics are drawn from Norman Ornstein, Thomas Mann, and Michael Malbin, *Vital Statistics on Congress, 1989-1990* (Washington, D.C.: Congressional Quarterly Press, 1990).

2. For an excellent summary of the campaign and what it was like see Richard Fenno, *The Presidential Odyssey of John Glenn* (Washington, D.C.: Congressional Quarterly, 1990).

3. For an introduction to the new politics of floor amending, see Steven Smith, *Call to Order: Floor Politics in the House and Senate* (Washington, D.C.: Brookings Institution, 1989).

4. Transcript, Office of the Press Secretary, November 10, 1987.

5. This unnamed aide is quoted in the *Washington Post*, January 11, 1988, p. A8.

6. Committee on Government Operations, *Department of Veterans Affairs Act: Report to Accompany H.R. 3471*, 100th Cong., 1st. Sess., 1987 H. Rep. 100–435, p. 8.

7. These figures are drawn from a U.S. Senate Governmental Affairs Committee memorandum written by Deborah Lessor, "Summary of Bills to Establish/Reorganize Cabinet Departments in the 95th–100th Congresses," February 26, 1988.

8. James J. Kilpatrick, "How Much for Veterans?" *Washington Post*, December 10, 1987, p. A15.

9. William Safire, "End of the Affair," *New York Times*, November 29, 1987, p. E17.

10. None of this would be possible without the tremendous help from the committee staff, most importantly the committee's chief clerk, who pulls all of the papers together, keeps the process moving, and provides just the right blend of hassling, encouragement, and prayer

to make the hearing come off. We at the Governmental Affairs Committee always believed our chief clerk, Mickey Sue Prosser, was the best in the Senate.

11. Earlier in the year I had learned the hard way that any senator or House member who wants to testify at a hearing may do so—I had told one senator's staffer there was no room for his boss at an upcoming hearing on financial management reform and was not so gently informed minutes later by our chairman that there would always be room for his distinguished friend.

12. "Department of the Month Club," editorial, *Washington Post*, December 14, 1987, p. A14.

13. "Veterans Stampede Congress," editorial, *New York Times*, December 14, 1987, p. A14.

14. *Congressional Record*, 100th Cong., 1st. sess., January 27, 1988, p. E68.

Notes to Chapter 3

1. It is important to note that veterans were not the only individuals barred from judicial review under one statute or another: federal employees were barred under the provisions of the Federal Employees Compensation Act. See Congressional Research Service, Library of Congress, "Congressional and Judicial Limitations on the Right to Judicial Review of Administrative Determinations under Various Federal Statutes," unnumbered report, June 10, 1986, by the American Law Division.

2. The original statute can be found at the Franklin Delano Roosevelt Presidential Library.

3. There is no evidence the plea was ever presented, but the telegram was sent on March 12, 1933, and can be found in the Franklin Delano Roosevelt Presidential Library in Hyde Park, N.Y.

4. These quotes can be found in the *Congressional Record*, 73rd Cong., 1st sess., June 1 and 2, 1933, and were researched by Philip Cushman, national president, Veterans Due Process, in a written statement presented to the Governmental Affairs Committee on April 11, 1988.

5. In 1973, for example, the VFW apprarently asked for nomination of a VFW candidate as administrator of the VA, even though the post was occupied by an able administrator, albeit a former American Legion official. According to an internal document to White House chief of staff Alexander Haig from Jerry Jones, a campaign functionary,

"During 1970 and 1971, Chuck Colson solicited the VFW's support for our Southeast Asia war policy, and recieved that support. He continued with VFW leaders during the 1972 campaign and got the organization's support for the President. Following the election, the VFW asked for a quid pro quo: the nomination of a VFW candidate as VA administrator. The agency had been headed by an American Legion member throughout the first term, and the VFW argued that it was time one of their people had the job." The effort fell through when the White House discovered that the VFW official involved, one Cooper Holt, who later became the VFW's executive secretary, had "over-represented" the organization's demands as part of an internal VFW political battle. It also didn't help that Chuck Colson became ensnared in the Watergate crisis. The memo was dated September 7, 1973, marked "EYES ONLY: ADMINISTRATIVELY CONFIDENTIAL," and is to be found in the National Archives' Nixon Project.

6. These data are drawn from internal data collected by the Board of Veterans Appeals, the highest review body within the VA prior to passage of veterans reform legislation in 1988. The document is numbered REPDISP2.F87 and is dated April 30, 1987.

7. This warning came in an internal VA document titled "Overview of VA's Position on Judicial Review" sent to all veterans groups. The document was undated.

8. Vietnam Veterans of America, *Guide to Veterans Benefits* (Washington, D.C.: VVA, 1987), p. 1-3. Thanks to Paul Egan for his help in understanding this and other puzzles at VA.

9. Ten million duplicate records were found in 1988. They covered the years 1940–45 and 1950–54, leaving eight million still lost.

10. This statement can be found in Section 3.102 of the regulations governing the VA benefits process (Title 38, Code of Federal Regulations, or *C.F.R.* for short).

11. This statement can be found in Section 3.102 of Title 38, *C.F.R.*

12. There is a deep literature on judicial review in the law journals. In particular, I recommend the following articles: Frederick Davis, "Veterans' Benefits, Judicial Review, and the Constitutional Problems of 'Positive' Government," *Indiana Law Journal* 39, no. 2 (Winter 1964); Scott Reisch, "211 in Progress: Must the Veterans' Administration Comply with Federal Law?" *Stanford Law Review* 40, no. 4 (November 1987); Sandra Murphy, "A Critique of the Veterans Administration Claims Process," *Brooklyn Law Review* 52, no. 3 (Fall 1986); Robert Rabin, "Preclusion of Judicial Review in the Processing of Claims for Veterans' Benefits: A Preliminary Analysis," *Stanford Law Review* 27, no. 1 (February, 1975); Tom Daschle, "Making the Veterans Admin-

istration Work for Veterans," *Harvard Journal of Legislation* 11, no. 1 (February 1984). I also strongly recommend a report by Frederick Davis for the Administrative Conference of the United States, "Judicial Review of Benefits Decisions of the Veterans Administration," Final Draft (Washington, D.C.: Administrative Conference, November 20, 1978).

13. This letter of March 17, 1988, came from William Fraser, of Advocates for Basic Legal Equality, Inc. Similar horror stories came from a variety of sources, including Veterans Due Process, Inc.

14. Concerns regarding the effectiveness of the VA process were voiced repeatedly over the 1980s by the Vietnam Veterans of America, among them the VVA Legal Services/Public Interest Law Clinic. At the height of the debate over the VA benefits process, attorneys at the Public Interest Law Clinic voiced their concerns to the Governmental Affairs Committee in a letter to the author, March 24, 1988:

"First, we have encountered problems with the Veterans Administration's file moving and tracking system. This problem area includes lost files. A related problem consists of lost or misplaced materials submitted to all levels of the VA. The third problem concerns the remand and audit processes of the VA. Fourth, there are problems with responses to inquiries about claimants' cases at all levels of the VA, including VA Medical Centers. Fifth, we have repeatedly run into problems because the standards concerning burdens of proof are not clear. Finally, a problem particular to represented veterans is that of confusion over power of attorney."

15. The fight over judicial review speaks to broader questions of how the courts and Congress relate. For an excellent introduction to the topic, see Robert Katzmann, *Judges and Legislators: Toward Institutional Comity* (Washington, D.C.: Brookings Institution, 1988).

16. These figures are drawn from *DVB Executive Briefing Book*, provided by the deputy chief benefits director for the Program Management, Planning and Analysis Staff, October 1987.

17. NARS was the direct descendant of the National Association of Atomic Veterans.

18. National Association of Radiation Survivors, et al., Plaintiffs, v. Thomas K. Turnage, et al., Defendants. Plaintiffs' Joint Trial Brief, United States District Court, Northern District of California, September 8, 1987, p. 2.

19. Gordon P. Erspamer, prepared statement to the U.S. House

of Representatives Committee on Veterans Affairs, May 20, 1986, p. 6.

20. Erspamer, prepared statement, p. 6.

21. Ronald Abrams, Documentation of Due Process/NARS v. Walters/Analysis/Suggestion Actions, September 25, 1986, p. 3.

22. The case was still pending when the Senate and House finally passed the Judicial Review Act of 1988, thereby rendering much of Erspamer's case "moot" or no longer relevant to the real world.

23. Subcommittee on Compensation, Pension, and Insurance of the Committee on Veterans' Affairs, *Operation of the Board of Veterans' Appeals*, U.S. House of Representatives, 100th cong., 1st sess., October 6, 1987, Serial No. 100-32, p. 7.

24. "White Paper-BVA Remands," undated, unpublished Veterans Administrations internal memorandum, received by Governmental Affairs in February 1988.

25. See G. Calvin Mackenzie, *The In and Outers* (Baltimore: Johns Hopkins University Press, 1987), for a set of readings on how the appointments process works and doesn't work.

26. Quoted in the *National Journal*, October 8, 1982, p. 1715; Nimmo was in trouble at the VA from the start, and not just because he ordered the costly refurbishing of his office at the very time the Reagan budget cut veterans benefits. He simply did not realize how tough the veterans issue was and how little authority a VA administrator actually had. "I didn't realize the size or complexity of the agency or the divergent pressures put on the administrator by so many interests and elements. I should have realized it but I didn't. I didn't realize the extent to which the veterans organizations were able to apply pressure. . . . I think the agency should be given Cabinet rank simply to balance the power equation." See also p. 1717 of the October 8 *National Journal*.

27. In fact, there was some evidence that judicial review would make no difference whatsoever and might actually encourage VA employees to ignore due process to an even greater extent because they knew the courts might eventually clean up their mistakes. See Charles Koch, Jr., and David Koplow, "The Fourth Bite of the Apple: A Study of the Operation and Utility of the Social Security Administration's Appeals Council," prepared for the Administrative Conference of the United States, Final Draft (Washington, D.C.: Administrative Conference, September 28, 1987).

28. The legislative history of judicial review is summarized in a Governmental Affairs Committee memo by Deborah Lessor, "Legislative History Highlights—Judical Review," January 25, 1988. The bill

passed as S. 330 in 1979, S. 349 in 1982, as S. 636 in 1983, and S. 367 in 1985. It also passed as part of S. 1651 in 1984. In each case, the bill died in the House Veterans Affairs Committee.

29. "Vets Rights to Sue for Benefits Pressed," Bill McAllister, *Washington Post*, February 19, 1988, p. A4.

30. "The Vets: Having It All," editorial, *Washington Post*, February 23, 1988, p. A14.

Notes to Chapter 4

1. The DAV figure comes from Board of Veterans Appeals data.

2. *Washington Post*, March 13, 1988, p. A4.

3. See Richard Harwood, "The VA Question," *Washington Post*, June 19, 1988, p. C6. Harwood also concluded that there "was a clear coincidence of viewpoint in the paper's editorial stance and its news coverage. . . . Was the news coverage tilted against the VA plan? Yes."

4. National Academy of Public Administration, *Evaluation of Proposals to Establish a Department of Veterans Affairs: A Report by an Academy Panel for the Committee on Governmental Affairs, United States Senate* (Washington, D.C.: National Academy of Public Administration, March 1988), p. 21.

5. "Cabinet-Making 101," editorial, *Washington Post*, March 16, 1988, p. A14.

6. Quoted in David Bonior, Steven Champlin, and Timothy Kelly, *The Vietnam Veterans: A History of Neglect* (New York: Praeger, 1984), p. 136. For an excellent introduction to the history of veterans policy and politics, see Gilbert Steiner, *The State of Welfare* (Washington: Brookings Institution, 1971). Steiner is one of the few observers of modern social welfare to even acknowledge that veterans policy might be part of the social safety net.

7. See "The Iron Triangle: July Near Miss Signals Vets Committee Shift," *Veteran* 6, no. 9 (September 1986), for the story; the *Veteran* is a publication of the Vietnam Veterans of America.

8. These positions are drawn from the Vietnam Veterans of America, *Veteran* 6, no. 9 (September 1986), p. 24.

9. Office of Program Planning and Evaluation, Program Evaluation Service, *Program Evaluations of Veterans Compensation for Service-Connected Disability* (Washington, D.C.: Veterans Administration, unpublished draft, c. 1984), chapter 7, p. 51.

10. OPPE, *Program Evaluation: Veterans Compensation*, p. 57.

11. At the VA, the internal adjudicatory process clearly gave the

benefit of the doubt to the original rating boards, whether by allowing those boards to make the first review of a veteran's appeal or by permitting the Board of Veterans Appeals to remand cases to the original board.

12. Veterans Administration Regional Office (VARO), Houston, *Compensation and Pension Field Survey Report*, December 14–18, 1987, p. A10.

13. VARO, New York, *Compensation and Pension Service Field Survey Report*, June 15–19, 1987, pp. 19–20.

14. VARO, Lincoln, *Compensation and Pension Service Field Survey Report*, November 2–6, 1987, p. A14.

15. "Featherweights," editorial, *Washington Post*, April 17, p. A16.

Notes on Chapter 5

1. The commission's key conclusions are summarized in the Federal Election Commission, *Advisory Opinion 1980–87*, September 15, 1980.

2. These tax returns, called a Form 990, are technically public.

3. See Leslie Maitland Werner, "Records of Presidential Transition Funds Released," *New York Times*, June 2, 1984, p. A9.

4. Lawrence Longley and Walter Oleszek, *Bicameral Politics: Conference Committees in Congress* (New Haven, Conn.: Yale University Press, 1989), pp. 158–59.

5. The numbering of sections works as follows: title by roman numeral, section by arabic number, (small letter), (arabic number), (capital letter), (roman numeral).

6. Just because we were all Democrats did not mean we got along. We owed a great deal to a member of Senator George Mitchell's personal staff, Steve Hart, for helping reduce much of the tension, and for acting as an intermediary between the two committees. As the only senator who sat on both the Vets and Governmental Affairs Committees, Mitchell, and his staff, could play that role most effectively. Bill Brew, of the Vets Committee staff, was always helpful, too. Finally, Senator Roth's staff, most significantly Mike Mitchell and Chip Copeland, was always working toward consensus on these issues.

7. Department of Veterans Affairs Act of 1988, Report of the Committee on Governmental Affairs United States Senate, Report 100–342 (Washington, D.C.: U.S. Government Printing Office, May 12, 1988), p. 21.

8. Report 100-342, p. 36.

9. Report 100-342, p. 20.

10. Report 100-342, p. 35.

11. Walter Oleszek, *Congressional Procedures and the Policy Process* (Washington, D.C.: Congressional Quarterly Press, 1989), p. 180.

12. Order nos. 615, 617, and 618 had already passed, but their numbers are never reassigned.

Notes to Chapter 6

1. For an overview of recent change in the Senate, including the rising concern with election, see in particular Barbara Sinclair's analysis in *The Transformation of the U.S. Senate* (Baltimore: Johns Hopkins University Press, 1989).

2. Conventional Wisdom Watch, *Newsweek*, June 6, 1988, p. 4.

3. Conventional Wisdom Watch, *Newsweek*, July 4, 1988. p. 4.

4. Sinclair, *Transformation of the Senate*, pp. 115–16.

5. Quoted in Sinclair, *Transformation of the Senate*, p. 130.

6. Quoted in Alan Ehrenhalt, "In the Senate of the '80s, Team Spirit Has Given Way to the Rule of Individuals," *Congressional Quarterly Weekly Report*, September 4, 1982, p. 2182.

7. See Charles O. Jones, *The United States Congress: People, Place, and Policy* (Homewood, Ill.: Dorsey, 1982), p. 321.

8. Sinclair, *Transformation of the Senate*, p. 126.

9. Sinclair, *Transformation of the Senate*, p. 128.

10. Sinclair, *Transformation of the Senate*, pp. 115–120.

11. Sinclair, *Transformation of the Senate*, p. 140.

12. In fact, the Court of Veterans Appeals proposed later in the process was modeled on the U.S. Tax Court (26 United States Code 7441 *et seq.*)

13. Alan Simpson, letter to Gene Murphy, national commander of the Disabled American Veterans, August 26, 1988, p. 2.

14. Bill McAllister, "Veterans' Appeal Bill May Advance," *Washington Post*, June 5, 1988, p. A6.

15. The story appeared on June 18, 1988, p. 1.

16. A "Dear Colleague" letter addressed to all senators, July 8, 1988.

17. Sinclair, *Transformation of the Senate*, p. 138.

18. I should add that we found working with the minority staff of the Senate Veterans Committee extremely pleasant, especially the staff director, Tony Principi, who would later become the first deputy secretary of the new department.

19. Steven Smith, *Call to Order: Floor Politics in the House and Senate* (Washington, D.C.: Brookings Institution, 1988), p. 239.

Notes to Chapter 7

1. See Lawrence Longley and Walter Oleszek, *Bicameral Politics: Conference Committees in Congress* (New Haven, Conn.: Yale University Press, 1989) for a history of conference committees, and the most detailed discussion available of how conferences work, who wins and loses, and the role of conferences in a bicameral legislature.

2. Longley and Oleszek, *Bicameral Politics*, pp. 158–59.

3. Longley and Oleszek summarize a host of studies that compare House/Senate conference scores and rightly conclude that "the recurrently posed question Who wins—House or Senate? may be of little relevance to the actual politics of legislation and to the more significant questions of which political and legislative interests prevail. Who wins in conference committee politics? is a significant question, but not when expressed in terms of chamber success scores or statistical counts." See Longley and Oleszek, *Bicameral Politics*, p. 87. It is my hunch that the only way statistical counts could be valuable is if they compared the same rough set of players over time, in which case the court would show that the two bodies even things out as best they can—that is, one body may prevail on a single conference, only to seek opportunites to let the other body prevail on the next. The hypothesis is simple: to the extent possible, the two chambers will even out.

4. These provisions were designed to prevent a non-confirmed chief of staff from running the department, as had been the case under the most recent administrator. It was perfectly logical for the Senate to insist that all top officials be subject to advice and consent, particularly since the Senate would do the confirming, and hardly surprising that the House didn't care.

5. John Manley, *The Politics of Finance: The House Committee on Ways and Means* (Boston: Little, Brown, 1970), p. 271.

6. Report of the Committee on Government Operations, U.S. Congress, *Investigation of the Disability Compensation Programs of the Veterans' Administration*, Report 100–886, 100th cong., 2d sess., August 18, 1988, p. v.

7. Committee on Government Operations, Report 100–886, p. 18. I knew the staffer, Mark Smolonsky, who wrote this report, and was delighted to see his handiwork and strength in the final conclusions.

8. For a review of the optimum forum for judicial review, see David Currie and Frank Goodman, "Judicial Review of Federal Administrative Action," *Columbia Law Review* 75, no. 1 (January 1975): 1–88.

Notes to Epilogue

1. Editorials, "Good News from Veterans Affairs," *Washington Post*, March 11, 1990, p. A14.
2. Letter from Charles E. Joeckel, National Adjutant, Disabled American Veterans, to Administrator Derwinski, August 17, 1989, p. 3; Derwinski courted the controversy, however, by appointing four veterans groups to the earlier search for a chief benefits director, appointing two as "persons who have experience in the management of veterans benefits programs or programs of similar content and scope," still leaving the DAV off the list.
3. Under the veterans administrative adjudication process, the Board of Veterans Appeals can make more than one "final" decision.
4. Gordon Erspamer made this argument on behalf of the National Association of Radiation Surveys and his other plaintiffs in responding to the government's motions to dismiss his case as moot following enactment of the Judicial Review Act. See National Association of Radiation Survivors, et al., v. Thomas K. Turnage, et al., "Plantiffs' Joint Response to Defendants' Notice of Filing VA Judicial Review Act," December 5, 1988, United States District Court, Northern District of California.

Notes to the Appendix

1. The business-tycoon style is drawn heavily from the work of Richard Cyert and James March. Written twenty-five years ago to debunk theories of firms as rational actors, *The Behavioral Theory of the Firm* (Englewood Cliffs, N.J.: Prentice-Hall, 1963), is still the best statement of how businesses really work in a world of "bounded" rationality.
2. This decision-making style is drawn from the garbage-can model of organizational choice. Interestingly enough, the garbage-can model itself was developed by Michael Cohen, James March, and Johan Olsen as a way of understanding how universities decide. Much as we think of universities as places to learn, they hardly make choices through careful deliberation. When it comes time to setting a university

budget, hiring a new athletic director, designing a new library building, or recruiting a chaired professorship, universities can be quite unruly.

Again, because universities are rarely able to decide about big issues in an orderly fashion, and because decision-making opportunities are so rare, any decision-making opportunity that does arise creates a magnet for all kinds of unrelated issues. The hiring of a new athletic director becomes a debate about minority recruitment in the Agriculture School; the new library becomes a struggle over housing for poor people in the neighborhood.

See Michael Cohen, James March, and Johan Olsen, "A Garbage Can Model of Organizational Choice," *Administrative Science Quarterly* 17, no. 1 (Winter 1972): 1–25; see also James March, "Decisions in Organizations and Theories of Choice," in Andrew Van De Ven and William Joyce *Perspectives on Organization Design and Behavior* (New York: John Wiley, 1981).

3. This notion of the Cabinet reorganization as a product of garbage collecting fits nicely with work by James March and Johan Olsen, the originators of the garbage-can model of organizationsl choice. As they argue, "reorganizations tend to become collections of solutions looking for problems, ideologies looking for soapboxes, pet projects looking for supporters, and people looking for jobs, reputations, or entertainment." See their article, "Organizing Political Life: What Administrative Reorganization Tells Us about Government," *American Political Science Review* 77, no. 2 (June 1983): 286. Clearly, the veterans groups and VA did not intend for this reorganization to be a garbage can—they wanted a small town or kingdom to prevail, thereby moving the bill quickly and surely through Congress. What the VA experience suggests is that garbage cans may not always be created spontaneously—that is, there may be a key role to be played by individual players who exercise a gatekeeping role, opening the "lid," so to speak.

Index